QOHELETH

Second Edition

Readings: A New Biblical Commentary

QOHELETH

Second Edition

Graham S. Ogden

SHEFFIELD PHOENIX PRESS

2007

Published by Sheffield Phoenix Press
Department of Biblical Studies, University of Sheffield
Sheffield S10 2TN

www.sheffieldphoenix.com

A CIP catalogue record for this book
is available from the British Library

Typeset by Vikatan Publishing Solutions, Chennai, India

Printed by Lightning Source

ISBN 13-digit 978-1-906055-08-0 (hardback)
ISBN 10-digit 1-906055-08-4 (hardback)

ISBN 13-digit 978-1-906055-09-7 (paperback)
ISBN 10-digit 1-906055-09-2 (paperback)

Contents

Preface to the Second Edition

I am delighted to have had the opportunity to reflect again on Qoheleth in light of the work of other scholars whose writings have in more recent years added so much to the understanding of this challenging book. While I have appreciated their approaches and conclusions, I have not felt compelled to change my basic approach to, nor understanding of, what it was that Qoheleth was attempting to say. Readers will note some modifications on individual points of exegesis and interpretation, but overall I felt that the contribution of my original approach was still worth consideration.

My gratitude to David Clines for believing that the commentary was worthy of a re-run. And my thanks to all who have found the original commentary of some help and for their comments.

Melbourne
Christmas 2006.

Preface

More years ago than I now care to remember, I was introduced to Qoheleth in a seminar at Princeton Theological Seminary. I still recall vividly my struggles with understanding the text, but even more so my frustration as I worked through the secondary material. It was there that I was drawn into the centuries–old debate about Qoheleth, its meaning and significance. My fascination with the book led to its becoming the subject of my doctoral dissertation, and I have not been able to put the book aside since. Numerous articles have preceded this attempt to write a commentary which makes more sense of the book than I was able to find in so much of the secondary materials. However, I have no illusions that I have answered all the questions it poses, nor that I shall now be free of the hold which this work has over my scholarly interests. Many readers will be aware of my basic approach to Qoheleth as reflected in those earlier articles. The commentary, however, permits those isolated articles to be seen in the fuller context of the book as a whole.

I am grateful to those who have responded to the earlier articles and who have encouraged me to continue with the commentary, Not only does Qoheleth provide a fascinating academic study, it more importantly offers profound insights into the real issues of faith in a broken and enigmatic world.

I wish to thank the Sheffield Academic Press for their willingness to publish the manuscript, and to the editorial staff for their assistance.

My wife, Lois, who has 'shared my life with Qoheleth' these many years, deserves far more credit than these few words can express.

Taipei,
September 1987

Abbreviations

AB	Anchor Bible
AJSL	*American Journal of Semitic Languages and Literatures*
BASOR	*Bulletin of the American Schools of Oriental Research*
BDB	F. Brown, S. R. Driver, and C. A. Briggs, eds. *A Hebrew and English Lexicon of the Old Testament* (Oxford: Clarendon, 1907)
Bib	*Biblica*
BKAT	Biblischer Kommentar: Altes Testament
BTB	*Biblical Theology Bulletin*
BZAW	Beihefte zur ZAW
CBQ	*Catholic Biblical Quarterly*
CBQMS	Catholic Biblical Quarterly Monograph Series
CJT	*Canadian Journal of Theology*
CTM	*Concordia Theological Monthly*
ETRel	*Études theologiques et Religieuses*
HAT	Handbuch zum Alten Testament
HSAT	Die Heilige Schrift des Alten Testaments
HUCA	*Hebrew Union College Annual*
ICC	International Critical Commentary
IDB	G.A. Buttrick, ed. *Interpreters' Dictionary of the Bible.* 4 Volumes. Nashville, TN: Abingdon, 1962
ITQ	*Irish Theological Quarterly*
JBL	*Journal of Biblical Literature*
JJS	*Journal of Jewish Studies*
JNES	*Journal of Near Eastern Studies*
JQR	*Jewish Quarterly Review*
JSOTSup	Journal for the Study of the Old Testament Supplement Series
JSS	*Journal of Semitic Stdies*
LXX	Septuagint
MT	Masoretic Text
NCBC	New Century Bible Commentary
NICOT	New International Commentary on the Old Testament
NJB	New Jerusalem Bible
NJPS	New Jewish Publication Society Version
OTL	Old Testament Library
RB	*Revue biblique*
REB	Revised English Bible
RHPhR	*Revue d'histoire et de philosophie religieuses*
RThPh	*Revue de théologie et de philosophie*
SBL	Society of Biblical Literature
SBT	Studies in Biblical Theology
SJOT	*Scottish Journal of Theology*
ThZ	*Theologische Zeitschrift*
VTSup	Vetus Testamentum Supplements
TDOT	*Theological Dictionary of the Old Testament*
TJT	*Taiwan Theological Journal*
TUMS	Trinity University Monograph Series
VT	*Vetus Testamentum*
ZAW	*Zeitschrift für die altestestamentliche Wissenschaft*
ZThK	*Zeitschrift für Theologie und Kirche*

Introduction

The interpretation of any document, whether a modern political pronouncement or an ancient religious text, is a task to which the interpreter looks forward with a great sense of excitement and challenge. To draw from that literary work its meaning then and now is a task not to be undertaken lightly, the more so when its possible impact upon both the interpreter and those to whom an interpretation is offered is taken into account.

Subjective factors inevitably influence one's interpretation, owing to the cultural separation, differing world views, geographical and historical distance, diversity of language and the like, which stand between the reader and the original writer(s). Yet at the same time, the interpreter must seek consciously to minimize his or her subjectivity. Our search is for the meaning intended by the original author or community whose work we are studying, insofar as that is recoverable by us using all the critical tools available. Additionally, one must recognize that the material now before us has had its own history within the communities which created and preserved it.

The difficulties which the book Qoheleth has occasioned the interpreter have a history extending back many centuries. It is a book which has proved particularly problematic for interpreters, so that views of its intended meaning are polarized. This situation is due, in part, no doubt, to the subjectivity and limitations of individual scholars, but the fact that this is a problem of such long standing points accusingly at the book itself. The book is difficult to comprehend. The reasons for this will become clear as we proceed.

The two well-known views of Heine—that Qoheleth is the quintessence of scepticism—and F. Delitzsch—that it is the quintessence of piety—make us immediately aware of the basic problem. The contents of the book appear to be so confusing that two *opposite,* and not just variant, interpretations seem possible. Either Qoheleth contains contradictory statements, or his diverse material forces the interpreter to choose to emphasize one aspect rather than another. The apparent confusion which results does not stem entirely from the presuppositions or limitations of modern scholars, but dates back to the early Jewish rabbinic schools who, according to the Mishnah and Talmud, were equally divided as to whether Qoheleth would 'render the hands unclean' or not. Qoheleth found itself listed among books acceptable for use within the faith community toward the end of the first century CE, simply because its beginning and end contained 'religious teaching'. However, it has rarely seen wholehearted acceptance, and this is largely due to the nature of the materials of which it is composed.

Consensus about the book, its canonical qualifications, and its meaning, has been lacking, and the same may be said with regard to other issues such as its possible unity and structure. However, more recently the book has been the subject of sustained scholarly interest, leading to a growing conviction that some of these earlier problems may now be better understood, if not fully resolved.

The Unity of Qoheleth

Alleged contradictions in the book led scholars such as Barton, Jastrow, McNeile, Podechard, and Siegfried to suggest that various redactional additions and glosses had been introduced into Qoheleth, and that they were in conflict with the original. The purpose of these additions was to make the work more acceptable to readers. Numerous presuppositions lie behind this approach, one being that there were various attempts by others to produce a more orthodox work; another that Qoheleth's work was overall one that required 'correcting'. Why these critics of Qoheleth's position would preserve those ideas that they wished to counter rather than simply expunging them, remains unanswered. Another attempt at solving the apparent contradictions has been to suggest that Qoheleth quoted more traditional sayings and then countered them with his own views, making the work an individual's dialog with the tradition. However Fox (1989) has shown that these approaches are fundamentally flawed since it is nigh on impossible to accurately identify alleged quotations. The circular nature of this issue of quoted material has been pointed out clearly by Good (1965: 170).

Other scholars such as Galling, Herder, Kroeber, Plumptre, Ranston and Weiser, saw the lack of unity throughout the book as originating in Qoheleth's own mixed and troubled soul as he vacillated between the extremes of faith and unfaith. This approach, likewise, depends upon first assuming that the material contains contradictions, and then attempting to explain psychologically what state of mind the author was in at the time. Both approaches are flawed. Loader has attempted to explain the tensions and contradictions in terms of their being intentional; they are meaningful polar structures in which statements A and B are both valid within the textual unit. He views the calls to pleasure as the way in which the practical tension can be overcome. More recently Krüger has noted that 'the book of Qoheleth in its present form can be fully understood as a coherent text' (2004: 16). This view depends on recognizing the book's 'discursive character' and on 'the possibility of an ironic playing around with the traditional genres and themes'.

To some extent, doubts about the unity of the book can be traced to an inadequate appreciation of a central feature of wisdom material in general. Because wisdom sayings are not able to encompass all the complexities of human experience in one pithy saying, wisdom literature tends to contain a number of apparently contradictory sayings. An example from Prov. 26.4-5 will make the point obvious. Being situationally governed, there are times or occasions when one kind of advice is appropriate and others when that same advice would be counter-productive. In such a circumstance, the opposite advice would be fitting. (See also the discussion by Sanders on the hermeneutics of true and false prophecy [1977].) In evaluating the material in Qoheleth we need to be clear that we have not overlooked this essential dimension. Inconsistencies in our human environment that seem to defy all logic or reason are so prevalent that true sages must find ways to deal with them. No one statement or advice will suffice to deal with the vast range of human experiences. If one is truly wise then the experience of inconsistencies in the world cannot be ignored, dismissed or explained away; rather they have to be confronted and from that encounter the best possible advice must be given. Simplistic sayings are not acceptable—the world, its warts and all, are to be laid out for further reflection. Such is the mission of Qoheleth.

It would be correct to say that most modern scholars now accept that Qoheleth (1.2-12.8) is the work of one sage. Evidence for this position resides in the peculiar literary style, the constant return to a chosen theme, the repetitions, phrases, and concepts which bind the work together. A strong advocate of the unity of the book is Loader (1979). He concludes, on the basis of his literary investigations, that there is not one contradiction in the original book (1.2-12.8); rather we have a masterly-arranged series of 'polar structures'. The possibility that Qoheleth quotes more traditional sayings and advice so as to raise questions about them, or that he is setting them up for rebuttal should not be dismissed despite the difficulty of identifying what is and what is not a quotation

Structure of Qoheleth

The conclusion that Qoheleth is a unitary work does not necessarily imply that it has a definable structure. In fact, even for those who are convinced that there is a demonstrable structure to the work, there is little agreement about what the structure is. Delitzsch has concluded that all attempts to show a plan or thematic development are doomed to failure. We first take note of those who have seen in Qoheleth little more than a collection of unconnected aphorisms. Most famous is the view of Galling (1932), but it is shared by others such as Hertzberg and Zimmerli, Fohrer and Ellermeier, to mention only some. Perhaps the most unusual solution is one offered by Bickell (1844). His rather extreme view was that the 'pages' of the original document became disarranged, and thus he took it upon himself to put the work back together in such a way as to display its 'original' form and structure.

There have been those who have believed that a progression in thought was present throughout the work, that Qoheleth moved steadily and logically from thesis to conclusion. A. Cardinal Bea (1950) believed that though not readily visible, a structure is nonetheless recoverable; a theme (1.2-3) is expanded in 1.4-2.26, the thesis being that nature, pleasure, and wisdom, cannot satisfy the human need, for wisdom cannot explain life's enigmas (3.1-7.24). This holds true despite the fact that wisdom has inherent practical value (7.25-9.17). Much earlier, in 1904, Genung had argued that Qoheleth could be divided into seven sections, all relating to the theme of enjoying life (see also Rainey, 1964). H. Ginsberg (1950, 1952, 1955) wrote several articles in defence of a structural unity in Qoheleth, while Vogel (1959) argued for a unified structure on literary grounds. Wright and Castellino (1968) presented detailed analyses of the book in an effort to demonstrate its structure. Subsequent to his earlier attempt,

Wright advanced a numerical thesis, based on the numerical value of select, though not necessarily key, terms in the book (1980, 1983). His hope was to prove the correctness of his earlier view about the overall structure of the work, but the theory is built upon such an arbitrary use of evidence that one cannot take it seriously. E. Glasser (1970) and F. Rousseau (1981) have presented further analyses of Qoheleth's structure, the former depending more on a thematic approach moving between *bonheur* and *sagesse*. Lohfink (2003) continues to maintain his view that the book contains a chiastic pattern with its central or pivotal section offering a 'Religious critique' in 4.17-5.6. More recently Krüger (2004) has noted that the 'structural signals in the text are too vague and ambiguous' to establish a clear and 'correct' division of the text. He makes the point that in actual fact the question of its overall structure has little relevance for the interpretation of the book. Rather, the many smaller units need to be seen in their own as well as the larger context, especially since the boundaries of the various units are not clearly marked.

It becomes clear from even a brief review of scholarly opinion that the nature of the material in Qoheleth and the way in which it is presented make the structure, if any, difficult to determine. Thus Loader (1979) expresses the conclusion many before and since have also reached, that we have neither a logical progression of thought through the work, nor merely a collection of separate sayings. We shall discover that there are, in the individual pericopes, structural features which suggest that the book is not devoid of a certain structure, however difficult a precise description of that structure may prove to be.

Thus we come to a mediating position in which the various blocks of material which comprise the book are seen as individually relating to a theme. This avoids the problem of defining the structure in terms of a logical connection between one unit and the next.

However, we need here to note another problem for those who would speak in these thematic terms, for the difficulty of determining the beginning and end points of many of the smaller components of Qoheleth is not a minor one. One only has to peruse the various commentaries and articles to realize that there is little consensus about locating these important points of transition from one thought unit to another. And when one realizes that the manner in which we divide the book will largely affect how we recover its theme and thesis, then the problem seems to grow. The lack of consensus about unit subdivisions rests largely on the inadequacy of criteria for making decisions about the smaller units of the book. So yet another problem faces the commentator, and the reader will understand why in the present commentary a deal of time is spent attempting to justify the decisions taken with regard to dividing the book into its component parts.

In the commentary which follows, it will be argued that a programmatic question about humanity's *yitrôn* or 'advantage' (1.3), together with its answer (negative), and the response which flows from that, provide a framework necessary for understanding Qoheleth's goal and the arrangement of his material to hopefully reach that goal. These three features of question-answer-response which are repeated throughout offer a basic framework for chs. 1-8, and allow us to accommodate all the intervening material. We see the examples from personal and social life contributing to the discussion of the question about *yitrôn* (1.3), and to its answer—there is no *yitrôn*—and leading into the advice that life as a gift from God must be enjoyed. Each subsection is relevant to the search for an answer to that basic question. As we move from ch. 8 into the final chapters, 9-12, there is a shift to discourse material in which the value of wisdom itself is appraised, especially in light of a life which is so marked by the enigmatic. The former, chs. 1-8, provide the setting for this final discourse.

Thesis and Purpose

The question of emphasis is fundamental in determining Qoheleth's thesis. We have already noted above the contrasting conclusions about the book which have marked scholarship in the past. Basically, these have come about because of differing emphases—does one stress the so-called 'vanity'-theme, or the call to enjoyment?

Clearly the recurrent *hebel*-phrase is, and should be, of major importance in the discussion of Qoheleth's thesis by virtue of its frequent use and central function. It is true to say that most scholars have determined that it represents the conclusions, the thesis, which Qoheleth wishes to convey, though Scott (1965) does admit that the thesis does not end at that point, but with the practical advice to find pleasure in life. Insofar as most scholars have assumed that *hebel* carries a negative connotation both inside and outside Qoheleth, they have supposed that the book's fundamental posture is that life is empty and void of meaning.

There are two questions one must ask. The one has to do with the meaning of *hebel* in the specific context of Qoheleth; the other is whether the *hebel*-phrase does in fact represent the book's focus and thesis. In Appendix A the reader will find a more detailed discussion of the meaning of *hebel*. Suffice it to note here that for Qoheleth the term has a very specific meaning: it identifies the enigmatic, the ironic dimension of human experience; it suggests that life is not fully comprehensible. It in no sense carries the meaning 'vanity' or 'meaningless'.

The second question is an even more significant one. Does *hebel* actually summarize the thesis of the writer? Admittedly it occurs frequently and at central points in Qoheleth, but Zimmerli has argued cogently that the term cannot be used to determine adequately what Qoheleth's stance towards life is. A term's frequency of usage is not the only criterion in fixing its importance for a book's thesis.

It will be argued in the commentary to follow that although the *hebel*-phrase occurs in many concluding statements, these are points at which the author answers his own programmatic question. They are not the point at which he offers his advice on how to live in a world plagued by so many enigmas. That advice comes in the reiterated calls to enjoyment in 2.24; 3.12, 22; 5.17 (18); 8.15, as well as in 9.7-10. We shall be looking not to a secondary element in the book's framework, but to the climactic statement, the call to enjoyment, as that which puts the thesis of the book. Thus the structure assists in our answering the question of the book's thesis. Its thesis, then, is that life under God must be taken and enjoyed in all its mystery.

As for the purpose of the book, we turn again to the structure as we have outlined it. The purpose then is seen clearly as a search for an answer to the programmatic question about *yitrôn* (1.3; 2.22; 19; 5.16[17]; 6.11). The question has to do with whether there is any *yitrôn* or 'advantage' to being wise in this world. The term *yitrôn* is another key term coined by Qoheleth. Its meaning is discussed in Appendix B. Briefly, it is the special term for the positive advantage here and in the future which the wise might expect from living according to the instructions of the wisdom tradition. This question of *yitrôn* is the one Qoheleth puts to a younger generation, urging them to reflect on the issues he will raise while they are still young. The importance of doing so while still a youth is that a direction for life is thereby established. Qoheleth's purpose, then, may be defined as calling on the next generation to ponder deeply the kinds of life issues to which there seem to be no complete answers, while at the same time holding firm, and positively accepting, life as God gives it. With this conclusion about the book's thesis and purpose, though for different reasons, Glasser, Good, Polk, Whybray, Witzenrath, Seow and others would basically agree.

One further note about the thesis and purpose of this book needs to be added at this point. Appendix B provides evidence that the key term *yitrôn* has a singularly significant meaning. One of the major themes which weave its way through Qoheleth's thoughts about life is that of death. It intrudes into life in an inexorable way, but it comes at its own time, and often before God's justice is seen to be exercised in situations where the person of faith would expect to witness it. Therefore, Qoheleth wonders whether there is any *yitrôn* at all, when it is demonstrably true that so often in this present life there appears to be no *yitrôn*. Certainly, there is some 'portion' available to the believer, but this hardly equates with *yitrôn*. The semantic field of the term *yitrôn* must be defined broadly enough to include the possibility of an 'advantage' beyond death for the faithful. Of course, dependent as he is upon the empirical method of observation and reflection, he cannot come to any final conclusion on this matter, but his thoughts are running in that direction.

If this thesis about Qoheleth is true, then the book we are about to study represents the earliest Old Testament document to express, albeit in a tentative manner, the thought that there might be something beyond death, at least for the wise. Qoheleth then marks one of the earliest formal steps in the formulation of the thesis of the resurrection to life beyond the grave, at least for the wise. In this respect, he is the forerunner of views shared by the Pharisees and Jesus two or three centuries later. However, as is obvious from the final discussion in chs. 9-12, Qoheleth in the end must confine his advice to living as a wise person in this present life, yet never losing sight of the inevitable end we face.

Who is 'Qoheleth'?

'Qoheleth' (see comments on 1.1) is the adopted name of the author of 1.2-12.8. He is an Israelite sage, who, according to the Editor's testimony in 12.9-10, stood firmly within the wisdom tradition. Evidence from the book's language and literary convention (the use of Persian terms such as *pardēs* in 2.5, *pitgām* in 8.11, and other Aramaic connections), indicates he was most likely a teacher during the second or perhaps as early as the third century BCE. The ancient tradition that it is a nom-de-plume for Solomon cannot be substantiated.

The Present Shape of the Book

In what has been discussed above, it has been made clear that 1.2—12.8 marks the extent of Qoheleth's original work, to which 1.1 and 12.9-14 have subsequently been added.

One may well ask about the remainder of the book, about 1.1 and 12.9-14. The general consensus is that these are editorial additions which have brought the book to its present and final canonical form. This is an important observation, for it reminds us that the document once produced by Qoheleth for his students, was preserved by them, no doubt for the value they saw in it, then commended to a second group by yet another wisdom teacher whom we dub the 'Editor'. This two-fold movement in the canonical formation of the book, ignoring for the moment the independent life of many of the quotations found within it, is important as we consider its life within the believing community of Israel. Whether these two communities or groups of wise were contemporaries or from successive generations is a question we cannot now answer with certainty, but at least we are pointed to the fact that Judaism of the time was a pluriform religion (see M. Stone, 1980; E. Ulrich, 2004).

While we recognize that there were at least two groups involved in Qoheleth's transmission, we need to be aware that others in the Jewish community may not have ascribed equal authority to Qoheleth's words. This is reflected in the debate about its worthiness for inclusion in the books acceptable for public reading.

Why was the original document provided with a Superscription and an Epilogue? Was it that the original work and its devotees were only a minority group whose views were not widely known? Was it that another sage wished to make available to a wider public the thoughts found in this work? Was it to add his own imprimatur to a textbook for use among his own students? Or was it to defend the ideas and suggestions within it against other and competing theologies as a valid minority viewpoint? The Editor certainly commends the honesty of Qoheleth's search, at the same time pointing to the disturbing nature of his findings.

There is a note of apologetic in this commendation (12.9-10), suggesting that the reason for the addition was to convince a sceptical majority of the worthiness of the views here expressed.

The Editor also makes the point (12.12-14.) that the pursuit of wisdom is an endless task, calling for a level of commitment and dedication similar to that exemplified by Qoheleth. We may sense here also that this work was meeting disparaging reviews among certain other Judaic groups, so that the Editor feels constrained to defend Qoheleth against them. He finally affirms the wisdom ethic: fear God and follow his commands. That is, God, and not man, will be the final arbiter of one's endeavours. The Editor is also stating that Qoheleth has not at any point abandoned faith, though some with narrower vision might have been convinced that he had.

The final shape of Qoheleth suggests clearly that the original work was preserved and handed on with a commendation to others by a second wisdom teacher. Although it might represent a minority view within the Judaism of that time, it nevertheless stands for the truth. Its probing after an answer to the perplexing question of death and *yitrôn* was quite revolutionary. It may well be that the difficulty many had in accepting this document was simply that it pushed too far beyond the norms not only of the wisdom tradition, but of other aspects of Israelite faith of the time. This would explain why an editorial addition was necessary to guarantee its wider circulation in the faith community. It is this which has assured it of a continuing place within the canon.

Appendix A

The Meaning of the Term *Hebel*

That Qoheleth expresses a basically negative view of life in this world is a conclusion dependent upon assigning to the term *hebel* a meaning equivalent to 'vanity'. Our task here is to examine the specific manner in which Qoheleth used the term in order to discover more exactly what semantic value the word carries in this book.

Hebel occurs 38 times in Qoheleth, and is important not only for this fact of its frequency (this represents more than half of all OT examples), but also for the fact that it is employed as a key term in concluding statements which climax many smaller sections throughout the book (e.g. 2.11, 17, 23). Additionally, we note the significant use of the term, in a functional role, in 1.2 and 12.8; here the compound forms *hᵃbēl hᵃbālîm... hebel* serve as the two inclusions which bracket the entire original work. For these reasons, we can appreciate how our understanding of the term will colour our reading of Qoheleth and our assessment of his message.

It is a fact that in its occurrences outside Qoheleth, *hebel* means something equivalent to 'vanity', 'nothingness', 'vapour'. This is the sense we discover from its uses in Deut. 32.21; Isa. 57.13; Jer. 8.19; 10.8; 51.18; Prov. 13.11; 21.6; Ps. 78.33, and many others; it addresses the notion of the uselessness, the powerlessness of idols, and the fruitlessness of much human endeavour. Our question must then be 'Does Qoheleth use *hebel* in this same manner?' So many scholars assume with R. Davidson (1983: 187-89) that this is so, that it seems almost impolite to doubt this consensus.

James Barr (1961: 171) has reminded us that words have meaning in specific contexts and in relation to the intention of those who use them. In a more modern context, we are all familiar with the way in which words assume new connotations and meaning with each generation, or with regional and geographical variations. This is so because language is a living and dynamic phenomenon, rather than something static and unchanging. Only by examining the ways in which Qoheleth actually employs *hebel* (or any other key term) can we determine what meaning he gives to the term.

While it might be possible to infer from some examples of the *hebel*-phrase that human life is vain, there are at least three factors in Qoheleth which must be part of the equation by which we determine its meaning. They are:

1. the painful scenarios to which the *hebel*-phrase is added as a response;
2. the meaning of the parallel and complementary phrases, "striving after wind", "a sore affliction", and "an unhappy business";
3. the calls to enjoyment which punctuate the book at key points.

We shall consider representative examples of the *hebel*-phrase in order to arrive at a contextual definition of its meaning.

1. Scenarios Which are Described as *Hebel*

a. 3.16-19. Qoheleth presents for reflection a human situation. Corruption and evil are found in places where one would expect to find exemplary justice and righteousness. This general observation could refer to the legal system, the royal household, or to the religious world. It is the problem of pervasive evil. Qoheleth's response is two-fold. In v. 17 he offers an orthodox theological response. He affirms that God will at some point bring justice to bear; the 'pus' will be cleansed from society, for all is under the control of a just deity. To introduce this 'solution' Qoheleth has used the phrase, 'I said in my heart (to myself)...' and it is the reiteration of this phrase at the head of v. 18 which indicates that the two comments in vv. 17 and 18 are actually parallel. Verse 18 then represents another and equally valid response to the dilemma of v. 16. On this occasion, Qoheleth suggests that the pervasiveness of evil works as a form of testing, the purpose of which is to prove to humankind that on at least this level it is on a par with the animal world. Like the animals, even 'sophisticated' humanity will die (cf. Ps. 49). To denote his feelings about this, Qoheleth calls upon the term *hebel* (v. 19).

The specific socio-theological problem highlighted here is a very basic one. Qoheleth suggests that one approach to this issue is to affirm one's religious beliefs yet more strongly (v. 17), or alternatively to leave the question open (v. 18). In the latter case, God's justice often appears to come too late, if at all. Those trapped in unjust situations may die long before God's justice is seen to be done. So it is this scenario, and the apparently insoluble theological problem which it throws up, to which Qoheleth responds with the *hebel* phrase.

Does this then mean that life is vacuous, or meaningless? Does the fact that there are no ready-made answers for the problem of v. 16 lead to the conclusion that therefore life is 'vanity'? If God's justice were to intervene, as v. 17 confesses, then clearly the problem mentioned in v. 16 would be resolved, and 'vanity' or 'emptiness' would be thoroughly inappropriate as evaluations of the situation. On the other hand, if one were to die before actually seeing divine justice work itself out, would that strip life of its meaning? Surely not! The term *hebel* in this context is the vehicle chosen to draw attention to an enigmatic situation, a theological conundrum. Consistent with what is spelled out in more detail later in the book, we find Qoheleth here impressing on his young readers the fact that we must live with many unanswered questions. It does not mean for one moment that life therefore is 'vanity'; rather, the pain of faith is living with many questions unanswered.

b. 4.7-8. A *hebel*-situation is the assessment which brackets the problem presented in these two verses. Pictured for us is the lonely workaholic, whose bank balance continues to rise as he climbs the corporate ladder. But to what purpose? He never stops to ask the important question: 'for what purpose am I doing all this'? This failure to ask a most basic question is something which Qoheleth finds difficult to comprehend; it is *hebel*. It is clear that the man in question gains a great deal materially from his endeavours. He does acquire some 'portion' (*ḥēleq,* 2.10 etc.), but to Qoheleth, this is far from enough, so the situation represents yet another of life's ironies.

c. 6.1-2. A theological problem of no small proportions is presented in the very brief case-study of 6.2. The author prefaces his description with comments about his feelings with regard to the situation (6.1): that it is *ra'*. (Throughout Qoheleth, *ra'* describes any painful or traumatic situation, rather than one which is morally corrupt or evil.)

Briefly, we are told of an individual to whom God has given all manner of material benefits. In the tradition of Deuteronomy (e.g. 7.12-15; 28.1-14) these benefits would be seen as unmistakable tokens of divine blessing and approval. Unfortunately, as Qoheleth describes the scene, this person is seen to lack a most necessary gift, the ability to enjoy those tokens. True, there is a bright side, in that these goods do bring joy to others, even if not to the person whose they are. This is a peculiar situation depicted by the word *hebel.* Would it then be correct to say that life was 'vanity' or 'empty' when from the Israelite perspective these goods were all tokens of God's pleasure? Those material benefits which are crucial to life cannot themselves make life meaningless. There is nonetheless a problem, an anomalous situation, brought about by the inability to enjoy what one has; it is an enigma, and Qoheleth does not offer any rationale for it. He merely opines that this kind of situation is *hebel.*

d. 8.14. Similar to the example provided in 3.16-18, this also draws attention to the anomalous dimension of life. Good things happen to bad people; bad things befall the good. Though not universal, this problem is sufficiently common to raise a serious theological question. Why does a just God allow this kind of thing to occur? We do not have the answer. Yet life does not thereby cease to have meaning, and become 'vanity'. In describing this scenario as *hebel,* Qoheleth's meaning is that life is enigmatic, and the sign of wisdom is that one can accept that.

2. Parallel and Complementary Phrases

Qoheleth on occasion adds several other phrases to the basic *hebel* phrase, the purpose being to emphasize and to complement the thought of the central phrase. The most frequent of these additions is 'a striving after wind' (RSV), *r*^{e}*'ût rûaḥ* (1.14 etc); but there are two others which deserve mention, 'a sore affliction', *ḥolî ra'*, and 'an unhappy business', *'inyān ra'.*

a. *r*^{e}*'ût rûaḥ*. The root *r'h* describes the work of the shepherd as he pastors the flock. An alternative rendering of the phrase would be 'shepherding the wind'. What Qoheleth describes is the attempt to bring the wind under control, to make it blow in a certain direction according to the dictates of the shepherd. From this perspective we see it as a delightful idiomatic phrase for attempting the impossible. Qoheleth shares God's humour at any foolish attempt to control the environment, his breath *(rûaḥ).*

b. *ḥolî ra'*. In 6.1 we meet a scenario which calls for much heart searching. The way in which Qoheleth presents this particular problem suggests that God has a direct hand in the fact that the person concerned does not enjoy the material wealth he has accumulated. It is for this reason, more than for any other, that the sage feels pain. As a complementary expression, it suggests an interpretation for *hebel* which emphasizes the anomaly in the situation described.

c. *'inyān ra'*. Descriptive of the sad soul frantically searching for wealth but neglecting the question of its purpose, this phrase again points to the fact that there are so many situations in life which defy our human comprehension, causing us painful moments of doubt.

It seems abundantly evident from the representative examples of *hebel* which we have investigated that Qoheleth does not mean to claim that life is empty, vain, and meaningless. As he addresses the next generation his point is simply that life is replete with situations to which even the sage, the philosopher theologian, has no answer. It is the word *hebel* that Qoheleth applies to describe these situations. That which is difficult to understand or explain, which is hidden from human investigation, is indeed deeply troubling, but that is all it is. To persist with the traditional gloss 'vanity', with its ambiguity—excessive pride, or worthlessness—lends such a negative cast to the term and thus to the book that it is to be avoided at all costs. See further under notes on 1.2.

3. Qoheleth's Call to Enjoyment

There is yet a third factor which must play its part in our search for the meaning of the term *hebel* as used by Qoheleth. It lies in the reiterated calls to enjoy life.

Despite past difficulties in establishing the structure of the book as a whole, this commentary will give reasons for claims that the book does have a general structure, in the sense that it moves from programmatic question through response to advice grounded on the preceding evidence. That this pattern recurs throughout the first eight chapters allows us to claim that Qoheleth is searching for an answer to his question, and in light of what he finds, or has himself experienced, he offers his summarizing call to enjoy the life which God gives (2.24; 3.12-13, 22; 5.18[19]; 8.15). This approach permits the conclusion that Qoheleth's purpose in writing is to be sought ultimately in the positive calls to his readers to receive thankfully from God the gift of life. This advice we find again in the discourse section

9.7-10, where Qoheleth urges the youth of Israel to enjoy the life and work which God apportions. These calls to enjoyment are actually theological statements of faith in a just and loving God, despite many signs which might appear contrary. Thus, from a structural standpoint, it is clear that Qoheleth's focus is upon an affirmative rather than a negative view of human life. Qoheleth comes to us as a realist, but one who never loses sight of the fact that life is God-given and for our benefit (see also Good, 1965: 176-83; Polk, 1976).

For these reasons, it is important to state clearly once again, that the term *hebel* in Qoheleth has a distinctive function and meaning: it conveys the notion that life is enigmatic, and mysterious; that there are many unanswered and unanswerable questions. The person of faith recognizes this fact but moves forward positively to claim and enjoy the life and the work which God apportions.

Despite accepting that Qoheleth does not see everything in life as futile and meaningless, both Murphy (1992) and Seow (1997) nevertheless continue to prefer the term 'vanity' as the most adequate term to render *hebel* in Qoheleth. The reason is basically that they accept it as a kind of 'code word' that is able to embrace the various shades of meaning found in the Hebrew term as used in Qoheleth. However, the negative connotations of the term 'vanity' must influence a reader's perception of the position Qoheleth adopts, and for that reason we see it as an unfortunate choice.

Appendix B

The Term "*Yitrôn*"

In the commentary to follow, arguments will be advanced to justify calling the question in 1.3 Qoheleth's 'programmatic question'. It is *the* question to which Qoheleth is seeking an answer. As he presents his reflections on the vast array of human experiences, he asks whether in and through them there is any *yitrôn* to be gained. It is vital for an understanding of this book that we be as clear as possible about the semantic field of this term.

In the midst of spectacular material success, a sure sign of divine approval according to the deuteronomic perspective, Qoheleth reveals that he was not able there to locate *yitrôn* (2.11). In a society pervaded by injustice, and where at times even God's justice was not evident, or in a world suddenly shattered by death's untimely intrusion, where does one find *yitrôn?*

The Hebrew root *ytr*, from which *yitrôn* is coined by Qoheleth, speaks of the profit or gain one might expect from commercial enterprise, the 'bottom line' which so interests the investor. However, 'that which remains over', in the context of Qoheleth does not appear to carry a material sense. The fact that Qoheleth actually creates this neologism, points towards its having a peculiar and circumscribed field of reference.

Yitrôn is used altogether ten times (1.3; 2.11, 13[2x]; 3.9; 5.8[9], 15[16]; 7.12; 10.10, 11); there are also related words, *môtar* (3.19), and a participial form *yôtēr* (6.8, 11; 7.11) which also functions as an adverb, as in 2.15; 7.16; 12.9, 12. Included in these eighteen usages of the root *ytr* are some which are too general to aid our definition of its parameters, such as 1.3; there is one in which the meaning is difficult to determine adequately (10.11), and there are several in which, for textual or grammatical reasons, its specific reference is far from clear (5.8[9]; 7.11, 12; 10.10). This leaves us with seven examples of *yitrôn* as a noun that will form the basis of our search for its meaning: 2.11, 13; 3.9, 19; 5.15[16]; 6.8, 11.

1. 2.11. Having summarized his extraordinary achievements in 2.1-10, Qoheleth, in the first formal response to the programmatic question, determines that *yitrôn* was not to be found in those considerable material and other attainments. Fame, fortune, and pleasure were all his; but to depict such achievements he selects the term *ḥēleq,* 'reward'. This would imply that *yitrôn* and *ḥēleq* are to be distinguished semantically. While their semantic fields include that which one gains from work and effort, the immediate impression from the example in 2.11 is that *yitrôn* is not dependent upon material success. Even if one were to argue that *yitrôn* refers to some deep inner satisfaction, which the wise might expect, one would have to take into account the additional fact that the *yitrôn* Qoheleth longs to know is not to be found 'under the sun'. If it is not equated with some worldly, measurable benefit, then it probably belongs to a somewhat different order. While undoubtedly not 'other worldly' in the full sense, Qoheleth is at least pointing in the direction of a *yitrôn* which transcends this present earthly experience.

2. 2.13. The comparative saying in this verse makes the point that there is an essential relationship between wisdom and the availability of *yitrôn*. Only the wise and those who pursue wisdom can expect to know *yitrôn*. 'Folly' (*siklût*) cannot provide anything akin to it.

3. 3.9. Another general expression similar to 1.3, this one has appended a discussion which aids in further clarifying the meaning of *yitrôn*. In addition to the moments of time which God's providence determines (3.1-8), there is also 'eternity' (*'ôlām*) resident in the human consciousness (3.11). While a great deal of ink has been spilled in an effort to define *'ôlām* more closely, it does appear clear that it must be distinguished from those moments of time expressed as *'ēt* or *ḥēpeṣ*. That *'ôlām* may refer to 'ignorance' or 'darkness' does seem to have support from what follows (see Scott, 1965), but this introduces a meaning which *'ôlām* does not generally demonstrate in other locations—1.4, 10; 2.16; 3.14; 9.6; rather, the meaning approximates to the traditional 'for ever'. Further, when Qoheleth uses the phrase *nātan lēb* (1.17; 7.2, 4, 7, 21; 8.9, 16; 9.1; 10.2) he is pointing to the reflective process. Combining these features, we arrive at the suggestion that 3.9, though a generalized phrase, does appear to speak of an awareness that the time and experience of this world are not the only dimensions with which we have to do, and that *yitrôn* is bound up with that 'eternal' dimension.

4. 3.19. Conscious of a pervasive lack of justice in society, Qoheleth ponders whether God will redress this situation. His answer in 3.17 is 'yes', but this he then balances with another observation: at times justice is not seen to be done before the demise of the offended party (see Appendix A). The question then raised is, does this redress occur after death? Qoheleth admits ignorance; he does not know whether beyond death there is some restoration made, so one cannot conclude whether humankind has any more *yitrôn* than the animals. From this comment it is evident that if Qoheleth could confidently pronounce some distinction between wise and fool, and between humankind and the animal world, beyond death, it would then be viable to talk about humankind's *yitrôn*.

5. 5.15(16). Is *yitrôn* possible for one born into an already destitute family? Again it is implied that *yitrôn* is not to be equated with material reward, otherwise one could not even pose the question in this manner. The bitterness of life for such a pauper would further suggest that any *yitrôn* possible would have to be beyond this life, for not only do the destitute lack material benefits, they also have little in the way of a sense of well-being. Nor would it be correct to project *yitrôn* into the psychological realm and conclude that in this case it meant 'a sense of self-esteem'.

6. 6.8, 11. In 6.1-11 we meet a prosperous but morose tycoon. Better off than such a person is a still-born child, is Qoheleth's perhaps surprising conclusion. Though both die, it is the child with whom the 'advantage' lies because he/she has already entered 'rest' (*naḥat*). The notion of 'rest' is similar to what Job speaks of in 3.11-19, as a post-death experience in which all the traumas of life are eliminated.

The above brief investigation indicates that the original commercial application of *ytr* is absent from Qobeleth's use of his term *yitrôn*. He has assigned it a metaphorical sense to speak of that which is nonmaterial. It might refer, in part, to an inner contentment which abides throughout an enigmatic life, but it seems also to incorporate the possibility of some experience beyond death.

The traditional view that at death all humanity, good and bad, wise and fool, passed to the netherworld, to Sheol, embodies an ethical dilemma, especially when justice is not meted out during one's earthly life. The deuteronomic view that God rewards the just and punishes the wicked eventually was seen to know too many exceptions for it to be accepted without some additional explanation or evidence. Israelite sages acknowledged that not always was God's justice visible to all. Where, then, did this dilemma lead?

The function of the word *yitrôn* which Qoheleth coined was to gather up all his hopes that there might be some just resolution of these many human enigmas. While Qoheleth cannot prove that there is a distinction between good and evil, wise and fool, beyond death, yet it is inherent in his belief in divine justice that something of that order must be considered. By focusing on the *yitrôn* of the wise and affirming its reality, Qoheleth is moving towards the view that to affirm God's justice requires that separate treatment be given the good and evil person. If it does not appear in this life, then perhaps the solution can only lie beyond death.

Unfortunately, like any sage methodologically dependent upon empirical observation, Qoheleth can only intimate his belief. By opting for the question-form (1.3 etc.), Qoheleth is indicating that he cannot prove that *yitrôn* will be granted beyond the grave, but he insists that it is at least a possibility, an extension of the goodness the wise may enjoy now.

If this is the semantic field of Qoheleth's term *yitrôn*, then we have uncovered a particularly significant area of OT thought. The NT clearly stands at a point where a developed thesis of life after death, with mutually exclusive fates for good and sinner, has arisen. Even though such a theory was not acceptable to all parties within Judaism, it is at least an established theological dictum by that time. Shrouded in mystery is the route by which such an understanding came about. If there is any basis for the viewpoint argued above with respect to the term *yitrôn* in Qoheleth, we now can claim that it represents one of the earliest stages in the process by which Israel arrived at such an understanding. It is further significant in that it identifies an Israelite sage as a prime figure in that discovery. Perhaps this will assist our re-evaluation of the sage and of the wisdom movement within the entire OT theological process.

Chapter 1

What is a Person's 'Advantage'?

1.1 Superscription

This introductory statement announces that the following discussion represents the work of one identified only as *Qoheleth,* apparently a title, but one which has defied precise definition. That it is indeed a title and not a proper name is further suggested by the addition of the definite article in 7.27 and 12.8. It is assumed that *qohelet* is the feminine participle of the root *qhl,* used frequently in the Torah to describe the gathered community of Israel, the 'congregation' (cf. Exod. 12.6; Num. 16.3). The significance of the feminine participle is that it describes one who holds an office, in this case, in the congregation of Israel. What exactly this person does in that office is not clear. The Greek interpretation of *qohelet* is *ekklēsiastēs,* usually rendered in English as 'Preacher'. As such it reflects a certain understanding of an office holder in the Christian church, rather than a Jewish liturgical functionary. The 'arguer' seems a more appropriate translation (cf. Neh. 5.7; Kugel, 1985: 236-37).

Who is this Qoheleth? The text implies that he is a royal figure from Jerusalem (cf. 1.12), a Davidic descendant. The term 'son of David' is a flexible term including generations of descendants, but the impression the verse gives is that it refers to Solomon. As it would have been a simple matter to refer to Solomon by name, if that were indeed the case, we assume that the allusion to Solomonic authorship is a literary device akin to that used later in the apocryphal 'Wisdom of Solomon' from the first century BCE. The purpose of this allusion is to heighten the authority of what follows by hinting that it is the work of 'Solomon', the archetype of Israel's wise men. For reasons already given in the Introduction, we know that this document is considerably later than Solomon and thus not from Solomon's hand. That 1.1 speaks of Qoheleth in other than an autobiographical style suggests that this verse is an editorial note to introduce the work; it is a superscription similar to those found at the head of many OT works, e.g. Prov. 1.1, individual psalms, and most prophetic writings.

1.2 The Theme

Five times in this verse we meet the key-word *hebel*. In all, this word appears 37 or 38 times throughout the book (there are doubts about the reading *hebl^eḵā* in 9.9, while *hkl* in 9.2 *is* read as *hbl* in the Septuagint. It will be argued in what follows that the MT in each of these cases should be retained. Thus *hbl* occurs 38 times throughout this book). In almost every example of its use, *hebel* is to be found as part of a summary or concluding statement. These two factors, frequency of use, and function, require that we be as clear as possible about the meaning of the word, for the way in which we interpret it will profoundly affect our understanding of Qoheleth's message. See Appendix A.

W.E. Staples (1943, 1955) pointed out that although in other OT documents *hebel* does convey a sense of 'emptiness', and 'unreality' (e.g. Jer. 10.15; Ps. 78.33), examination of Qoheleth's usage of the word indicates that such a meaning is inappropriate here. Staples recommends the meaning 'mystery'. E. Good suggests 'irony' (1981: 182). In describing incomprehensible situations as *hebel,* Qoheleth certainly does not mean that human life, in its many facets, is without meaning and futile; rather, he determines that life is enigmatic (cf. 2.22-23*),* not fully within our power to comprehend. There is also a dark side to life's incongruities, though it is not always or over-ridingly so (see Polk, 1976). For Murphy (1992, lix), and Fox (1998, 225-38) 'absurd' as proposed by Barucq is a better term to use as it focuses on what is incomprehensible about human existence, what Fox calls 'an affront to reason'. Yet Murphy continues to render *hebel* as 'vanity' for its value as a 'code word' in Qoheleth. Seow (1997: 102) also retains the term 'vanity' since he would maintain that there is no 'adequate alternative' in English that is able to render its breadth of meaning, and varying nuances. The real difficulty with retaining the traditional term 'vanity' is not only the fact that it is ambiguous, referring to an individual's excessive pride or arrogance, as well as that which is vain in the sense of worthless. The more troubling fact is that both meanings represent a negative set of values and so give an overall cast to the book that is misleading.

Miller's suggestion (1998: 437-54) is that *hebel* functions as a symbol with three referents: insubstantiality, transience, and foulness, by which he means those things that offend his sense of justice. These three senses, he suggests, are constructed into 'a single symbol embodying all three'. Specific contexts indicate which sense is intended. This is similar to the view of Fredricks (1993) who regarded *hebel* as a symbol for that which was transient and temporary.

The phrase *hᵃbēl-hᵃbālîm* is a superlative, expressing that which is totally beyond human comprehension and explanation. The *hebel* phrase in v. 2 sets the tone of the book, and it is balanced by a similar verse in conclusion at 12.8. Coming from a wise human whose responsibility is to teach others how to cope with life, this inclusio is a solemn warning that even the sage does not know everything (cf. 7.23-24). Despite that, Qoheleth claims that 'all is *hebel*'. The precise meaning of 'all' here is probably to be confined to the realm of human activity (Seow: 103). The recognition of the limitations to our understanding is an important starting-point in the task of coming to terms with human life. For Crenshaw, however, who renders *hebel* as 'futile,' the superlative form is simply 'the ultimate futility.'

1.3 Putting the Question

From the outset, Qoheleth makes clear what his purpose is. He is examining human life and work with a view to ascertaining whether or not there is any 'advantage' (*yitrôn*) in it. The question in 1.3 is the programmatic question for the entire book (contra Miller, 2002).

We note that this question recurs on several occasions. We find it again in 2.22; 3.9; 5.10[11], 15[16]; 6.8, 11. With few exceptions the form of the question in each case varies little. Not only do we find the question put regularly, we also note that there is a response to the question. Qoheleth concludes that there is no advantage to a person 'under the sun' (2.11). That is to say, *yitrôn* is not located in this world. However, having determined that such is the case, Qoheleth must, as a counsellor, give advice that is more constructive. This is forthcoming in 2.24; 3.12, 22; 8.15, where we note the form 'there is nothing better ... than...', and in 5.17[18] and 9.7-10 in slightly expanded forms (see Ogden, 1979). In other words, we may state that Qoheleth's discussion of human life not only begins with the programmatic question, but constantly refers back to it. In this way, the question, together with its conclusion and the accompanying advice, provide us with a framework into which the many individual observations and reflections are placed. This has important implications for our interpretation of the book, for it demands that each smaller unit be placed in this context of question-response-advice. Only then can we be more certain that we have grasped Qoheleth's intention.

Another matter that is determinative for our interpretation of Qoheleth is the content, the semantic field, of the word *yitrôn*. The word 'advantage' (*yitrôn*) comes from the root which expresses the idea that there is something that 'remains over', or 'excess'. Only in Qoheleth do we find this particular word, and it occurs ten times. It is used along with another term, *yôtēr*, from the same root and with the same nominal sense in 6.8, 11 and 7.11 (*yôtēr* has an adverbial function in 2.15; 7.16; 12.9, 12). In Appendix B a fuller discussion of the issue will be found. Suffice it here to note that *yitrôn* is Qoheleth's special term for wisdom's reward both here and after death. The term is necessarily lacking in precision, for Qoheleth is searching, questioning, rather than making dogmatic pronouncements. Dependent upon observation for his conclusions, he, like all other wisdom teachers, must remain tentative about that which resides outside the sphere of empirical research. Thus, his thoughts about what happens at or after death are placed within the question-form that introduces the framework for the opening chapters. In the commentary that follows we shall proceed with the assumption that the book is probing after an answer to the question of what remains to the wise person both in life, in one's toil in life and after death.

Our question in 1.3 also contains other vocabulary which is seminal to Qoheleth's thought. One such term is *'āmāl*, 'work', 'toil,' which speaks both of the action of working as well as of the outcome of or reward for such work. The second is the phrase 'under the sun', *taḥat haššemeš,* Qoheleth's favourite term for this-worldly existence. This phrase, found only in Qoheleth in the OT, is also known in third-century BCE Phoenician inscriptions. It will recur in the response to this question in 2.11.

1.4-11 A Poem

Before launching into a discussion of the question posed in 1.3, Qoheleth quotes a poem, the theme of which is the endless round of activity within nature. That this endless round of activity is 'pointless', as Crenshaw opines (1987: 61-65), passes a negative judgment on a movement that is value-neutral. The world is and remains, yet within it there is a flow, a cycle of regular and unceasing activity. Such cyclic motion may give the impression that certain occurrences are actually new and novel. Qoheleth suggests that what appears new is but the recurrence of some aspect of the past; it is new only to the one who newly experiences it.

What might be Qoheleth's purpose in quoting such a poem? We have no way of determining whether the poem is his own creation or whether he is drawing upon another source, but we can ask about its function. We presume that it is to set the stage for the discussion which commences in 1.12. Let us turn first to the details of the poem, bearing in mind that we are also seeking to answer the question of the poem's function at this point in Qoheleth's work.

1.4 The opening word of the poem is *dôr,* translated as 'generation'. The two participles 'going' and 'coming,' indicate regular movement. Over against this regular flow, there stands the earth immovable (1.4b). A clear contrast is intended (against Fox, 1988: 109). What are the two objects being contrasted? The second object, the earth, is obvious. The first element, *dôr,* may refer to generations of humankind replacing one another on the earth, and most commentators adopt this view. However, the two participles which describe the cyclic movement in 1.4a are, in vv. 5-7, applied to the cycle of nature, to the sun, wind, and streams. Thus the principle that we find in 1.4a is exemplified in 1.5-7 (contra Glasser, 1970: 23-24). We ought also to note that *dôr* in its original meaning refers to circular motion. Thus we can determine that v. 4 contrasts a circular movement within nature with the steadfast and immovable earth (Ogden, 1986). It is this opening line which marks the poem's theme, one which will be illustrated in the thoughts which follow. Seow (1997: 106) points out that *dôr* in combination with the verbs *hlk* 'go,' speaks of death, thus the coming and going of the generations speaks of the cycle of life as one generation replaces another.

1.5 The first illustration of cyclic movement is the sun with its daily progress from rising *(zāraḥ)* to setting *(bā')*. Having set, the sun is then described as panting (Hebrew *šô'ēp* means 'pant', 'long after') back to its original place ready to start the new day. It is an expression full of vitality, the two participles *šô'ēp* and *zôrēaḥ* portraying constant movement. Whether this movement is wearying or bears a sense of eagerness and longing is not a question to be settled unequivocally, as 'panting' is used in both senses in the OT (cf. Ps. 56.2; Isa. 42.14). Unfortunately our text leaves us without clear guidance as to which view approximates to Qoheleth's. Only for those who, for other reasons, adopt the view that Qoheleth's basic position is a pessimistic one, is it clear that the sun grows weary of this constant round. The emphasis implicit in the use of participles is upon the constancy of movement.

1.6 Here it is the wind *(rûaḥ)* which provides the second illustration of cyclic movement. We meet in this verse the participle *hôlēk,* 'going', repeated from 1.4a. The circular motion is made more clear by the use four times in this verse of the root *sbb,* 'turn', 'go around', and of *šûb,* 'return'. Whereas the sun moves from east to west, the wind is pictured as blowing from north to south. Thus vv. 5-6 cover all compass points. That this movement is wearisome, as some commentators have suggested, is not a thought present in the text.

The note about the *rûaḥ* returning (*šûb*) suggests a thematic connection between this opening portion of the book and its closing section in which the spirit/breath returns to God who gave it (12.7). That theme is what Carasik (2003) has described as typical of Qoheleth's over-riding view of the world.

1.7 Yet another incessant movement is presented, this time rivers flowing to the sea. Again the participle *hôlēk* appears, reinforced by the verb *šûb,* 'return'. For all the fresh supply constantly flowing into it, the sea is not filled. This is a remarkable feature of the never-ending motion within nature: it does not move toward completion; it knows only constant and cyclic motion. It is tempting to think that Qoheleth has in mind the Dead Sea, which, though it has no outlet, daily receives fresh input from the many streams that feed it, yet without filling it. Qoheleth sees a parallel in the sun's mysterious return to its starting point, with that of the stream which, having emptied itself into the sea, continues to be replenished, like the Jordan, to sustain the cycle. The phrase *'el māqôm* in both v. 5 and v. 7 provides the link between sun and stream. The emphasis is once more upon the constancy of the movement, consistent with the thesis of 1.4a.

1.8 The thought expressed in this verse by *y^e^gē'îm,* translated 'weariness', is for many commentators that which brings to the poem its tired and negative attitude towards the cycle within nature. We need to clarify its meaning, for apart from *y^e^gē'îm,* the text gives no other reason for adopting such a negative view.

The root *yg'* is used also in 12.12 where it speaks of exertion, endurance, toil, together with what that toil produces, namely the fruit of one's labour. It does not speak of easy acquisition, but of effort. At the same time it suggests that there will be something to show for the effort expended. This meaning would be appropriate for 12.12. Is it equally apposite in 1.8?

The text of v. 8a is brief, It states that 'all things/words *(dᵃbārîm)* are *yᵉgēʿîm*. As this poem uses many participial forms it is likely that *yᵉgēʿîm* is a participle rather than an adjective. In this case it can describe that which is toiling along towards some goal. That there is in mind a circular movement is not in doubt; that it is one which is wearying in the negative sense, or 'fruitless repetition' (Murphy, 1992: 8), takes us beyond the generalized form in which the text comes to us.

The remainder of v. 8 consists of three structurally parallel phrases, a fact which requires that we see them as parallel in intent.

A human	is not able	to speak
An eye	is not sated	with seeing
An ear	is not filled	by hearing

Each phrase offers a concrete illustration, this time from human life, of the continuous operation of mouth, eye (cf. also 4.8) and ear. Admittedly the first phrase is enigmatic, but because of the parallel structure, we may use the remaining two phrases as a means of defining the meaning of the first. Although there are potential situations that are contrary, the eye never reaches the point that it cannot take in more, nor does the ear become so filled with sound that it cannot accept any more impulses from the outside world. Eye and ear are not like containers with limited capacity. Similarly, the mouth is unable to finish speaking, in the sense that it has limitless potential for uttering sound, even if it cannot speak of anything new (v. 9). From these three observations it is clear that the ceaseless activity which has already been exemplified in the natural world of sun, wind, and stream in vv. 5-7, is true also of the human world. To see these three phrases as epitomizing the 'fruitless nature of human activity' as Murphy does (1992: 9) adds a value judgment that is not present in the text.

Thus the thesis of 1.4a is demonstrated in 1.5-8.

1.9-10 The immovable steadfast world, within which nature pursues its regular course, is the subject of 1.4b. Under different imagery, vv. 9-11 will relate to this theme.

Two parallel clauses stress that the future is the past. What will transpire in the future is that which has already been. Again the notion of cyclic recurrence, expressed through the existential verb 'be', relates expressly to the thesis of the permanence of the world. This general principle will be applied theologically in 3.14-15, so that we are better able to understand Qoheleth's thought. (Note how the two verbs *'āśāh*, 'do', and *hāyāh,* 'be', are used together in both passages.) The earth is unchanging because of the enduring nature of God and of what he does. Past, present, and future are all of one piece, indivisible. Thus Qoheleth is able to claim that nothing 'under the sun' is new.

'Newness' is not a category for describing this-worldly matters. This cryptic statement requires explanation. Qoheleth has asked (1.3) whether *yitrôn* is attainable 'under the sun'. He now suggests (v. 10) that 'under the sun' is not the appropriate place to look for *yitrôn* (cf. 2.11). For that which is completely novel we must step outside this world and think in broader other-worldly terms. One who observes something apparently 'new', actually is appreciating for the first time a fact long since in existence. To claim that something is novel indicates one's inexperience and thus folly. One schooled in the traditions of the sages would have learned that those in the past also encountered and pondered such questions. We note that the word 'already', *k^{e}bar,* is peculiar to Qoheleth in the OT.

1.11 Consistent with the theme of past and future in vv. 9-10, v. 11 speaks of former people *(ri'šōnîm)* and people yet to come *('aḥ^{a}rônîm)*. Of these two groups, Qoheleth suggests that there is no remembrance *(zikrôn)* of persons by succeeding generations. One cannot expect to live on in the collective memory, and thus have an 'after life'. Such hope is illusory.

Are we in a position now to know why Qoheleth quotes this poem? I suggest that the poem is to justify Qoheleth's present study. Qoheleth's point of departure is the fact of human existence. Life is a permanent feature of the world, even though we may trace within it an ebb and flow, as in the examples from nature. In a natural environment marked by permanence, by cyclic flow, humanity seeks to comprehend life—that which is seen as 'new' is actually the 'recurrent past'. Newness, be it of ideas or events, is not to be sought 'under the sun'. The pity of it is that just as we have failed to remember the past, so future generations will likewise fail to recall us and our achievements. We have no abiding place, no permanence in this world. This situation sets the stage for Qoheleth's discussion of *yitrôn*. He indicates that we cannot depend on answers from the past; each generation must itself face the question of life and meaning. Each generation facing the same questions as those in the past is another expression of the cycle of life; a challenge certainly, but not a fruitless one.

On this basis, we conclude that 1.4-11 argues the necessity of undertaking the following examination. Qoheleth will now go on to record his personal attempt to answer the question of life's meaning in the hope that it might be of some help to others.

1.12-18 The Quest

This brief section finds Qoheleth advising of his serious and personal pilgrimage in pursuit of an answer to the motivating question of 1.3. It gives the appearance of being in two parallel parts (vv. 13-15 and vv. 16-18), both of which conclude with an aphorism. However, the expressions used in each segment are not sufficiently alike to allow that conclusion to be pressed.

1.12 An autobiographical statement from Qoheleth, this verse differs from 1.1, which is an editorial statement. As regards content, however, 1.12 varies little from 1.1—Qoheleth does claim that he was 'king over Israel' rather than over Judah, and this clearly is meant to indicate the time of the united monarchy, the time of Solomon more specifically. It also leaves the impression that the author once was king but now has ceased to reign. The most satisfactory explanation is that the author is speaking of the time when Solomon was king, thus making even clearer the fact that Solomonic authorship is a literary convention. Qoheleth uses the accepted form of a royal declaration, one generally acknowledged as having Egyptian antecedents (see Crenshaw, *Old Testament Form Criticism*, 1974: 256-57), but perhaps modified in line with wisdom's conventions. Some scholars have suggested that this may well have been the initial introduction to the book, but this cannot be proved.

1.13,14 Qoheleth devoted his mind to the investigation of what transpires on earth (v. 13a). It is to be a comprehensive study of everything that is done under the heavens (*'al kol-'ᵃšer naʿᵃśeh taḥat haššāmayim*) The tool for this investigation was 'wisdom' (*ḥokmāh*), by which he means the inherited tradition of the wise men together with its method of observation and reflection. We are left with the clear impression that the object of his research refers to all human activity, rather than to situations in the natural world, a fact which correlates with the basic question asked in 1.3. In parallel with v. 13a is v. 14a. The scope of the investigation is comprehensive, embracing 'all the deeds they do under the sun.'

The latter half of each of these two verses establishes a temporary conclusion, temporary because it is still a long way from Qoheleth's final statement. However, by suggesting at the outset of his report what his initial response to the human situation is, we are at once allowed to feel something of the pain and frustration which accompanied his investigation. He tells us that everything he has observed is *'inyān ra'*, translated as 'unhappy business' (RSV). The root *'ānāh* (II), which is unique to Qoheleth in Biblical Hebrew, links with an Aramaic term describing one who is occupied with some task. The noun *'inyān*, therefore, is one's work; the qualifying term, *ra'*, suggests pain (cf. 2.23). When describing human action, *ra'* may comment on its moral value—it is an evil (cf. 3.16). On the other hand, if *ra'* is applied to what God does, it may be used as a parallel to *hebel* (cf. 2.21), in which case it forms part of the vocabulary of frustration. Our life, including the work God gives us, lies within the realm of that which we cannot fully comprehend, the enigmatic. The thought that work is what God gives us, is one which will recur in most of the 'nothing is better... than...' phrases (2.24; 3.13; 5.17[18]; 8.15).

The second and parallel temporary conclusion (v. 14b) uses the balanced phrases, *hebel*, 'enigma', and *r^{e}'ût rûaḥ*, 'striving after the wind' (RSV). This latter expression suggests the shepherd attempting to herd the wind as he would herd the sheep and goats. In other words, he is attempting something beyond his power to control. The interim conclusion is profound—human life and work, those elements that are God-given and that furnish our being and identity, are ultimately outside our power to understand as fully as we may wish.

1.15 To emphasize the point made, Qoheleth quotes an aphorism which carries the same theme—certain realities cannot be changed. Its structure consists of two parallel cola each with a noun + *lô' yûkal*—infinitive construct with prefixed preposition *l^{e}*.

That which has been twisted (*m^{e}'uwwāt*—pual participle of *'āwāh*) cannot be straightened out, nor arranged in neat order (*tqn*). Similarly, if something is missing or absent (*ḥesrôn*), there is no way in which it can be measured. Within the wisdom tradition, from which we presume the saying to be drawn, *'āwāh* may portray one whose mind is perverted (Prov. 12.8; Job 33.27) or foolish, while *ḥāsēr* is applied to those who lack understanding (Prov. 6.32; 7.7; 9.4 in the phrase *ḥ*^a^*sar-lēb*). Although the quotation has this pejorative background, the function it serves in its present location is that of supporting the interim conclusion that humans have to work within certain limitations. These limitations are, like the fool, a reality which we cannot change.

1.16 This verse opens with one of Qoheleth's frequent expressions for the reflective portion of his investigation—'I said to myself' (2.1; 3.17, 18). He considers his many achievements in the field of wisdom, determining that he has reached heights greater than any previous royal figure in Jerusalem (cf. 2.9). That Qoheleth was a royal personage seems implicit in the phrase 'all those who were before me over Jerusalem'. However, we have already seen (1.12) that this is essentially a literary device. If he were Solomon, the tradition behind the claim is recognized, but in reality there were only two previous occupants of the Jerusalem throne, so that this royal claim is rather a hollow one. The other unusual feature of his vaunting assessment is that he claims to be wiser than any previous figure—a claim based on a premise already determined as false (1.9-11).

Qoheleth additionally boasts that his heart (*lēb*, 'mind') has 'seen' (*rā'āh*) much wisdom and knowledge. This expression is peculiar to Qoheleth (2.12; 9.13).

1.17 In terms reminiscent of v. 13, Qoheleth presses on with the story of his search. On this occasion he is not investigating human work, but more the intellectual dimension. The verb *yāda'*, 'know', is inseparable from the experience of life, rather than speaking of acquired information, and so Qoheleth testifies to his personal undertaking to experience the entire world of wisdom and folly. The tendency to divide human awareness so simply into 'wisdom' and 'folly' is a device which the wisdom tradition used to sharpen its presentation of advice. Qoheleth has thoroughly investigated both. His interim conclusion about this task is that it also is like trying to 'shepherd' or control the wind—it is a task for which human beings do not have the resources. Qoheleth in v. 14 has used the phrase *r*^e^*'ût rûaḥ*, but here uses a slightly different form, *ra'*^a^*yôn rûaḥ*. We presume that the root meaning is the same and that these are parallel ideas.

1.18 Closely bound to the preceding sub-section by its use of keywords (*da'at, ḥokmāh, yāsap*), this verse has every appearance of an aphorism (as v. 15). The purpose of the quotation is made clear by the introductory *kî*, 'because,' which links it to the previous verse as its explanatory or supporting evidence. As for structure, we note two parallel cola (cf. v. 15)—verb + wisdom term + repeated verb + noun.

Having set himself to explore wisdom, Qoheleth came to the conclusion, similar to that expressed in the tradition, that to gain more knowledge and wisdom was at the same time to add to one's burden (cf. 12.11-12). Nothing of value can be gained without some measure of hardship and suffering.

At this point in Qoheleth's report we have no specific information about what he discovered, so that we are as yet unaware of the basis for such a conclusion. However, the statement itself alerts us to look for forthcoming evidence that illustrates the point made. This we shall find in places such as 2.12-17, 20.

One might be tempted to think that Qoheleth in v. 18 has reached an impasse—especially if we see the keyword *hebel* as expressing futility and meaningless activity—or that he would be justified in abandoning his pursuit. However, that is not what happens. Qoheleth actually moves forward from this position to search for a way or ways in which, within the limitations acknowledged, he and all others must operate. He must press ahead with the attempt to discover whether there is or is not some *yitrôn* for the wise in this world. There is a level of commitment in Qoheleth's search for wisdom that borders on the compulsive. As a sage he knows that there are no ready answers to the issues that confront the human species, but he can do no other than press ahead with his search despite the difficulties and frustrations that await him. His dedication to this task is caught up in the phrase with which 1.13 and 1.17 open—*nātattî 'et-libbî,* 'I devoted my mind to...'

Chapter 2

The Quest for 'Advantage' Begins

2.1-11 Testing Pleasure

2.1 The opening phrase, similar to 1.16, shows Qoheleth musing about the best way to begin his investigation into life's 'advantage'. The first aspect of life he intends to explore is 'pleasure' (*śimḥāh*). Such exploration is not a self-indulgent flight, but a scientific undertaking—note the verb 'test' (*nsh*)—pursued in a detached manner. The phrase *rᵉ'ēh bᵉṭôb* is rendered 'enjoy yourself' by the RSV, but we must admit that this is a rather loose translation. The verb *rā'āh* is one of Qoheleth's key words, and regularly applies to his observation of life. It speaks of more than casting a casual eye over things; it connotes a scientific and empirical examination of the realities of human life. As for *ṭôb*, we note its frequency in the book as a whole; it represents another central concept. Used here, it carries no moral content, but identifies all that is of advantage, all that is positive and good. In this note Qoheleth reminds himself to look closely into the 'better', happier aspect of life and the good it produces.

As a result of his investigations, he determines that pleasure is ultimately *hebel*, which is to say, it is frustrating since it cannot provide the *yitrôn* for which he was seeking. The section thus opens with a general verdict that will be supported in the following verses, and rounded off with the final conclusion in verse 11.

2.2 Qoheleth elaborates on the response to this research. As for 'laughter' (*śᵉḥôq*), and 'pleasure', he failed to find in them anything of 'advantage'. Actually, he believed them to be folly (*mᵉhôlāl*), what Crenshaw characterizes as 'calculated irrationality'. Pleasure was enjoyable, but still unanswered was the question of its function and value. The phrase, 'what use is it?' (RSV) may be better rendered, 'what is this (i.e. pleasure) going to accomplish?' *(mah-zôh 'āśāh)*.

2.3 The investigation (the verb *tûr* speaks of exploration and spying out; cf. 1.13; Ezek. 20.6) into life's *yitrôn* continues in accordance with the dictates of wisdom. There is a note of apologetic here as Qoheleth does not wish to be misunderstood as hedonistic. The significance of the participle *nôhēg*, 'lead', is that it identifies an on-going process, the key role played by his intellect as he pursued the experiment. But what exactly is it that Qoheleth does to 'cheer his body with wine' (*limšôk bayyayin 'et-b^eśārî*)? The verb *māšak* means 'to draw', or 'attract', but such a meaning seems inappropriate here. Hence the suggestion (Delitzsch and others) that we translate it as 'stimulate', or 'refresh' on the basis of a later Jewish usage (Talmud—*Ḥagigah* 14a). Seow (1997: 127) argues for a meaning 'induce', or 'to lead along'. For Lohfink (2003: 51) it means 'bathe (my body)'. Qoheleth partakes of wine to see whether this kind of involvement will prove to be folly or not (*'āḥaz b^esiklût*). (The noun *siklût* is found only in Qoheleth: 2.3, 12, 13; 7.25; 10.1, 11) The experiment is to persist to the point where Qoheleth is able to discover finally what is good or beneficial to a person during life. The word 'good' is nominal, with the meaning' good things', and is related to Qoheleth's several references to the benefits of eating, drinking, and enjoying the work that God gives (e.g. 2.24; 3.12 etc.).

2.4-6 Another aspect of Qoheleth's research was to establish a name for himself (*higdaltî*) as a builder. This would fit well with the image of Solomon, whose building programme was legendary (1 Kgs 7; 9.10). Vineyards were planted, gardens and parklands established (*Pardēs*, 'park', is a Persian loan-word, which in Greek becomes *paradeisos*, 'paradise') and in them various fruit trees were planted reminiscent of the Edenic Garden in Genesis 2. This allusion to Eden is clearly evident in the vocabulary used, but what Verheij notes (1991: 113-15) is that Qoheleth is claiming here not just to be a king like Solomon but to be as God. If this view can be sustained, then the results of Qoheleth's endeavours are quite the opposite of what God was able to do in creation—for Qoheleth, all was *hebel*.

Pools for ornamental and water-storage purposes were built. In an arid climate, water storage in rock-hewn cisterns was of vital importance. Archaeological evidence from cities such as Hazor and Megiddo, and Hezekiah's tunnel into Jerusalem, testify to water's importance in the life of the community. Qoheleth, however, claims to have constructed these pools mainly for ornamental purposes, as testimony to his wealth, power, and position.

2.7 His elevated position in society was evident also in the number of servants, male (*ʿ^{a}bādîm*) and female (*š^{e}pāḥôt*), he employed. Children of these latter (*b^{e}nē-bayit*) were further signs of blessing and prosperity. Cattle and sheep added to his prestige, they being customary measures of wealth and status in society. Of these latter he possessed more than any previous resident of Jerusalem (cf. 1.16). The implication is that there were many such persons, thus enhancing even more Qoheleth's reputation.

2.8 Further evidence of Qoheleth's material wealth is seen in his 'bank account' (*s^{e}gullāh*)—he amassed (*kns*) gold and silver (see also 1 Chron 29.3). The source of this great wealth is not indicated, but Qoheleth appears to imply that it came from conquests as tribute, as well as from revenues paid by subject rulers and provinces (*m^{e}dînôt*). The use of *m^{e}dînôt*, 'cities', is generally limited to later OT books as it is an Aramaic word (cf. Esth. 1.1, 3, 22; Dan. 8.2; 11.24), descriptive of political divisions in the Babylonian and Persian empires.

Other trappings of royal office are implied by the words 'singers' and 'concubines'. These are symbolic of *taʿ^{a}nûgôt*, the life of luxury (cf. Mic. 2.9), the full phrase referring to those things treasured by people. However, the precise meaning of the final term *šiddāh w^{e}šiddôt*, which the RSV translates as 'concubines', is not entirely certain. It perhaps refers to sensual and erotic pleasures, and one can understand this claim if the life of Solomon provides the model for Qoheleth's presentation (1 Kings 7). However, Seow (1997: 131) points out that the more likely explanation is that it refers to a box for holding the treasures. As a *hapax* its meaning will remain in dispute.

Thus in 2.4-8 Qoheleth catalogues various areas in which his achievements are more than considerable. The purpose, however, is clear. He is testing each area for life's *yitrôn*. His many achievements could be described as *ṭôb*, as good things in and of themselves. The motivation for the investigation, and the thoroughness with which it was undertaken, cannot be questioned, and Qoheleth deliberately makes these exhaustive claims to assure the reader that the conclusions which follow are not without foundation.

2.9-11 In summary form, Qoheleth refers back to his endeavours and achievements detailed in vv. 4-8. Two verbs already used in a similar manner in 1.16 (*gdl*, 'be great', and *ysp*, 'surpass'), together with the phrase 'more than all who preceded me in Jerusalem', describe his singular success. He adds, as he does in 2.3, that this entire programme was an experiment conducted throughout according to the guidelines set by wisdom (*'ap ḥokmātî 'āmᵉdāh lî*). Use of the word *'md*, 'stand', indicates his firm resolve, or perhaps better, wisdom provided the foundation and solid basis from which he worked.

Whatever he laid eyes on, or whatever his eyes craved to see (*šā'ᵃlû 'ēnay*) he was happy to acquiesce to (*lô' 'āṣaltî mēhem*), denying himself nothing (*lô' māna'tî*) in the way of pleasure. Qoheleth affirms that this 'work' of plumbing the depths of pleasure, indeed had its 'reward', *ḥēleq* (cf. 3.22; 5.17[18]; 9.9). Pleasure provides an immediate sense of enjoyment, and Qoheleth appreciates that. However, that is not all he is looking for. In v. 11 Qoheleth speaks of the reflective process which must follow any such experiment. This process is depicted by the verb *pānāh*, meaning 'to turn one's face towards', 'to look', and thus 'to consider' (cf. Job 6.28). Upon reflection, Qoheleth concludes that the 'portion' he derived from his work was, in the final analysis, *hebel*; it was like trying to 'shepherd the wind'. Thus *yitrôn* is elusive, a meaning that *hebel* seems clearly to carry at this point. Here under the sun *yitrôn* was not to be discovered. In fact the phrase 'under the sun' (cf. 1.13) in this context serves to emphasize that even to expect to find *yitrôn* on earth or during one's lifetime is wrong-headed. The rhetorical connections between 1.3 and 2.11 indicate that the latter stands as the first formal response to the fundamental question about *yitrôn* with which Qoheleth's search began (1.3). In terms of the structure of the work to this point, it becomes obvious that all the material intervening between 1.3 and 2.11 serves the purpose of leading us from the question to its answer.

Several key words have been used in 2.9-11, words which will occur again in similar concluding statements, so it is important for us to spend a moment clarifying their meaning. One key word is 'toil' (*'āmāl*), used for the first time in 1.3 but mentioned four times in this segment, and used altogether fifteen times in this chapter (half of the total uses in the book). In view of the parallelism in v. 11, we can determine that Qoheleth understands 'toil' in terms of the physical work in which one engages to sustain life. It describes whatever one does in the pursuit of pleasure (2.10); it also provides a source of enjoyment (2.24). Though at times 'toil' may prove difficult and require effort (2.22), yet throughout the book Qoheleth would have us believe that it has none but a positive value.

A second important keyword here is 'portion' (*ḥēleq*), sometimes translated 'lot' (3.22; cf. Wis. 2.9). Qoheleth uses the word principally in conjunction with 'toil'. From its several occurrences (2.10, 21; 3.22; 5.17[18]; 9.6, 9; 11.2) it is obvious that it refers to the accomplishments or pleasure derived from doing the work God intends for us. Its compass, however, is limited, for although in toiling a person may obtain a 'portion', it is very much this-worldly and distinct from *yitrôn*. And ultimately it is *yitrôn*, 'advantage', he seeks. Additionally, one's 'portion' does not provide enjoyment as an inevitable end (6.3); it is subject to risk (5.12-13), and has to be left to one's heirs at death (2.18-19). These are severe limitations indeed, but certainly not such that make it 'meaningless and worthless' as Krüger (2004: 67) argues.

2.12-17 Testing Wisdom and Folly

2.12 This verse opens with Qoheleth's only other use of the verb *pānāh,* with the meaning 'to consider', 'to face' (cf. 2.11). On this occasion Qoheleth resolves to observe two opposing values: wisdom, and madness *(hôlēlôt)* or folly *(siklût).* The latter is the more frequently-used word for describing wisdom's antithesis (cf. 2.3, 13; 7.25; 10.1). 'Madness' *(hôlēlôt)* is equated with evil in 9.3, but otherwise it is used always in association with folly, and has a negative value. Despite this, in order that his investigations be as thorough as possible, Qoheleth launches an investigation of both wisdom and folly. The procedure, as before, is not that of abstract reflection, but of the practical testing of both life styles. That madness and folly is a hendiadys, indicating 'inane folly', is Fox's conclusion (1977: 183).

Following this introduction, Qoheleth adds a rhetorical question, apparently intended to strengthen his case by justifying his methodology *(meh hā'ādām šeyyābô' 'aḥ^{a}rē hammelek 'et '^{a}šer-k^{e}bār 'āśûhû).* The question is not without problems for the interpreter. Literally the question runs, 'What is the man who follows the king who has already done it?' With its meaning unclear, we turn to suggestions drawn from other textual traditions. These argue for the addition of *ya'^{a}śeh* after *hā'ādām* (see RSV). On this rendering, the implication would be that if the 'king' conducted this kind of experiment, then those who succeed him would be best advised to follow his example. Alternatively, they would not need to repeat the experiment as they could draw upon the king's own experience. Yet the question still appears odd. Seow (1997: 134) has noted that the addition of the verb 'do' is unjustified, quoting with approval Coats' point that the form *meh hā'ādām* is a self-deprecatory phrase, 'who is the person...?'. To better understand its significance, we turn to v. 18, where a like phrase, *'ādām šeyihyeh 'aḥ[a]rāy,* is used. In vv. 18-21 Qoheleth deals with doubts about the wisdom of the one who succeeds him and who inherits or gains control of his goods. Thus the question and answer in v. 12 represent the ideal he would hope to see realized that subsequent royal figures will also pursue the quest for life's meaning. Krüger (2004: 68) interprets the intention here as emphasizing the unique accomplishments of which Qoheleth boasts. The question also introduces the discussion of death and its implications.

2.13 What did Qoheleth 'see' or learn from his research? He saw that wisdom and folly were as distinguishable as day from night (cf. Prov. 6.23; Gen. 1.3-5). The use of the word *yitrôn,* 'advantage', at this point is important, for having determined that pursuit of pleasure and material success could never lead to *yitrôn* (2.11), Qoheleth asserts that *wisdom* offers the only hope for its attainment. In the light of what is to follow, this verse has the ring of a confession of faith, but it is a faith tempered by the reality of death as the final end of every creature.

2.14 The wise person is one who walks in the light—Hebrew idiom here speaks of having 'eyes in one's head'; eyes open, the sage has knowledge and acts accordingly. By contrast, the fool is likened to one who stumbles in the dark, uninformed, and a danger to himself and others. Despite such an obvious contrast, Qoheleth has to admit that both wise and fool face the same 'fate' (*miqreh*). Qoheleth's response is introduced by *yāda'tî gam '[a]nî,* a forceful expression, meaning 'Even I can recognize that...' It gives the impression that he is reluctant to face the fact of this common end for all. What is this common fate which both fool and wise alike must face? On the basis of what follows in vv. 15-17 and 3.19 (see also 9.3), it is unquestionably 'death' to which he is referring rather than mere 'contingency' or 'chance'. As the book unfolds, we discover that the most persistent problem which Qoheleth faces is that of death, the universal and unavoidable end that relativizes all distinctions between wise and fool.

2.15 As he ponders the inevitability of his own death, Qoheleth recognizes that being wise can do nothing to prevent or to forestall that event despite the faith statement of some that the wicked and foolish perish early (Prov. 10.27 and the deuteronomic tradition generally). Thus the next question for him is, 'what value does wisdom carry if I, like the fool, must die also?' In the text itself there are some difficulties. What the RSV renders as 'so very (wise)' is the word *yôtēr*. The other uses of this word in 7.16 and 12.9 have led to the view that here also the meaning is adverbial. It is just conceivable that v. 15b could be rendered, 'why have I been wise? Have I then some advantage?' However, in view of the uncertainty surrounding it, we shall remain with the interpretation familiar from the RSV.

Qoheleth answers his own question (v. 15c)—it is a mystery (*hebel*); there is no final answer!

2.16 Wise and fool share one other prospect: after death they are little remembered (cf. 1.11; 9.5, 13-16). The statement is set forth here as a bald fact. After death there is no permanent memorial to either the wise man or the fool. One dies, and is forgotten. This sentiment is expressed also in Ps. 49.10-20, in one of the so-called wisdom psalms, and flies in the face of sayings to the contrary (e.g. Prov. 10.7). Qoheleth almost plaintively cries that death is blind to the merits of the wise over the fool, taking issue with any who would claim otherwise; death is utterly impartial and indiscriminate. The bond between wise and fool in their common death is highlighted literarily by the reiterated phrase *heḥākām ʿim hakkᵉsîl.*

2.17 If wise and fool stand so clearly divided in life, but are bound together at death, what implications are there for Qoheleth's investigations?

Qoheleth pours out deep feelings of revulsion at this situation—'I hated life' (cf. Jer. 20.14, where Jeremiah rues the day of his birth). 'Life' is here expressed as a plural, *ḥayyîm,* to indicate that it is the totality of human life that is in mind. He is appalled at all that happens on earth, a situation he can describe only as *raʿ*. This term may denote what is immoral or evil, but may be applied equally to that which is intolerable, or distressing. He further adds the *hebel* phrase from 1.14 to draw greater attention to the enigmatic nature of such a situation and to his inability to comprehend it. Qoheleth is pained not only by the heavy burden (*ʿālay*, 'upon') of the universality of death, but by his own inability to explain it. This is particularly so when wisdom is of such demonstrable value in life itself. We see in this crisis Qoheleth's urgent need to find some solution to the apparent injustice of death's impartiality—clearly *yitrôn* is not to be found before or at death. Thus he leads the reader to question along with him whether perhaps after death there is a *yitrôn*.

2.18-23 Is Toil Worthwhile?

2.18-19 As in 2.11, where Qoheleth concludes that 'pleasure' produced only a 'portion' or limited enjoyment, so here. The testing of wisdom and folly leave other unanswered questions.

The keyword in this section is 'toil' *('āmāl),* that process of labouring and accumulating a reward. Under shadow of death, Qoheleth accepts the fact that what he accumulates from his work must be left for another to inherit. The pain of this situation resides not so much in the fact that another will be master of (*šlṭ*) that for which Qoheleth has toiled, but in the fact that the heir may be either wise or foolish (cf. Ps. 39.6). Over this matter Qoheleth cannot exercise any control. The question, 'who knows...?' (v. 19), is actually an affirmation that nobody knows, least of all Qoheleth himself, whether the heir will act wisely or not. The sense of frustration (*hebel*) which Qoheleth expresses is almost tangible. It is also bound closely with the idea that there is no memorial to the wise man—the heir may dismiss from his mind the wise conduct exemplified in his predecessor.

In v. 12 Qoheleth raised the question of what one who 'came after the king' would do. The idealized answer he offered was that such a person would pursue the same course as himself. In v. 18 he repeats the idea of one who comes after him. However, here in v. 19, his confidence that the heir will be wise having been undermined, the more positive attitude of 2.12 has dissipated. Hence the cry that this situation is *hebel.*

2.20-21 In a recall of sentiments from v. 17, Qoheleth reacts to this situation. He turns (*sbb*), either for the first time or yet again, to despair. The word 'despair' (*lᵉya'ēš*) is a piel infinitive, an intensive form allowing Qoheleth to express the depth of his feelings. It is a term rarely used in the OT and is found only in 1 Sam. 27.1; Isa. 57.10; Jer. 2.25; 18.12; Job 6.26. His despair is not directed against life itself in this instance so much as it is against 'toil', his work and its reward. The cause for despair we read in v. 21. Qoheleth points to the example of one whose work depends upon wisdom, knowledge, and skill. ('Skill', *kišrôn,* used only here and in 4.4 and 5.10, has a root meaning of 'prosperity'.) This three-fold expression speaks of one with the highest of qualifications, so one might expect that the rewards from his toil were not inconsiderable. However, all gain would ultimately fall into the hands of an heir who did not exemplify those same high qualities (*lô' 'āmāl bô*). The translation of this latter phrase depends upon the meaning given to the preposition *bô*, literally 'in it.' Two possibilities present themselves. In parallel with the first part of the verse, *bô* refers back to the tripartite instrumental phrase. Thus the heir did not work with the same wisdom, knowledge, and skill. The second possibility is that *bô* means *for it,* that is to say, he did not work for what he inherited. Although this latter is probably the most widely accepted interpretation, the first possibility is preferable because Qoheleth appears intent upon making a distinction between one who works wisely and one who does not. Of this situation Qoheleth opines that it is an enigma. Even more so, it is a disaster (*rā'āh rabbāh*).

At this point Qoheleth appears to have abandoned himself to a thoroughly pessimistic spirit. But is this where he remains? Can we take this statement as an accurate reflection of his mind? No. We must, as he did, keep things in perspective, and that perspective is provided by the overall structure of 1.3-2.26 and its question-answer-response format. Although at this juncture in his presentation, Qoheleth gives the impression that he is drowning in self-pity, he in fact rises from that point to the positive thoughts expressed in the climactic words of vv. 24-26.

2.22-23 As this first section of Qoheleth's report concludes, he repeats the question which has been his direction throughout. Its form, to all intents and purposes, is the same as 1.3, for minor variations are not significant ones, despite the fact that the keyword *yitrôn* is absent. He asks what he has achieved by all the physical and mental toil he has exerted. The question is put in general terms, as he asks it for all who are pondering the meaning and value of life—*meh hōweh lā'ādām*, 'what is there for any person who...?' The use of *hōweh le*, a participial form (cf. Neh. 6.6), enables Qoheleth to highlight what one currently has as a result of toiling. What the RSV translates as 'strain', is the word *ra'yôn lēb*. From the root *r'h*, this noun form has been used in 1.17 to portray the attempt to 'shepherd' the wind (RSV 'striving). In this context Qoheleth applies the term to mental activity, asking what measurable results there are from the physical and mental effort applied to all his investigations outlined in 2.1-21.

The physical and mental aspects of the question in v. 22 are paralleled in v. 23, where Qoheleth portrays the never-ending ('day' and 'night') struggle to analyse and comprehend. 'All his days' may speak either of the duration of his life, or mean 'all day long.' The pain (*mak'ôbîm*) he senses may be either mental or physical, and here the word stands possibly as the predicate in a nominal sentence, as does 'vexation' (*ka'as*) which accompanies the noun *'inyān*, 'business'. Thus Qoheleth speaks of labouring all day, then at night when his mind seeks rest he finds none, his experiences and observations inhibiting sleep. Such a situation is beyond Qoheleth's power to comprehend.

Thus in 2.12-23 Qoheleth has focused on two major issues: (1) the utter impartiality of death which strikes both wise and fool alike, and (2) one's inability to determine how an heir might use one's accumulated and hard-earned goods. These are issues which have little to do with one's own accomplishments during life. His point becomes clearer. Material reward for hard work cannot prevent or delay death. After death, one's heir is completely free to use the inheritance in whatever way he or she pleases. Thus to place ultimate value on such material things is folly. Surely there is something more available to the wise man not only during this life but also beyond death. This is where one must look for *yitrôn*.

2.24-26 Qoheleth's Advice

The significance of this section for interpreting Qoheleth's message is especially great, and it is so for two reasons: one is its content, the positive advice it offers; the other reason is structural, by which is meant that it stands as the response which Qoheleth makes both to the programmatic question (1.3; 2.22) and the negative answer he offers to that question in 2.11. Thus from 1.3 to 2.24 the author moves, via this structure, from problem to solution. Yes, life has its problems and its frustrations, its dark side, but it also provides some tangible reward to the worker. Despite the fact that life has this enigmatic dimension, is fraught with problems and pain, to Qoheleth's mind there is only one possible attitude to adopt: enjoy what God gives.

The form of expression in v. 24 (*'ēn ṭôb...*) will be found again in 3.12, 22 and 8.15, with its sentiments expressed in a variant form in 5.17[18] and 9.7-10 (see Ogden, 1979). In inviting the reader to enjoy his toil, Qoheleth utilizes three principle verbs, 'eat' (*'ākal*), 'drink' (*šātāh*), and 'take pleasure in' (*śāmaḥ*). Qoheleth justifies this advice on the grounds that this is the divine intention for us; it is God's gift (v. 25).

As each call to enjoyment follows a similar and basic pattern, our next question has to do with the reason Qoheleth advocated these particular activities. Each represents a fundamental activity, hardly high-minded or 'spiritual'—or are they? Eating and drinking are vital to the sustaining of life. (In the Lord's Prayer we are also invited to request that our daily 'bread' be provided regularly.) When the OT portrays the promised land as 'flowing with milk and honey' (Deut. 6.3), we note a similar sentiment. God provides us with what is basic to our survival—we are therefore to eat, drink, and take pleasure in these activities, as well as in the toil and its rewards which are additionally part of the divine bounty. Qoheleth is life-affirming because he envisages human life in all its mystery as a gift of God. He may at times feel despair, and on occasion 'hate' life both for what he sees and experiences in it, but these are only passing responses. His final and decisive response, and thus his advice to all, is 'take and eat', for God has given you life. Presumably this is also the attitude which will, because of its wisdom, lead to *yitrôn*.

Owing to the appearance of an unusual verb, *ḥûš,* in v. 25, some MSS (LXX, and Syr.) have amended the text at this point to conform to that of v. 24, *šātāh*. However, as *ḥûš* means 'to enjoy'; the alteration is not called for. Seow (1997: 140), however, argues that its meaning here is similar to an Arabic term meaning 'to gather, glean'. Another odd feature of the text of v. 25 is the reading *mimmennî,* 'from me', which seems inappropriate. It is better to read *mimmennû,* 'from him'.

If v. 25 is Qoheleth's justification for the advice in v. 24, the status of v. 26 requires clarification. Both verses begin with the particle *kî,* which suggests that v. 26 runs a parallel course to v. 25. The reference to 'joy' as divine gift in both further cements their relationship. In v. 26 we detect two contrasting situations, the one 'good' *(ṭôb),* the other sinful *(ḥôṭe');* the sinner or fool works for the welfare of the good person. For Crenshaw (1987: 90), following Ginsberg, the two contrasting terms take on a different meaning in this present context, akin to 'fortunate' (*ṭôb*) and 'unfortunate' (*ḥôṭe'*). What exactly is implied by the phrase, 'gathering and heaping' *(le'ᵉsôp wᵉliknôs)* is unclear (cf. also *kns* in 3.5). Our basic problem here is one of consistency, for v. 26 appears to claim that God's gifts are essentially for the good (= wise, pleasing to God) person's enjoyment, while the fool

(= sinner, offensive to God) works for the benefit of the good. This statement contrasts with that of v. 21, where the gifts of God to the wise are actually enjoyed by the heir, and that without his working for them; in fact, the wise is working for the sake of the heir, who may well be a fool. Such an apparent inconsistency has led to the suggestion that v. 26 is not the view of Qoheleth but of a more 'orthodox' editor who attempted to balance the original statement with something more acceptable (Podechard, 1912). However, we must recognize that in this book there are many such contrasting viewpoints set alongside one another (cf. 3.17,18; also Gordis, 1968: 95-108). The wisdom tradition knew full well that no single statement could encompass all truth. Thus it is most likely that 2.26 with its deliberately positive note, is intended to heighten the notion that on occasion the wise is actually better off than the fool, and this is despite his occasional bad experience noted in 2.21. Neither 2.21 nor 2.26 can represent the totality of truth, but each may be true given certain circumstances. The purpose of v. 26 is to lend support to the advice contained in the section vv. 24-25.

The situation outlined in v. 26 is, like that of v. 21, difficult to comprehend (i.e. *hebel*). This section also reminds us that the word *hebel* can be applied to either negative (v. 21) or positive (v. 26) situations, indicating clearly that the traditional rendering 'vanity' is most inappropriate.

Chapter 3

All in God's Time

As we progress from ch. 2, in which Qoheleth highlighted his own considerable achievements, we notice that in ch. 3 the emphasis moves to what God does. This transition is significant as it reflects the issue with which Qoheleth is grappling, namely humanity's place in God's world.

3.1-15 God's Control of Events

This section has a distinctive theme—time—which separates it from the previous chapter. Its terminal point we are able to fix at 3.15 on the grounds that vv. 16-22 address a different subject. Despite this radical change within the chapter, there are elements which 3.16-22 share with 3.1-15, such as the time reference in v. 17, and this fact assists us in uncovering the reason for the two sections being juxtaposed.

Within 3.1-15 we observe minor subdivisions which carry the argument. In 3.1 an introductory statement is followed in vv. 2-8 by a catalogue of 'times'. Our programmatic question from 1.3 reappears in 3.9, then Qoheleth turns to observe (v. 10), and to draw conclusions from his observations (vv. 12, 14). The final verse is reminiscent of thoughts in the opening poem (1.9).

3.1-8 The 'Time' Poem

3.1 Every earthly event (*ḥēpeṣ*) occurs at a determined moment of time. Underlying this introductory statement is the conviction that creation is marked by an orderliness which originates in the divine plan and will. This concept is one of the basic building blocks of wisdom theology (cf. Zimmerli). There is here also an echo of the order and innate goodness of creation as expressed in Genesis 1 (cf. also Sir. 16.24—17.14).

Every event (*ḥēpeṣ*) has its time (*'ēt*). In stating this principle, Qoheleth reveals an up-beat, positive attitude, *ḥēpeṣ* coming from the root *ḥpṣ*, 'to find pleasure in'. Even though in later OT literature the word has a more general meaning, 'matter', and although in the following poem both good and evil are together included in its compass, nevertheless the impression given in v. 1 is that when events rest in God's hand, it is not something to cause alarm. Two terms are used here for 'time'. The first, *zᵉmān,* is a word in late Hebrew connoting 'appointed time', the root *zmn* meaning 'to purpose', 'devise' (cf. Esth. 9.27; Neh. 2.6). The second term, *'ēt,* describes moments or points of time.

3.2-8 The 'poem' with which Qoheleth illustrates the principle enunciated, contains a series of twenty-eight contrasting elements (see Loader, 1979: 29-33). Of these, all but the final pair are expressed by means of *'ēt* plus the infinitive construct. The effect of this literary feature is to produce a poem with reiterated vowel sounds, especially the long 'o' vowel characteristic of the qal infinitive construct. That the poem was originally an independent work and is here quoted by Qoheleth is most likely in view of the fact that most of the concepts and verbs of which it is composed are not found elsewhere in the book. For Blenkinsopp (1996: 57) it represents a passage 'cited but not authored by Qoheleth as a foil to his own distinctive and untraditional views about human existence'. It almost certainly comes from within the wisdom tradition, and, as Crenshaw suggests ('The Eternal Gospel', p. 34), is onomastica-like in form (see also Whybray, 1989: 66). Qoheleth quotes this poem partly to introduce once again the programmatic question in v. 9, and partly in illustration of the thesis of v. 1.

The paired actions in v. 2—birth, death; planting, uprooting—relate to the initial and terminal points of the life-cycle. In the case of birth and death, they are events over which human beings have no control. Humans are born and die at a time not of their own choosing. The activities of planting and uprooting or 'harvesting' are the beginning and end points of normal agricultual activity. They also may allude to human life *per se,* to human endeavour or work. These paired actions pick up the theme of death already raised in 2.12-17. (The uprooting of what has been planted may refer literally to the process of harvesting, as Dahood has argued, but the more basic sense is what Krüger [p.77] has called a 'hostile' act.)

Verse 3 has a chiastic relationship with v. 2 in the sense that destructive actions or end-events in v. 3—killing, demolishing—are placed before the constructive actions of healing and building.

Presumably killing and healing are paired actions directed against a fellow human being, while demolishing and constructing are architectural activities.

Similarly in the balanced clauses in v. 4, weeping and lamenting appear first, with expressions of joy—laughing, dancing—constituting the second matching pair in the latter half of each clause. Emotional responses to differing situations are the focus here.

The first pair of contrasts in v. 5a, b is not completely intelligible, for it speaks of 'stones' (*'ᵃbānîm*) to be 'scattered' (*šlk*) or 'gathered' (*kns*). The stones may be literal stones, in which case some mundane reference is intended, such as clearing a field of stones in preparation for planting, or the gathering of building materials. However, in the Midrash *Qoheleth Rabbah,* the two actions specified are understood as having a sexual reference—there is a time when sexual activity is appropriate and times when it is not. We have no way of determining with any precision what the phrase means, though we should note that it remains within the pattern of contrasting actions of which the poem is composed. Nor are we required to use v. 5c, d for the explication of v. 5a, b, as no other paired actions operate in parallel fashion in this poem. In the second half of the verse, the contrasting nature of the items listed is abundantly clear—embracing (*ḥbq*) and refraining from embracing (*rᵃḥōq mēḥabbēq*).

Searching out something (*bqš*), and its antithesis, giving up something (*'bd*) or destroying it, open the list in v. 6. The search alluded to could refer to acquiring property and losing it. The second pair has to do with keeping or holding on to something (*šmr*) as contrasted with sending it away (*šlk*, hiphil).

In v. 7, tearing (*qr'*) and sewing (*tpr*) are juxtaposed, followed by maintaining silence (*ḥšh*) and speaking (*dbr*). The tearing and sewing have been related to the practice of tearing one's clothes in mourning and then repairing them once the period of mourning was over. The poem then comes to a close with love (*'hb*) and hate (*śn'*), war (*milḥāmāh*) and peace (*šlm*), in chiastic order. Crenshaw (1987: 96) notes the chiastic pattern in these four activities.

In each paired action in 3.2-8 the emphasis is upon the antithetical nature of the activities. In seeking the meaning or significance of the poem as a whole, it is unnecessary that we assign a meaning to every element. This approach is justified not only by the general structure of the poem with its multiple contrasts, but also by the fact that each action in the poem stands without any specific context, making the contrasts themselves more stark. Nor is there any discernible pattern in the arrangement of these opposites. The poem illustrates the thesis of v. 1, that time and event are correlated. It would be going too far to suggest that each event is evaluated—this latter is the feature of the poem in ch. 7 with its many comparatives. Rather, the poem in ch. 3 makes the simple point that life is composed of many different events which, in the evaluation offered in v. 11, will be described as 'beautiful'. By illustrating this with events which stand at either end of a spectrum, Qoheleth embraces all actions that lie between those extremes. The contrasts then have an inclusive value, meaning that *everything* in life has its appropriate time, the point made so forcefully in v. 1.

Within a world ordered in this fashion, human beings must live, and Qoheleth's task is to provide advice relevant to the one who seeks to order his or her life. The question which he asks again in v. 9 (cf. 1.3) is raised against the background of a world of order. Thus the poem functions as a means of introducing further discussion of his underlying question about *yitrôn*. As in ch. 1, the poem and the question are related. In ch. 1 he first puts the question, then uses the poem to foreshadow his thesis; in ch. 3 it is the poem which comes first because he wishes to take up the issue in a different context. Here he asks whether one can find any *yitrôn* in a world which stands under divine discipline. Every event is under God's control; if so, then where does *yitrôn* lie?

3.9 Putting the Question Again

The form in which the programmatic question recurs here differs in some respects from that in 1.3 and 2.22, in that it lacks the indirect object. Here the person whose possible *yitrôn* is the subject of enquiry is *hā'ōśeh*, the 'doer', or 'worker'. On the basis of the pattern which typifies the *mah yitrôn* clauses (see Ogden, 1979: 343), we conclude that *hā'ōśeh* is identical to the *hā'ādām* used in the other examples. Thus, an individual's life as *'āmāl*, 'labour', in a world under divine orders is also the concern here. This is Qoheleth's question, and we need to bear this context in mind as we proceed with our interpretation.

3.10-15 Reflections on Time

In structuring his presentation, Qoheleth first ventures his observation (v. 10), then offers two conclusions arising therefrom (vv. 12-13, 14-15).

3.10-11 Qoheleth has observed the task (*'inyān*) which God has appointed for humankind. In 1.13, which contains much the same thought as this verse, we note the addition of *ra'*, expressive of the pain and hardship of the human endeavour. There is no comparable qualification in 3. 10, though the thought probably persists. What specifically is the 'task'? It is God-given, and in the present context presumably refers to the matter of living responsibly in a world of divine ordering, although in 2.26 the *'inyān* which God gives is the work undertaken by the sinner for the benefit of others. This suggests that at least in that particular context, *'inyān* depicts an arduous and personally fruitless task.

It is in v. 11 that we seek further elaboration of the task which Heaven assigns, and here we discover that *'inyān* is not necessarily to be construed as painful labour. God's world has both order—this is the significance of the reiterated *'ēt*—and beauty or goodness (*yāpeh*). This is the context in which humanity labours. The noun *yāpeh* can in this context also refer to the appropriateness of the moment, so that what God does takes place at times most appropriate to himself, if not to human beings. In addition, Qoheleth suggests that God has put *'ōlām* in *their* heart. First of all, to what does 'their' refer? If v. 10 and v. 11 are related, 'their' can only refer to the 'sons of men' in v. 10. Our second question relates to the meaning of the term *'ōlām*. That it is a temporal concept seems to fit the context, but scholars have differed in their opinions. If *'et* and *z^{e}man* speak of moments of time, then *'ōlām,* the new dimension of temporal awareness which God imparts, must refer to something in the time-spectrum lying beyond those moments, those extremities of time addressed in the poem. Qoheleth uses the term *'ōlam* on other occasions (cf. 1.4, 10; 2.16; 3.14; 9.6), all of which accord with the general OT usage, that is as a reference to the 'eternal' dimension, whether past or future. It is what Murphy notes as 'a divine, not a human, category' (1992: 34).

Those scholars who find this approach unacceptable suggest that *'ōlam* may speak of the sum total of time (Gese, 1962: 149; McNeile, 1904: 62, 99). For Ewald and Volz, *'ōlām* had a spatial meaning (cf. also Gordis, 1968: 231). For other scholars, textual emendation provides the solution; thus, Dahood would like to read *glm,* 'darkness', 'ignorance' (1952: 206). Others, like Scott, determine that *'ōlam* here means 'obscurity', on the grounds that the root meaning of *'lm* is 'that which is hidden'. For Whybray

(1989: 74) also it is 'ignorance'. These would also contend that the second half of the verse supports such views. Some would wish to read *'āmāl*, 'toil', in lieu of *'ōlām*. Although the following clause (v. 11b) does state that we are unable to find out what God plans, nevertheless, given the temporal setting of the chapter, we should resist any attempt to offer a solution which falls outside such a field of reference. Thus we shall accept the meaning, 'a consciousness of the eternal'. Of the seven other occasions upon which Qoheleth uses the verb *nātan* with *lēb* (1.17; 7.2, 21; 8.9, 16; 9.1), the meaning is 'to ponder', 'take cognizance of', with *lēb* denoting one's 'mind'. Thus, in addition to observing the order of moments of time, we have also been given, according to Qoheleth, an awareness that there is something which transcends these limits, namely, the eternal. The problem for Qoheleth, however, lies not in the word *'ōlām* itself, but in the fact that being aware of such a 'time', we can discover nothing about it.

In this context, *lō' māṣā'* marks its first appearance in the book, but it will occur with increasing frequency as Qoheleth pushes further in his discussion of what humans cannot find out.

The meaning of the phrase *mibbᵉlî 'ᵃšer lō'* is something of a conundrum, yet its importance must be acknowledged, for the meaning we assign to the phrase will influence how we view the divine actions. If we are happy to render the phrase as a purpose clause, the implication is that God deliberately intends that facts about our world will never be known to us. If we see the phrase as a result clause, then Qoheleth is reminding us of the limitations in our comprehension of divine activity. This latter is the more appropriate one (cf. Jer. 2.15; 9.9-11; Job 4.20 for examples of the use of *mibbᵉlî* + participle).

The reference 'from beginning to end' (*mērō'š wᵉ'ad-sôp*) coordinates with vv. 1-8 and the extremities which characterize the poem. Thus, humanity cannot discern the entire sweep of the divine plan.

3.12-13 The question of *yitrôn* having been raised again in 3.9, Qoheleth must provide yet another answer. This he does in 3.12 (cf. 2.24) using the first of two introductory markers (*yāda'tî*). The background is that of the problem set forth in vv. 10-11. If humanity cannot comprehend fully the 'eternal' dimension and all that God does, then what advice can the sage offer? Again we note the appearance of the 'There is nothing better... than...'-form which counsels enjoyment of life. In v. 13 we discover what 'enjoyment' means in this context. There are three component parts: eating, drinking, and working. All are recognized as divine gifts (*mattat-'ᵉlōhîm*) basic to normal healthy life, and are to be enjoyed as such. The appearance three times in this section of the verb 'give' (vv. 10, 11, 13), all with God as subject, helps clarify Qoheleth's point. What, he asks, should be our response to all that God gives? We can do no other than accept his gifts gladly and use them as the donor intended.

3.14-15 A second response is also introduced by *yāda'tî*, 'I know'. If vv. 12-13 stressed what a person could do, this second response emphasizes what God does. This feature is made additionally clear by the fact that both verses conclude with a statement beginning with *wᵉhā'ᵉlōhîm...*, giving the impression that the initial statements in each verse anticipate that final clause.

In the case of v. 14, God's actions are eternal (*lᵉ'ōlām*). Qoheleth knows enough of God's doings to make this affirmation. Earthly events are marked by fixed moments (3.1-8), they are time-bound. God's actions, on the contrary, transcend this world and time. Thus the *'ōlām* divinely placed in the human consciousness is that which links us to the realm of the divine, even though we are unable to describe it in detail. Qoheleth insists that we have some knowledge of these divine deeds: they are complete, needing nothing by way of addition (*'ālāw 'ēn lᵉhôsîp*), nor can anything be subtracted from them (*mimmennû 'ēn ligrōa'*; cf. Deut. 4.2; 13.1[12.32] where it refers to the completeness of the law as it stands). In light of the question in 3.9 about *yitrôn*, what is the significance of the statement about God's eternal actions? It would appear that Qoheleth is forging a link between a person's *yitrôn* and the eternal acts of the deity. He has already made clear that *yitrôn* is not to be sought in this world (2.11). Qoheleth seems to be moving towards the thought that humanity's *yitrôn* and God's eternity are somehow bound together.

God's work is also complete and purposive. The final clause of v. 14 suggests that what God does in this eternal realm is worked 'so that' certain things may result. This is the function of the so-called relative *še*. What is that purpose or result? Our text reads, *yir'û millᵉpānāw*, but it requires some explanation. That mankind might 'fear in his presence (before him)' is a standard interpretation (cf. RSV and most commentators). How correct is such a view? The verb *yir'û* could be the qal imperfect of *rā'āh*, 'see', or of *yār'ē*, 'fear'. Unless some other criterion is present to help us make the choice between these two alternatives, we are probably dependent upon quite subjective factors for our selection. As to the subject of the verb, we must depend upon contextual indicators—thus we presume it is the *b^{e}nē-hā'ādām,* 'humanity' in v. 10. Is humanity to 'fear from his presence', or to 'see (what proceeds) from him'? In view of the fact that the opening verb in this pericope is *rā'āh*, and since Qoheleth is discussing what humanity can or cannot discover of the divine activity, it is entirely reasonable that an interpretation which accords with this wider context be adopted. Thus: 'God has done (this) so that they might see (what proceeds) from him'. On this reading, *mill^{e}pānāw* relates to 'him' as the source of all action, and it dovetails with the unit's overall stress upon the deeds of the deity.

3.15 In 1.9 we have already met thoughts akin to those now expressed in 3.15. However, the translation of 3.15, like that of 3.14, is contentious. The initial *mah,* an interrogative, may also be used in the sense of 'whatever'. Thus a possible translation is 'whatever has been, already is, and (whatever) shall be, already has been'. In this manner. past, present, and future are bound together. Such an understanding indicates that the thought of v. 15a and that of v. 14a run along similar lines, for if what God has done is complete and eternal, then past, present, and future form a unity.

The concluding phrase, *hā'^{e}lōhîm y^{e}baqqēš 'et-nirdāp*, presents further problems for both translator and interpreter (see Salters, 1976: 419-22). So we have translations such as Scott's, 'God sees to what requires (his) attention', and Gordis's, 'God always seeks to repeat the past'. Both are representative of attempts to clarify a very obscure Hebrew sentence. The verb *y^{e}baqqēš,* 'seek', in the imperfect suggests frequency or habitual action. What is it then that God seeks? According to the RSV, it is 'that which is driven away'. This is an empty tautology. The sense of the word *nirdāp* is far from obvious, especially as the only OT use of the niphal participle *nirdāp* is the one in our text. Taking as our starting point the fact that vv. 14a and 15a seem to run parallel, we assume that the second part of each verse bears a similar relationship. The subject of both clauses is God; the syntax is similar—the subject is followed by a verb and a related clause. This leads to the suggestion that *še* in v. 15b is a truncated form of *'et-'^{a}šer,* parallel to the *še* of v. 14b. The verb *bqš,* 'seek', in later OT material has an extended meaning, 'request', 'ask'. It is entirely conceivable that *bqš* here is of the same order. Furthermore, if the second half of v. 15b is a relative clause rather than an object-clause, then *nrdp* may be either a niphal perfect or a qal imperfect first-person plural. I would therefore propose a translation as follows: 'God requests that it be pursued' or 'God requests that we pursue (it)'. It is not God who does the pursuing or seeking, but ourselves, a meaning according more closely with the tenor of the book as a whole. The remaining question is to what does 'it' refer? On the basis of advice tendered in 3.12-13, 'it' would be the pursuit of the enjoyment of God's gifts and of what God does. Or perhaps, God asks that we follow the *'ōlām* set within our consciousness.

3.16-22 The Problem of Injustice

Qoheleth cites another observation of the human situation, and in doing so gives us a further insight into his methodology. He first mentions an anomalous situation typical of human society. He reflects upon that situation, and from it draws a conclusion. Thus, 'I saw..., and said to myself...' (cf. 4.1-2).

In this section we discover two reflections (v. 17 and v. 18) both of which are introduced by the same phrase, *'āmartî 'ᵃnî bᵉlibbî*. Each reflection consists of a motive clause introduced by *kî* (vv. 17b, 19). The second response is the longer of the two and leads to a closing observation (v. 22) drawn from the process of reflection. The structure of the section is both obvious and logical.

Keywords are a significant component in this pericope. The major concepts of evil, judgment, and justice found in v. 16 recur in v. 17, indicating the essential link between the observation and his reflection. The phrase 'a time for every matter' (*'ēt lᵉkol ḥēpeṣ*) in v. 17c binds the response to the theme of the chapter by reiterating 3.1 as an inclusion. In the second reflection (vv. 18-22), the operative words are 'humanity' (*bᵉnē-hā'ādām*) and 'beast' (*bᵉhēmāh*), together with the three-fold use of words which describe what these two have in common—'one' (*'eḥād*), 'fate' (*miqreh*), 'breath' (*rûaḥ*).

The general structure of the pericope, its keywords and concepts are vital signs to observe as we seek its interpretation.

3.16 The verse falls into three parts: the introduction to the observation, and the observation itself which is presented in two parts: (a) *mᵉqôm hammišpāṭ*, 'the halls of justice', and (b) *mᵉqôm haṣṣedeq*, 'the place of righteousness'. The latter halves of both

(c) are identical, *šammāh hārāša‘*, ‘there was wickedness’. The focus of Qoheleth’s vision is the halls of justice, which he notes are marred by corruption *(rāša‘)*. The expression used is a generalized one so that we are to assume a typical court scene. Qoheleth’s concern with injustice in the world gives us a glimpse into his soul; it is from this concern and the theological discord which it signals, that we learn of his motivation for pursuing the issue of one’s *yitrôn* (cf. 8.10-14).

3.17 Qoheleth’s initial response is to offer what we might call a ‘standard answer’. An orthodox reply to the predicament in v. 16 would draw comfort from the fact that God will judge at the appropriate time (*‘ēt*) and hopefully overturn the injustice. It is obvious that the statement in v. 17 represents a traditional response, but that it does not reflect Qoheleth’s own convictions is a further conclusion which some scholars are tempted to draw (e.g. Rankin, Scott *et al.*). These scholars would see vv. 18-22 as representative of Qoheleth’s own deep feelings, not those noted in v. 17. Generally they regard this verse as a gloss (see Crenshaw, 1987: 102).

However, a conclusion that vv. 18-22 are Qoheleth’s views over against v. 17 fails to appreciate two important features of this work. The first is that although Qoheleth may represent even an extreme position on the faith spectrum, the fact that he raises disturbing questions does not mean that he has abandoned one of the more central tenets of that faith, namely that God is just. He may fail to see that justice operating in many cases but he still appears to hold to a God who will judge with justice. The second feature of Qoheleth’s presentation is that he often sets two opposing responses alongside one another in order to highlight some of the anomalies of human existence (cf. 2.13-14, 15; 9.17, 18). Thus, 3.17 gives expression to an orthodox opinion, one which we have no reason to believe Qoheleth does not share. The hope that God will intervene on behalf of the victims of injustice is predicated upon the fact that God has determined the ‘times’ (3.1), that he is in control (9.1), and that all will work out satisfactorily in the end. Without this important faith statement the following response would lose its value as the opposing reality which creates the anomaly Qoheleth is addressing. That is to say, on the one hand Qoheleth firmly believes that God will act in judgment upon human injustice, yet at the same time he must acknowledge that on many occasions divine justice *is not seen to be done.* This is usually because death intrudes unexpectedly.

The final word in this verse, *šām,* 'there', has been another point of debate. Most scholars—and their views are reflected in the RSV rendering—prefer that we read *śam,* 'appoint', in its place. Such a change is not inconceivable, but if we allow for some deliberate correspondence between v. 17c and 3.1, then we are best advised to retain the nominal form rather than introduce a verb which would destroy the parallelism. Thus *šām* should be retained as a reference back to 3.16 and the place where the perversion of justice was noticed.

3.18 The re-use of the introductory formula *'āmartî 'anî belibbî* indicates that in vv. 18-21 we have a second and concurrent response to the situation identified in 3.16. Its basic theme is carried by the keywords 'humanity', 'beast', 'fate'.

We must deal initially with the numerous problems of syntax in this verse before moving on to an exposition of its meaning. The phrase *'al dibrat,* 'concerning the matter of', occurs in 7.14 and 8.2 as well as in Ps. 110.4. There follows an infinitive construct *lebārām* from *brr,* 'to separate', 'sort through'. This infinitive requires translation as a regular perfect, though perhaps with an emphasis upon the divine purpose which is the thrust of the infinitive. Seow (1997: 167) suggests that the verb *lebārām* really means to 'to choose them' or 'to test them'. A second infinitive, *lir'ôt,* speaks further to the question of the sorting process. Our problem here is that if we retain the qal infinitive, its subject is of necessity God himself. The following pericope indicates that God's intention is to help humanity see that it shares with the rest of creation a common terminal point, death. Therefore, to read *lar'ôt* (hiphil) would be the more appropriate. The two concluding words, *hēmāh lāhem,* are redundant. The duplicate *hēmāh* may be a dittograph, though there seems no reason for adding *lāhem.* A second view, that these words are indeed original has been maintained (Delitzsch, Herzberg, Lauha, Crenshaw) and rendered 'in and of themselves'. This latter adds nothing to the meaning of the verse, except perhaps to lay greater emphasis on the preceding material. Despite the problems inherent in the verse's syntactical peculiarities, the tenor of the verse is clear: humans and beasts share a great deal in common. The basis for this conclusion (note the parallel *kî*-phrase in v. 17) is the fate which they share.

3.19 The fate (*miqreh*) of human and beast is one. To leave the reader without any doubt as to what that fate is, Qoheleth explains that both die. In 2.16 a similar thought has already been voiced, though on that occasion it was the fates of the wise and the foolish which were set together. Not only do human and beast share a like fate, they also share *rûaḥ*, that 'spirit' which animates them. Thus in life as in death no distinction is possible, with the resultant conclusion that their *môtar*, 'advantage', is also common.

The word *môtar*, 'advantage', is used only this once by Qoheleth (cf. Prov. 14.23), though it derives from the more frequent *yôtēr*, *yitrôn*. Does *môtar* convey a concept similar to or distinct from *yôtēr*? Why has Qoheleth used this highly unusual form? On the assumption that a different form probably has a unique significance, we derive from the context clues for its possible interpretation. Qoheleth's point is that because of this shared fate, humanity has no more *môtar* than the animals. The phrase gives the impression that Qoheleth believes that humanity ought to be somewhat distinct, but any possible distinction is negated by the shared experience of death. Therefore man cannot be said to have any 'advantage' over the rest of creation. Qoheleth admits that there is nothing unique about humanity if its end is the same as that of the lower elements of creation. It is that uniqueness which Qoheleth denotes by the term *môtar*, to demonstrate what 'extra' benefits ought to inhere in being human.

Verse 19 concludes with the *hebel*-phrase. Whether the phrase functions as a motive clause to explain why no difference exists between humankind and animals—they all are *hebel*—or whether it has another function has to be determined. The *hebel*-phrase almost always operates as a concluding statement rather than as a motive clause. This usage pattern is important, and ought to be given due weight. Thus, we should understand the *kî* in this verse as asseverative rather than introducing a motive. This interpretation would be rendered, '*indeed,* everything is enigmatic'. The transitoriness of human existence and the fact that no distinction is made between humans and animals calls forth the *hebel* conclusion. It makes no sense to argue that *because* all is *hebel,* therefore all have one fate, death.

3.20 The theme of the unity of human and beast in death continues in v. 20 with the use of the keyword *'āpār*, 'dust'. It is applied here to the destination (*māqôm*) of 'all'. All are from dust, and will return thereto at death. Though Qoheleth here does not utilize the term *miqreh,* it seems obvious that the meaning of v. 20 is the same in amplification as that of v. 19. The creation tradition visible in Gen. 2.7 and 3.19 colours this verse. The three phrases of which v. 20 is composed each begin with *hakkōl,* and thereafter exhibit a similarity of structure. This pattern has the effect of heightening the notion of common death which 'all' share. Verbal forms here are also not insignificant. The participles *hôlēk*, 'going,' and *šāb,* 'returning', speak of current action. 'All' are in process toward that final dusty destination. We should note also the re-use of central terms ('all', 'place', 'go', 'return') from 1.7 in this verse, even to the extent of *hlk* and *šûb* in participial form.

3.21 Our common end is the grave, yet the question remains whether the human spirit follows an independent course thereafter. Qoheleth's frustration, the source of the enigma, is thus not death itself but the intrusion of death such that justice is pre-empted, or that the expected distinction between humankind and our animal companions is not apparent. The interrogative 'who knows?' in effect asserts that nobody knows whether the human spirit ascends to some final destination while that of the animals travels in the opposite direction. The significance of the phrase 'going up' is presumably that it mirrors the notion that the divine dwelling place is in the heavens, while the abode of the dead is portrayed as 'downwards' and away from God. Thus the real issue for Qoheleth is what happens *after* death, and whether at that point any final solution to such problems as injustice on the life-side of death is possible. It is apparent that Qoheleth believes some distinction is required, even though it presently lies beyond proof, beyond empirical testing. Qoheleth's term *yitrôn* holds within it hope for some post-death resolution.

3.22 Qoheleth observes. This phrase leads directly into the concluding remarks. He observes that there is nothing more rewarding (*'ēn ṭôb min*) than that one should enjoy one's work (*yiśmaḥ hā'ādām b^{e}ma^{ca}śāw*). The thesis rests on the presupposition that this is an attainable goal, one which is our God-given 'portion' (*ḥēleq*). In a second *kî*-clause Qoheleth offers yet another reason for this advice. The interrogative 'who will bring him ... ?' is actually a pointed claim that 'nobody will bring him to see' what might happen after he has gone—either on earth or in Sheol, it makes no difference. It is fruitless to attempt to look beyond death for there is no tangible evidence on which to base an opinion. Yet despite this limitation we detect a clear note of hope in Qoheleth's presentation. There is something 'after him'

(ʾaḥ^a^rāw), beyond this life, believes Qoheleth, and that is part of our *yitrôn.*

Verse 22 with its 'there is nothing better than'-form is a parallel to 2.24 and 3.12, and for that reason is significant in tracing the book's overall structure. The form is one of the building blocks for the entire work, that component which carries the advice Qoheleth offers, dependent upon the preceding observations and reflections. As a conclusion, it represents Qoheleth's entirely positive perception of life as divine gift which, if we do not enjoy, we squander.

Chapter 4

Mathematically Speaking

4.1-12 Mathematically Speaking

Qoheleth continues in ch. 4 his report on the testing of life. At first glance, he appears simply to follow on from where he concluded in ch. 3. However, there are certain unique features of 4.1-12 which catch our attention, and which give this chapter its special character and identity.

Chapter 3 drew to a close with the advice that life should be enjoyed. That would suggest that the pursuit of an answer to his basic question of life's *yitrôn* had reached another turning point. We might, then, expect a repetition of the *yitrôn* question as occurred in 3.9, but we find no reference to *yitrôn* again until 5.15[16]. Chapter 4 seems, therefore, to be something of an insert. Its own structure (see below) and theme alert us to its individuality, but we must not lose sight of the fact that it relates to the overall work as part of Qoheleth's continuing empirical testing of life.

Structurally we note three observations in vv. 1-2, 4-5, 7-8, rounded off with conclusions in vv. 3, 6, 9. Each conclusion has two features: (1) The 'Better' proverb; (2) a mathematical theme using the numerals 1 or 2 (see my article, 1984: 446-53). This opening trilogy of sub-sections is followed by three conditional clauses in 4.10-12a, bearing a mathematical theme. The entire unit is then brought to an end with a numerical quotation, v. 12b.

The structure of this section is consciously planned, and is set out below to aid our interpretation.

As far as the general content is concerned, the three observations relate to (1) oppression in the community (similar to 3.16); (2) toil; (3) the enigma of an apparently meaningless working life. In subsections two and three the keywords are *hebel* (vv. 4, 7, 8) and *'āmāl*, 'toil' (vv. 4, 6, 8, 9). The conditional clauses of the fourth sub-section (vv. 10-12) have a common theme, namely the value of having fellow-workers or supporters.

4.1	Again I saw	Observation A
4.3	Better than both is	Conclusion A
4.4	Then I saw	Observation B
4.6	Better is one handful	Conclusion B
4.7	Again I saw	Observation C
4.9	Two are better than one	Conclusion C
4.10	For if they fall, one with	Condition 1
4.11	Again, if two lie together	Condition 2
4.12a	And, if one man	Condition 3
4.12b	A three-fold cord...	Final conclusion

4.1-3 Outnumbered by Oppressors

4.1 The society in which Qoheleth lived, like all human communities, was not without its problems. Its injustice was noted and reflected upon (3.16-21). In ch. 4, another problem which concerned Qoheleth was that of oppression, the work of powerful elements in society. 'Oppression' (*'šq*) occurs twice in v. 1, on the first occasion as an abstract noun (cf. Amos 3.9; Job 35.9), and on the second as a passive participle. The concept occurs only on two other occasions in Qoheleth (5.7[8]; 7.7). Qoheleth's major concern at this juncture is for the one who is the victim of others' oppression, a fact which is evidenced by the reiterated phrase *'ēn lāhem m^enaḥēm,* 'there was no one to comfort them'. The oppressed are not only mistreated, their plight and tears are ignored by the rest of the community. In the second of the reiterated phrases, the word 'them' refers back to the suffix on the passive participle *'ōš^eqēhem,* 'those who oppress them'. In other words, the reiterated *'ēn lāhem m^enaḥēm* refers to the one group, those who have been oppressed. On the side of the oppressors is power (*kōaḥ*), indicating that the privileged class misuses its authority to further its own interest. A brief sketch is given of the little care which society shows towards the victims of an oppressive ruling caste.

4.2 Having described the situation he knew, Qoheleth ponders its significance. The opening word of v. 2, *šabbēaḥ,* is most likely an infinitive absolute used in place of the finite verb, 'I rejoiced'. On the basis of his analysis, Qoheleth determines that those who have already died are better off than those still alive. The contrasting pair, 'dead' and 'living', in this context must refer respectively to those oppressed persons whose life has passed, and those who are still living under the hand of the oppressor. Qoheleth believes that those who have been released from oppression by death have a relative advantage (cf. also 6.5; 7.1). If Qoheleth's thoughts are moving in the direction of the possibility of *yitrôn* after death, then this statement makes good sense. Qoheleth's immediate concern is not that of removing oppression, but of exposing the reality of an unjust world and of reflecting on the painful lot of the oppressed person. Lying behind this concern is the pressing issue of divine justice.

4.3 It is in v. 3 that we read Qoheleth's conclusion, drawn as a result of reflection on the situation portrayed in v. 2. Although one might determine that even death is preferable to living under oppressive regimes, Qoheleth takes the matter further. He suggests that one not yet born is even better placed than one who has died. The reason is presumably that the unborn has not had to encounter the question of oppression. Unfortunately, those not yet born will nevertheless have to deal with life in a world that is full of oppression and, ultimately, death. As a sage responsible for observing and commenting on the human condition, Qoheleth's pain at having to watch oppression work its hardship on certain community members, is something he would wish others to be spared. However, the irony is that none has any choice about being born, and so this third option further underscores the inescapable conclusion that what is 'good' or even 'best' is not within human power to enjoy.

The first occasion of the use of the 'Better'-proverb in this book is something to note. It is a significant literary form in Qoheleth both for its frequency (most OT examples are found here) and for its functional role. (On the use of this form, see G. Bryce, 1972: 343-55; Ogden, 1977). The 'Better'-proverb serves here in v. 3, and in most cases in Qoheleth, as a concluding device. The characteristics of the form and of its role allow us to affirm that v. 3 is Qoheleth's personal conclusion with respect to the observation in vv. 1-2. We also note that it is a numerical type of proverb utilizing the numeral 'two' (*šᵉnēhem*) to speak of the above-mentioned 'dead' and 'living', then adding a third condition as the most preferred one, to elevate the unborn above the oppressed whether they be dead or still alive.

4.4-6 How Much Toil is Too Much?

4.4 'Toil' (*'āmāl*) and 'skill' (*kišrôn*) are the objects of Qoheleth's deliberations in this section. He expresses the belief that 'rivalry' (*qin'āh*) provides the incentive for the effort expended in work and in the sharpening of proficiency. There is nothing in the context nor in the two terms themselves to suggest that the challenge to excel is unheathly, though that is always a possibility. However, Qoheleth does allow that it is a mysterious inexplicable drive, an enigma (*hebel*), which knows no bounds.

4.5 Qoheleth cites a situation which is in direct contrast with v. 4; it describes a fool who is idle—that is, 'he folds his hands', unwilling to work (cf. Prov. 6.10-11; 19.15)—and as a result destroys himself or 'eats himself'. However, on this latter phrase see Whybray (1982) and the argument that it may mean that he still has food to eat (so also Lohfink, 2003: 69-70). But the term 'fool' (*k*[e]*sîl*) always carries a negative evaluation and so it seems unlikely that 'eats himself' could have such a positive sense. The participial forms *ḥōbēq*, 'fold', and *'ōkēl,* 'eat', denote a perpetual state, attitude, or life-style on the part of the fool. Qoheleth finds nothing commendable in the fool's attitude, though at this point, the saying is quoted principally as a counter-point to the observation in v. 4.

4.6 The third component in this sub-section (v. 6) is Qoheleth's conclusion drawn from the above contrast. It, too, is couched in the form of the comparative 'Better'-proverb (cf. v. 3). The numerical values 'one' and 'two' are used, the conclusion reached being that 'one' measure (*kap* = palm, handful) is of higher value than 'two'. This conclusion is justified because the lesser amount represents something beneficial (*naḥat,* 'rest' - here as 'peace' or 'security'), while the higher amount is a burden (*'āmāl*, 'work'). The intriguing thing about Qoheleth's presentation in v. 6 is that it is the 'rest' which is commended, whereas in v. 5 it was condemned. This reversal indicates that the positive evaluation of 'work' and the negative attitude to 'rest' are not absolute values; they are purely relative. 'Rest' is of advantage when indulged in appropriately and not taken to excess. The same is true of work—too much work may become a burden (cf. 7.16-17). Seow (1997: 180) has suggested that 'the comparison is not between an amount of rest and twice the amount of toil, but an amount of anything with peace *vs.* anything with toil'.

4.7-9 The Purpose of Work?

4.7-8 Introducing this section is the phrase found also in 4.1. It marks Qoheleth's concern with yet another life situation, one which, like many others, is enigmatic (*hebel*). On this occasion he describes a solitary individual toiling ceaselessly. He pursues riches (*'ōšer*), but having gained them, fails to derive any satisfaction (*śāba'*) from them. We note the concept of 'eyes not being satisfied' repeated from 1.8. Nor does the worker ponder the purpose, the goal of his unremitting labour; he gives no consideration to who will actually benefit from his toil, in contrast to 2.18-22. Qoheleth perceives such an individual aimlessly questing for wealth as beyond his comprehension.

The solitariness of the individual worker is described in terms of 'one without a second' (*yēš 'eḥād wᵉ'ēn šēnî*), and as one without 'son' or 'brother'. The term *'ēn*, 'without', used three times in this verse, highlights the theme of isolation.

4.9 Here in the 'Better-proverb with which the section closes, the numerals 'one' and 'two' appear again. However, their use differs from that of 4.6, for 'two' are better than 'one'. The 'one' of v. 9 is clearly the solitary worker whose case history is given above. 'Two' is better because when there are two persons involved there is the possibility of sharing what one gains, of mutual assistance (*yēš lāhem śākār ṭôb ba'ᵃmālām*). This allows for some purpose to enter one's working life. To Qoheleth's mind, unless the gain from work is something to be shared with others, life remains without meaning and purpose. Thus a different perspective on work is offered from that given in 4.4-6. The competitive spirit which drives one to greater performance needs to be balanced against the danger of compulsive action. When work becomes an unreflective drive for riches, it ceases to have meaning. On the other hand, when kept within bounds and its benefits shared with others, work has worth.

From the viewpoint of wisdom, mathematics is an imprecise science. 'One' may exceed 'two' in value (v. 6), though not always (v. 9). Their relative values are determined by the nature of the elements in the comparison.

4.10-12 The Advantage of Numbers

The particle *kî*, 'because', binds this section to the preceding one by providing the basis for the argument that 'two' are better than 'one', v. 6 notwithstanding.

This sub-unit consists of three conditional clauses, each commencing with the particle *'im*, followed by an imperfect verb form. Each clause offers a self-evident example of the advantage 'two' have over 'one'.

4.10-12a First of all, in v. 10 Qoheleth posits a situation in which two persons fall. When one person can assist the other, any problems associated with the fall are minimized. The second and equally simple illustration (v. 11) is of two persons sharing a bed on a cold night. They keep each other warm (cf. 1 Kgs 1.1-2), whereas a person sleeping alone may struggle to be warm on a cold night. Thirdly, in v. 12a, a single combatant meets two opponents. In a one-to-one situation, each combatant has the possibility of victory. However, should one combatant have to face two opponents simultaneously, the likelihood is very great that he or she will be defeated. Yes, 'two' are better than 'one'.

4.12b The entire unit 4.1-12 is brought to a conclusion in 4.12b, not with the 'Better'-proverb noted in each of the previous segments, but with an aphorism about a plaited rope—*haḥûṭ hammᵉšullāš lō' bimmᵉhērāh yinnātēq,* 'A three-strand rope cannot be broken easily'. Again the theme is the strength or advantage in numbers. Here the numeral 'three' appears for the first time, perhaps significantly as the sum of the other two digits. The form *mᵉšullāš* is the pual participle of the root *šlš*, meaning to divide into three parts (cf. Gen. 15.9; Ezek. 42.6). The advantage which can accrue from quantitative difference is thus highlighted.

The thesis of v. 12b relates to the first section of the unit (4.1-3) as well. If the oppressed person lacks supporters, or conversely, if the oppressor has a numerical advantage and greater strength, then the oppressed person is better off in the grave. Companionship, whether in oppression, in toil, or in life generally, may redeem an intolerable situation, as well as give it meaning and purpose.

Qoheleth in this section has drawn upon numerical sayings as a peculiar form of presentation. The numerals have a representative rather than absolute value, so we note that the operation of the numerals themselves in this chapter differs from that which we find in other numerical wisdom sayings such as Prov. 6.16-19 and 30.18-31. In these latter, the numerals have real number value, whereas in those examples from 4.1-12 the numerals denote 'less' and 'more', 'little' and 'much', even 'alone' and 'in company'.

Among the OT 'Better'-proverbs, these are the only three examples using a numerical basis for evaluation. We determine that this is a unique variation on the basic 'Better'-proverb form, and one which may almost certainly be attributed to the literary creativity of Qoheleth.

The thrust of this section 4.1-12 comes through clearly. In a world of oppression, of injustice, and of striving, to face life without companionship and support is decidedly painful. Death may indeed be preferable. However, a different perspective is possible if there are others willing and able to share our burden and to participate with us in confronting this enigmatic world, to minimize its frustrations and pain. Commitment to and with the poor and oppressed is the concrete shape of the 'good news'.

4.13-16 The King and The Youth—A Comparison

Few passages in the wisdom literature arouse the kind of search for historical incidents or personalities as background that this passage does. Jewish tradition going back to the Talmud has sought to identify specific individuals referred to in a veiled manner in these verses (Gordis, 1968: 243). Most modern scholars, however, would see this attempt as misguided given the general nature of wisdom writing and of Qoheleth's presentation in particular (Lauha, 1978: 92). The conclusion is thus that two characters referred to in this unit are typical or representative figures, they are mere exemplars and not historical individuals (cf. Zimmerli, 1967: 185; Murphy, 1992: 42). However, I would wish to depart from this general consensus and suggest that in the case of 4.13-16, Qoheleth is alluding to two well-known historical personalities honoured by the wisdom tradition. They are used as examples of the thesis of v. 13 (see Ogden, 1980: 311-15).

Unlike other segments of the book where the 'Better'-proverb comes at the end of the pericope, Qoheleth varies his presentation here and places the saying at the head of the unit. The thesis of v. 13 is then upheld by citing two examples (v. 14). The second portion of the unit (vv. 15-16) offers a separate observation, and to indicate that separateness, Qoheleth moves to first-person speech. The theme in this case is that the sage generally receives neither recognition nor reward.

4.13 The 'Better'-proverb draws a comparison between two extreme figures. On the one hand, there is a king. His social position, combined with his seniority in years, under normal circumstances would place him above all others in the community. On the other hand, there stands a youth who is poor. Both qualities would place him at the other end of the social spectrum from the king. In drawing a contrast between these two personalities, the 'better' of the two would, by traditional definition, be the royal person. However, Qoheleth reverses this logic, and he does so by introducing the criterion of wisdom (cf. also Sir. 11.5-6). Though young, poor, and inexperienced, the youth is *wise;* though experienced, wealthy, and privileged, the king is a fool, refusing to heed advice (*lō' yādā' l^e^hizzāhēr 'ôd*).

4.14 Two examples, introduced by *kî* and *kî gam,* are cited in support of this thesis. The first speaks of one who went from prison (*bēth-hāsūrîm*) to the throne (*limlōk*). Records in the OT do not contain reference to any known person who actually followed this path so precisely, though some, such as Joseph, Jehoiachin, and Daniel, may come close. That no OT personality exactly fits this 'prison-to-throne' motif, would seem to support the theory that the examples cited are typical or representative only. However, the term *mlk* not only refers to royal leadership; it also may describe the work of the *counsellor* (cf. Neh. 5.7; see also de Boer, 1969: 53-56). Qoheleth does not draw upon the regular term for counsellor (*yô'ēṣ*) at any point in this document, but he does use the term *mlk* in 10. 16, 17, 20 with a meaning parallel to that of 'counsellor'. The OT does contain a story of a young man of outstanding wisdom, Joseph, who was released from prison to serve as Pharaoh's advisor. One further piece of evidence that Qoheleth has the Joseph story in mind is his use on several occasions (7.9; 8.8; 10.5) of a term *šallit,* used on only one other occasion, in Gen. 42.6, as a term descriptive of Joseph's office as counsellor. It also is parallel to the phrase *'āb l^e^parōh* (Gen. 45.8; see also de Boer, 1969: 57-58).

Thus in this first example, Qoheleth suggests that the poor but wise youth takes precedence over the foolish king in a manner similar to the young Joseph who came from prison to the position of counsellor (*mlk*) to the Pharaoh.

The second illustration Qoheleth offers is from the David tradition. Our evidence for this link is the term *rāš,* 'poor'. In 1 Sam. 18.23, the young David questions the wisdom of Saul in making him a member of the royal family by marriage. David's objection is that he is too 'poor' for such a position. In the telling of the David story the term *rāš* is a significant one, occurring at 2 Sam. 12.1, 3, 4. That it is an important one in the wisdom literature is evidenced by its use twenty-two times in Proverbs, twice in Qoheleth, and only on six occasions elsewhere, three of which concern David. The allusion implicit in the participle *rāš* is that it is a wisdom idiom for David. Like David, the maligned and the poor, any youth can rise to prominence provided he or she is wise. Wisdom is that quality which ultimately determines true greatness, and thus can elevate one above those whose worth is judged in terms of wealth, privilege, and social position.

4.15 Normally the use of 'I saw...' *(rā'îtî)* marks the beginning of a new unit in Qoheleth (cf. 3.10; 4.4; 6.1 etc.). We have no reason to think that this feature differs in 4.15. So our attention is directed away from 4.13-14 for the moment, and to a new situation beginning with v. 15. In this Qoheleth again tenders a personal observation in which he notes the multitude living ('moving about', *m*ᵉ*hall*ᵉ*kîm*) on earth. He sweepingly surveys human society, very different in focus from the veiled historical references in v. 14. Within this moving mass of humanity attention is focused on a young person. The contrast between the general and the particular is further achieved by the verbs used: the mass is 'walking' *(m*ᵉ*hall*ᵉ*kîm),* while the youth is 'standing' *(ya'*ᵃ*mōd).*

Two problems of interpretation may be taken up. The first relates to the meaning of the term *taḥtāw*. It has been customary to see this as a reference to the youth taking the place of the king mentioned in v. 14, *taḥtāw* meaning 'in *his* place' (cf. Loretz, 1964: 71; so also Crenshaw, Lohfink, Krüger). K. Galling (1932: 296) believed the phrase 'under the sun' indicated Egyptian influence, the sun being a reference to Pharaoh. As Loretz points out (p. 69), this theory lacks all concrete evidence. However, the separation of v. 15 from the preceding examples suggests that the pronominal suffix on *taḥat* does not refer to either person in v. 14, but rather that it is a parallel to the phrase *taḥat haššemeš* in v. 15a. Thus the youth does not stand 'in the king's stead', but both he and the masses are 'under the sun', or 'under it'.

The other difficulty for the interpreter rests with the term *hayyeled haššēnî,* literally 'the second young person'. There is no reason why this should be linked with the youth mentioned in v. 14, as the contrast in this second half of the unit is between the youth and the rest of humanity, not with the king mentioned earlier. Thus, the term most likely means 'another youth', but one unrelated to the youth mentioned in v. 14 (contra Murphy).

4.16 The human parade mentioned in v. 15 is endless; there was no end to all 'who were before them' *(lipnēhem).* To whom does the suffix 'them' refer? Assuming that this sub-section is linked with the thought of vv. 13-14, Gordis (1968: 245-46) believes it refers to the youth and the king. However, if v. 15 truly addresses a new context, 'them' most likely relates to the crowds and the youth of v. 15a. Qoheleth suggests that later generations *(hā'aḥ^{a}rônîm)* will 'not rejoice in him'. In the context, 'him' indicates the youth. As to the form of the rejoicing, we face another difficulty; we presume it means some kind of public acclaim or adulation. Thus Qoheleth appears to be arguing that in the on-going parade of human history, there are some 'unsung heroes' whose wisdom the crowds fail to recognize or heed, or that no matter what position one holds, in time one's reputation and popularity are completely forgotten. This situation Qoheleth laments as an enigma (cf. 9.15).

The significance of wisdom, its importance for determining one's real value as a person, even if not guaranteeing one's social position, to Qoheleth is obvious. However, Qoheleth is forced to concede that the rest of society has never recognized the outstanding wise youth, presumably because they have been blinded by other criteria such as wealth and social status. This grieves Qoheleth and his frustration is expressed in the enigma (*hebel*) phrase and its parallel with which the chapter closes.

Thus 4.13-16, consisting of two parts, refers to youth. It is possible, Qoheleth claims, for a young person to exhibit wisdom, and thus to demonstrate a superiority over those who lack wisdom. In Israel's own history there were two such figures, Joseph and David, who could be called upon as illustrative of this point. Despite the later rise of both Joseph and David, the fact that virtually no recognition is given to young sages, is an indictment of the values of a society content to honour any old fool who has wealth or social position. What an enigma!

Chapter 5

On Religion and Possessions

The most obvious feature of this chapter is the variety of subjects with which it deals. In 4.17-5.6 (5.1-7) we encounter a topic rarely discussed by the wise of Israel, namely cultic concerns. We note the reference to God (Elohim) on six occasions in the opening subsection (cf. also 3.10-15). Qoheleth takes up the subject of oppression again in vv. 7-8 (8-9), along with the inability of material things to provide satisfaction (vv. 9-11[10-12]), and in vv. 12-16 (13-17) an unfortunate situation (*ra'*) is cited, leading up to the use once more of the programmatic question in v. 15(16). The suggestion which flows from consideration of these various issues, namely that life should be enjoyed, is presented in 5.17-19 (18-20).

If we are correct in theorizing that Qoheleth is still vitally interested in pursuing the question of *yitrôn,* then these various sketches of the human scene are all equally important to completing the picture. Within a world marked by human folly, oppression, and material success which fails to provide satisfaction, where does *yitrôn* lie? Qoheleth in this section takes us further along the road of his pilgrimage in search of the answer.

4.17-5.6 (5.1-7) Attitudes in Worship

Throughout this section Qoheleth moves from the reflective mode characteristic of the previous section to imperative, using four admonitions relating to cultic activity. Each is supported by a motive clause, and in addition there are quotations or comments which add force to the appeal. Thus 4.17(5.1) "Guard...," 5.1(2) "Be not rash...," v. 3(4) "pay...," v. 5(6) "do not say...," all express admonitions, and 4.17(5.1)c; 5.1(2)b, 5.3(4)b, and 5.6(7) provide supporting arguments in motive clauses (see L.G. Perdue, 1977: 180-87). The other literary feature is the 'Better'-proverb in 4.17(5.1) and 5.4(5). Spanenberg (1998: 61-91) has further clarified the rhetorical unity of this section, structured around an admonition, followed by a prohibition, with motivation and completed by adding advice or reason for the prohibition.

The tenor of the admonitions and the mention of the fool on three occasions would suggest that Qoheleth is concerned that people avoid the kinds of mistakes the fool might make in this cultic area. Frequent use of vocabulary relating to verbal communication (*'āmar, dābar, peh, qôl, nēder*) focuses the issue about the dangers of incautious speech to which the fool is especially prone.

4.17(5.1) The opening imperative, 'Guard your foot...' (*šᵉmôr raglekā*) is a figurative usage, the foot substituting for the worshipper's conduct, urging the hearer to caution, literally, 'watch your step'. The use of the verb *šmr* in this context approximates to that of Prov. 21.23, where the sage also counsels caution in speech. Qoheleth argues that it is necessary to be prudent when one approaches sacred space. The term *bēth-'ᵉlōhîm* could relate to either the Temple or the synagogue; we are not required to be specific, though the text does speak of offering sacrifice. The admonition sets the tone for the following discussion.

The 'Better'-saying which Qoheleth draws upon argues the case. The offering of a sacrifice (*zābaḥ*), though of undoubted importance in Israel's cult, is here relativized. Being present to hear and then respond obediently (*šm'*) to divine or priestly instruction is better than coming to offer a sacrifice. This is not a view unique to Qoheleth—see 1 Sam. 15.22; Amos 5.22-24; Hos 6.6. (In this sentence the infinitive absolute, *qārôb,* functions as an imperative.) This evaluation is especially directed to the fool who is in danger of hasty bumbling. The undergirding argument follows.

The *kî,* 'because', introduces a clause which has presented difficulties for interpreters. Literally the clause reads, 'for they do not know to do evil (*kî 'ēnām yôdᵉ'im laᵃśôt rā'*). Does this mean that they do not know *how* to do evil, or that they do not know *that* they are doing or have done wrong? The infinitive *laᵃśôt* could be rendered in either way. Perhaps the key lies with the word *rā'*. Normally Qoheleth uses *rš'* or *r'h* when speaking of moral evil (cf. 3.16, 17; 8.10 etc.). The form *ra'* generally describes an enigmatic situation or calamity (e.g. 5.11; 6.1 etc.). If we consider this usage and its application to the present example, it is more likely that *ra'* describes something disastrous rather than some moral collapse (cf. Job 2.10; Isa. 45.7; Prov. 6.12-15). This would be even more obvious if what is being criticized was the action of a thoughtless fool, for he/she is less morally culpable than one who sets out deliberately to defy the law. The verb 'know' in this context refers to realizing or recognizing certain facts (Isa 59.12). The following translation is therefore suggested: '... because they do not realize that thev are creating havoc'. Injudicious action, failing to 'listen', will inevitably lead the fool into many a calamitous situation before God.

5.1(2) The note of caution is given here in two negative commands: 'Do not speak rashly', and, 'Do not let your heart (mind, *lēb)* rush to bring up a matter in the divine presence'. The latter command is similar to that in 4.17(5.1), where the divine presence is described as the 'house of God'. Regardless of the nature of the matter, be it intercession, lament, or praise, the principle Qoheleth enunciates is that of caution. It is better not to let your heart run away with you. Of course, the fool is more open to this possibility, for the fool rarely thinks before acting.

The second element in this verse offers the basis for the admonition: *kî hā'ᵉlōhîm baššāmayim wᵉ'attāh 'al-hā'āreṣ*. The vast gulf fixed between humanity and God is sufficient for Qoheleth to counsel the fool not to rush in with a word which is at once hasty and ill-considered. 'Few words' (*dᵉbārîm mᵉ'aṭṭîm*) are one of the indelible signs of the wise, for they speak only after sufficient reflection (Prov. 10.14, 19). The distance between human beings and God is not merely geographical, but indicative of the essential difference between an all-knowing God and an earthly being with all the limitations which that implies. Qoheleth's focus is on the divine transcendance. Gordis's interpretation (1968: 248) that the distance between earth and heaven expresses the divine lack of concern with human affairs, is a view without adequate support in the text. Even less can one agree with Lauha (1978: 99) that God is a despotic figure. All the text requires of us is the recognition that humans are earthbound in every sense of the word. One's conduct reflects one's state and status, be it divine or earthly.

5.2(3) In order to justify the call for caution in speech and for less hasty talk, Qoheleth offers this proverbial statement. The contrast with 5.1(2) and its advocacy of few (*mᵉ'aṭṭîm*) words, lies in the reiterated use of *rab,* 'much', 'many'.

The two halves of v. 2(3) are in parallel; thus, the 'dream' and the 'voice of the fool' form a balanced pair. Both are accompanied by, or typified by, 'much business' (*'inyān*) and 'many words'.

Determining the specific meaning of the aphorism, like so many statements which have little or no contextual setting, is always problematic for the interpreter. Here, the first half of the verse indicates that one activity, in this case dreaming, is associated with much work. Some commentators suggest that the aphorism is quoted in full, although the first half is irrelevant to the setting, with only the second half indicating Qoheleth's point. However, there is nothing in the first half of the saying that is inconsistent with Qoheleth's own views. It would seem that Qoheleth's point throughout is that certain tasks demand considerable energy for their performance. Furthermore, dreaming can indicate a fertile mind and undisciplined action, resulting in the failure to realize the dream. For Crenshaw this means that 'frenetic business has lingering effects that disturb sleep, causing dreams' (1987: 116). However, it is difficult to see that dreams might result from disturbed sleep. Perhaps the implication is that these are bad dreams, though such a reading does not fit the text that we have. Seow has pointed out that dreams are often figurative for that which is ephemeral and illusory (1997: 198) and so here it is virtually synonymous with the key word *hebel*. In the parallel example, the 'voice of the fool' is associated with much talking, and in this context this must be seen as a criticism, especially in contrast with the few words of the wise (v. 1[2]). The aphorism serves to support Qoheleth's case for wisdom: do not speak rashly like the fool, for it is both laborious and as fruitless as dreaming.

5.3(4) The second admonition relates to the making and fulfilling of vows (*ndr*), and appears intended to make more specific the general admonition of 4.17(5.1). The passage demonstrates a close affinity with Deut. 23.21-23. Vows in Israel were undertaken for various reasons: e.g. to invoke God's help (Jdg. 11.30-31; 1 Sam. 1.11), or to express, in a wide range of forms, one's devotion (see further, G.H. Davies, 'Vows', IDB, IV: 792-93).

The initial *ka'ašer*, 'whenever', in compound with the following imperfect, has a frequentative sense. In the original deuteronomic form (Deut. 23.22), the clause began with a simple *kî*. Consistent with the wisdom preference, Qoheleth omits the divine name, YHWH. Qoheleth also prefers the negative particle *'al* to the deuteronomic *lō'*. The principle, supported by both texts, is that any vow made should be fulfilled (*šlm*), that religious commitments must be regarded with due seriousness (cf. Ps. 66.13-14).

It is in the motive clause that Qoheleth adds his own justification for the admonition. In Deuteronomy 23 the reason advanced for fulfilling one's vow was that God so required it, and one should endeavour to avoid the sin of non-compliance. Qoheleth's view differs slightly: he argues that God finds no pleasure in fools *(kî 'ēn ḥēpeṣ bakk^{e}sîlîm)*. In both traditions, the deity is seen to take very seriously the fact that a vow has been made, and so expects its fulfilment. Qoheleth uses this example to typify foolish behaviour, so in his advice he calls for the completion (*šlm*, piel) of vows made as conduct befitting the wise.

5.4(5) A concluding 'Better'-proverb underscores the point made. It assumes two possibilities: not making a vow (*lō'-tiddôr*), and not fulfilling a vow made (*lō' t^{e}šallēm*). Of these two, the first is preferable. This attitude is similar to that in Deuteronomy 23. Problems arise only when a vow is taken but not completed.

5.5(6) This third admonition gives the impression that it is an alternative call for vows made to be carried out, rather than general advice to be judicious in one's speech (contra Zimmerli). This conclusion stems from the fact that Deut. 23.22-24 uses the terms 'mouth' (*peh*) and 'sin' (*ḥṭ'*) when admonishing a person to think first about whether one is able to complete a vow before taking it upon oneself. Thus it appears that the Deuteronomy 23 passage forms the background for this statement. We can therefore determine that Qoheleth concurs in this priestly advice.

The nature of the sin of which Qoheleth speaks may differ from that in Deuteronomy 23. Qoheleth hopes that the zealous devotee can avoid the need to confess at a later date that, because the vow could not be fulfilled, the vow was made in error (*kî š^{e}gāgāh hî'*). The term *š^{e}gāgāh* appears frequently in Leviticus (4.22, 27 etc.) and Numbers (15.22ff.) always with the sense of an inadvertent error. In Numbers, inadvertent sins find atonement through priestly intercession. Thus the 'messenger' (*malāk*) of whom Qoheleth speaks is almost certainly the cultic functionary or priest to whom such confession of failure and of impulsively made vows would have to be made (cf. Mal. 2.7; see also Salters, 1978: 95-101).

The second half of the verse adds a rhetorical question, 'Why should God be angry with you?' The interrogative *lāmmāh is* functionally similar to the particle *pen,* 'lest'. Retribution for sin is the thought behind this question, (cf. *qṣp* in Deut. 9.19 etc.) specifically that God should frustrate one's efforts (*ḥibbēl* *'et-ma^{ca}śeh yād^{e}kā*). Kugel, however, views the phrase *ma^{ca}śeh yād^{e}kā* as meaning one's personal possessions. The passage generally is addressed as a warning to the fool. Qoheleth senses that whatever the fool might accomplish, all is put at risk because of an inability to carry out an ill-advised vow or promise made.

5.6(7) The opening *kî* is seen by Gordis (1968: 249) as an asseverative, rather than as the particle introducing a motive clause. Our problem in interpreting this verse lies not in the introductory particle, but in the nature of the sentence. It has been supposed by most commentators that the text has been corrupted at an early stage, but that it might be a nominal clause, as Gordis suggests, is entirely plausible. Thus we can render *b^{e}rōb ḥ^{a}lōmôt wah^{a}bālîm ûd^{a}bārîm harbēh,* 'in the many dreams, frustrations, and profusion of words . . .' This would then lead into the final clause which calls upon the wise to 'fear God' (cf. 7.18). Such an understanding would imply that the first half of the verse identifies three valueless activities, activities which typify foolish conduct. There are some texts which in place of the MT *'et-'^{e}lōhîm* in the second half of the verse, read *'attāh* (LXX etc.). Emendation is not necessary, as the final *y^{e}rā',* an imperative, already implies the addressee is 'you'. Qoheleth's point is that many activities are in vain, and that such are the actions of the fool. Contrariwise, the sage fears God, and it is this which Qoheleth advocates as the only life-style which will satisfy.

5.7-8(8-9) Another Look at Injustice

5.7(8) These two verses are notoriously difficult both to translate and to interpret. They can be isolated from their context on the basis of their vocabulary and thus of their subject matter, though like the preceding section, this one also contains an admonition and a motive clause.

Aware from the outset that we will have difficulty in determining its precise meaning, let us nonetheless begin an examination of the text to isolate the problems.

The opening particle *'im* indicates a potential situation, one in which the poor (*rāš*) are oppressed. The term *'ōšeq* is a participle describing the one who oppresses. Then Qoheleth adds a term *gezel,* 'robbery', applied to the violent removal of law and justice. The combined use of *gezel* and *'ōšeq* occurs elsewhere in Ps. 62.11(10) in a context of lamentation. The rare word *m^{e}dînāh* is thought to be a loan word from Aramaic meaning 'province, city', but it is significant in that it is derived from the root *dîn,* 'judgment'. It refers then not only to geographical areas, but to areas delimited for juridical purposes. The term *bammᵉdînāh* can thus be rendered, 'in a (specific) legislative district'.

The admonitory phrase is *'al-titmah,* 'do not be amazed', and the object of that admonition is the situation (*'al haḥēpeṣ*) just mentioned. In this clause the term *ḥēpeṣ* appears to have a slightly different nuance from the one it has in 5.3(4).

The motive clause v. 7b is something of a conundrum. Three times the word *gab* is used. It speaks of height, but whether we should translate it as 'exalted' or even 'haughty' (arrogant) is very much a subjective judgment. The syntax of the verse is also complex. The use of *min* in the phrase *gābōah mē'al gābōah* is perhaps for the purpose of expressing the comparative: 'higher than the high', or 'more exalted'. This status is afforded the one described as 'the keeper' (*šōmēr*), though what specifically he 'keeps' is not identified. Does it have any connection with the opening admonition in 4.17? Is it the one who is the antithesis of the plunderer in v. 7a? If so, the 'keeper' is the one who preserves justice. This latter possibility would appear logical, in which case the verse as a whole would mean that despite the abuse of justice, one should not be duly concerned, because the one who preserves justice is actually the more highly exalted one. He is in fact the most exalted one, this being the force of the plural *gᵉbōhîm*. He stands above those who oppress the poor and ravage society.

The above interpretation departs from that of most other commentators as a perusal of sources will demonstrate. Others generally see an hierarchy of officials with each level more rapacious than the other. For Kugel (1989: 32-49) it refers to the perversion of justice because of bribery. On such a basis, this verse takes on a very resigned air, alluding to the very sorry state of human society with its institutionalized injustice. Murphy (1992: 51) suggests that it may be an 'ironic' observation about dishonest bureaucracy—that one should not expect anything better from such operators.

5.8(9) The first thing we note about v. 8(9) is that it lacks all signs which might indicate its relationship with its context. Beyond this, the problem is one of meaning. There exists no consensus about the meaning of the sentence (see e.g. Zimmerli, 1967: 191; Rankin, 1956: 58-60), a nominal one in which the personal pronoun *hû'* (Qere) substitutes for the verb 'be'.

To apply the term *yitrôn* to the earth, as happens in this verse, is unusual, for elsewhere it is used only in conjunction with human endeavor. Thus its specific intent is not evident. Could it be a reference to the produce of the land? This would certainly accord with the final term, 'a cultivated (*ne'ebad*) field'. (For the use of the niphal participle *ne'ebad*, see Deut. 21.4; Ezek. 36.9, 34) Perhaps it is the use of *melek*, which is our major problem, because it seems not to belong in this context, regardless of whether it means 'king', or 'counsellor'. Murphy's suggestion is that the king may be some kind of corrective to a society's rapacious officials, but how this works to the advantage of farmers is not stated (1992: 51). Krüger (2004: 115) understands it to mean that the king is the one who stands at the pinnacle of a society in which everyone strives for personal gain and advantage. Seow (1997: 204) argues for a different division of the MT consonants that removes the reference to the king and offers a translation 'the advantage of land is in its yield, that is, if the field is cultivated for (its) yield'. In other words, those with land should focus on what it produces rather than seek to enlarge their land holdings. Apart from the more general sense of a society in which individuals strive for purely personal gain, we should probably simply admit that this is one of those verses whose meaning we may never fully understand.

5.9-11(10-12) Things Cannot Satisfy

This section stands apart from the preceding material by virtue of its different subject matter, as well as on literary grounds. Its theme is that abundance of material things cannot provide what life requires for its satisfaction. The reiterated 'much' in vv. 10(11), 11(12), the use of the verbs 'satisfy' (śba) in vv. 9(10) and 11(12), 'eat' in vv. 10(11) and 11(12), and 'sleep' (v. 11[12]), provide the focus for the section. Also we should take note of the frequent use of participles, and the absence of the admonitory form so frequent in the preceding section, as important literary features that make the section readily identifiable.

5.9(10) Beginning our examination with the concluding phrase (v. 9[10]c), we discover that Qoheleth is presenting for our consideration yet another situation that he believes to be beyond explanation (*hebel*). To describe it, Qoheleth chooses parallel clauses, the subject of which is the one who loves (*'ōhēb*) money and riches. Some differences between the two parallel clauses require comment.

The initial participle *'ōhēb*, 'the one who loves', would be more intelligible if prefaced by the definite article, bringing it closer to the form *mî 'ōhēb*, 'whoever loves' in v. 9(10)b. In the second clause the prefix *b* on *hāmôn*, 'wealth', is unnecessary and perhaps is a dittograph. The latter half of the verse, if parallel to the first, lacks the verb *śb'*, 'satisfy'. Despite these minor variations, the meaning of the statement is unequivocal: determined pursuit of money will never meet one's deepest personal needs (cf. also 6.7). That this is an aphoristic statement seems likely. To it Qoheleth has appended his own reflection, namely that this is an enigma. It is enigmatic given that deep human longing for the security which wealth appears to offer. However, the issue here is not so much wealth *per se* but the insatiable pursuit of wealth and material possessions. Perhaps more significant is the doubt expressed in this verse about the deuteronomic thesis that material achievements are one tangible proof, among many, of the divine blessing (cf. Deut 7.12ff.). Qoheleth is now saying something similar to what he has already affirmed in 2.11, that *yitrôn* does not lie in the pursuit of or possession of these material items. Greed can only lead to one's destruction.

5.10(11) The theme of abundance conveyed in the root *rbb* has been a feature of this chapter (see vv. 2[3], 6[7]). On two more occasions in v. 10(11) it appears, bearing the message that acquiring more things is not necessarily the way to satisfaction. The initial *birbôt* is a temporal expression, 'when things increase'. The word *haṭṭôbāh* refers to 'goods', the collective notion being implicit in the feminine form. Thus, the more one has, the more one needs, or as Qoheleth expresses it, 'the more goods we have, the more mouths we have to feed'. The phrase 'those who eat it' can refer generally to those for whom the wealthy person is responsible, though Seow (1997: 219-20) opines that it is more likely to be the greedy persons themselves. While this might be argued, the phrase seems to refer to a group of people other than those who accumulate the wealth, leaving the wealthy person with nothing more than additional responsibilities.

On the basis of this aphorism, Qoheleth puts a question. He asks whether there is any *kišrôn*, 'ability', or 'gain' (cf. 4.4) to those who are owners (*ba'al*) of these goods, other than to be able to look at what they have acquired, and then to see it disappear as others consume what they have acquired. This word *kišrôn* is a late word describing what is suitable or advantageous. Indisputably, the amassing of goods is an achievement, a momentary pleasure, but that is all it is.

5.11(12) The present section closes with an observation, perhaps from within the tradition, that the worker (*'ōbēd*) sleeps soundly (*mtq*, 'sweet ') regardless of how much or how little he has eaten. In contrast, the rich person's surfeit (*śb'*) prevents sleep. Here the 'worker' presumably indicates one who is poor and so is an employee of those who are 'rich'. There is both a social and an economic gap between the two. We can understand why Qoheleth suggests that the worker has the advantage: a surfeit can become burdensome, a source of worry and of insomnia (*'ēnennû manniaḥ lô lîšôn*) while being poorer at least allows one to sleep well at night free of worry about one's possessions. A surfeit, whether of food or goods, may hinder sleep. A second factor here reinforces the argument in v. 10(11) that gain is always accompanied by increased costs such that any potential advantage in having more is quickly 'swallowed up'—a case of Parkinson's Law.

The entire section 5.9-11(10-12) holds together thematically: abundance or surfeit can be a liability. The message to those who continued to measure success in material terms, or who sought *yitrôn* within those parameters, is clearly that *yitrôn* is unrelated to any attempt to amass material possessions.

5.12-16(13-17) Further Evidence of the Pain of Riches

The passage is illustrative of the principle enunciated in 5.9-11(10-12), that riches may prove to be a liability rather than an asset. The term *'šr* in 5.11(12) provides the keyword for the next section as *'šr* recurs in vv. 12(13) and 13(14) and in the following section, 5.18(19). The other term characteristic of this section is *ra',* 'calamity'. Qoheleth's purpose in citing this case is to bring the theme of materialism's inability to answer human need into direct relationship to his search for *yitrôn* (5.15 [16]).

5.12(13) A 'sickly evil' (*rā'āh ḥôlāh*) exists on earth: it is the potential danger (*rā'āh*) of having too much wealth (*'ōšer*). A careful individual hoards (*šmr*, cf. 4.17) his goods, but discovers that in the process something untoward has happened, namely, the savings are lost. The term *ba'al,* 'owner', links with v. 10(11) above (note that this term is often used in the plural with singular meaning).

5.13(14) What was the rich man's problem? Those very riches he guarded so carefully vanished (*'bd*) on account of *'inyān ra'* (cf. 1.13; 4.8), that is to say, in a venture which may have been morally questionable, or simply unfortunate in its outcome.

Either interpretation of the phrase *'inyān ra'* is possible. Thus, no matter how much careful attention one gives to amassed wealth, there is never any guarantee that it cannot be lost through misfortune or through business failure. (Lohfink's suggestion that it was a bank failure is without foundation.) That Qoheleth has in mind the former predicament, misfortune, appears the more likely in view of his quotation from Job 1 in v. 14(15).

In v. 13(14)b what is arguably a second and independent situation is introduced. This is judged to be independent of the preceding one because of its distinctive vocabulary (*b^e^yādô, m^e^'ūmāh, šebbā', hlk*), and of its theme of entering and leaving the world naked in v. 15(16). It is the re-use of the phrase *rā'āh ḥôlāh* in v. 15(16) which suggests that a second situation is in mind. The implication of this view is that the subject of the verb *hôlîd,* 'bear a child', in v. 13(14)b is not the rich person spoken of above, but rather it is some other anonymous person. If this view of what is clearly an ambiguous text can be sustained then it follows that the focus of the verse lies not with the subject of the verb, that is the father, but with the child born into the world. The problem for interpreters is that the antecedent of the verb *hôlîd* appears to be the person mentioned in the first half verse, while the phrase 'he has nothing in his hand' could apply to both the child and the father. Perhaps all we can safely say about the illustration is that a father with nothing to hand on to his heir, regardless of the circumstances that bring about such poverty, impacts upon the child born.

5.14(15) Likewise the individual's nakedness (*'ārôm*) at birth symbolizes material poverty. Qoheleth here quotes from Job 1.21. That he will return 'going as he came' (*yāšûb lāleket k^e^šebbā'*) indicates that as one enters or leaves this world, one's material possessions have no significance. When we depart this world we are literally 'naked' and no tangible benefit arises to us from our life of labour (*ba'^a^mālô*), for those things we have acquired cannot be taken with us. We leave this earth as we entered it, empty-handed, as Job remarked. Rankin (1956: 60) would have this verse refer to the father (so also Murphy, 1992: 52) rather than to the child, though in fact it could refer to either. It states a general truth applicable to all humanity.

5.15(16) By using the term *gam,* 'also', and repeating the phrase *rā'āh ḥôlāh,* 'a sickly evil', we assume that v. 15(16) relates back to the second situation (contra Gordis, 1968: 253), that at birth and death humankind stands naked.

Why does Qoheleth consider this calamitous? Loss of former wealth, or the fact that at death one's gains from a life of toil have no further usefulness or significance, is problematic to our writer. But why? It seems that he is incensed that after all the struggle to acquire things, death comes along and robs us of them all. Of course, here Qoheleth is thinking purely in material terms, but for him the fact remains that to lose all one's hard-earned wealth for whatever reason, be it the result of poor business acumen or because of death, is a calamity. It appears that all that has transpired between birth and death counts for nothing.

It is for that specific reason that Qoheleth once again must ask the programmatic question, 'What is one's *yitrôn* under such circumstances?' We seem to have toiled for nothing other than the air we breathe (*rûaḥ*). *Yitrôn* cannot be identified with anything material, but is a term which reaches out for some less concrete 'benefit' to humanity, especially one which will not be stripped away by death. The concept of *yitrôn* must extend beyond death and be non-material if it is to meet all Qoheleth's criteria. It certainly can incorporate one's earthly 'portion', but is not restricted to such materialistic bounds.

The idiom *kol 'ummat še-* is an Aramaism, and means 'exactly' though the proper text should perhaps be *kî l*^{e}*'ummat* (cf. LXX *hosper gar).* The use of the imperfect form *ya*^{a}*mōl* stresses the unending nature of human toil.

5.16(17) One of the more problematic verses in the book, v. 16(17) generally defies satisfactory interpretation and so any explanation and translation must be tentative.

The subject of v. 15(16) is 'he', which we presume can mean humanity in general, but in this context may refer specifically either to the father or to the son he sired, or to both (v. 14[15]). If this be so, then v. 16(17) further explains the phrase 'toiling for wind' in v. 15(16). All human beings spend their lives (= days) 'eating in darkness' *(b*^{e}*ḥōšek yō'kēl).* Here we have a figurative use of the noun 'darkness' along with the verb 'eat' in a context that can only carry a negative connotation (cf. 2.14; 6.4; 11.8). What specifically 'darkness' figures is a difficult question to answer other than to see it as a reference to some kind of personal trouble and/or pain. The alternative reading *wā'ēbel,* 'and in mourning', in lieu of *yō'kēl* should be followed.

Verse 16(17)b opens with a verbal form *kā'as,* 'be angry', though the syntax probably requires a noun, 'anger'. 'His sickness' (*ḥolyô*) constitutes another minor textual difficulty in that the suffix 'his' cannot be adequately explained. The final term *qeṣep*, 'resentment', accords well with the notion of 'anger' in the same clause. Thus v. 16(17)b contains references to emotional reactions, anger and resentment, and we must presume that they, along with the illness, are induced by a life of hardship. They are all part of the 'sickly evil' which is the focus of this section. A more accurate translation and interpretation do not at this stage seem possible.

5.17-19(18-20) Good Advice for Hard Times

From a decidedly pessimistic tone, the focus in this final section moves from the darker side of human experience to an up-beat theme. It is this latter which epitomizes his message. Against the background of the traumas facing humanity, Qoheleth repeats the question, what is one's *yitrôn?* As he has done when previously proffering his advice, so also here, Qoheleth invites his readers to enjoy what God gives. The theme and vocabulary of this section are something we have met already in such passages as 2.24; 3.12-13, 22. In them we are urged to take a healthy and vigorous grasp of the life which God gives.

5.17(18) Qoheleth in his own experience, and from observation of others', is aware of the frustrations and unanswered questions which life throws at us. In response, he could have allowed these difficulties to occupy the forefront of his mind and to poison his outlook. That he does not do so is testimony to his almost boundless optimism, and it is that warmth and that courage which flow through these words. Here he suggests that there is only one way to meet life's enigmas: one must eat, drink, and search out the good things in one's life of toil (cf. 8.15). This response is grounded in his theology: God has given us life, and to enjoy it is our 'portion'. The thought promoted in this refrain is significant not only for its content, but also for the fact that it occurs in other statements which bring to a conclusion the discussion of *yitrôn*. Thus in 2.24; 3.12, 22; 8.15 we find similar responses, indicating that this basic attitude stands as Qoheleth's most profound and positive response to the search for meaning (cf. also Whybray, 1980: 15-16).

The reference again to humanity's portion (*ḥēleq*) reminds that human experience and toil provide some measurable reward (cf. 2.10; 3.22). At the same time, we are conscious that this material 'portion' is too restricted to provide Qoheleth with the *yitrôn* he seeks.

A troublesome point of syntax in this verse is in what the RSV translates as 'to be good and fitting'. The problem is that the so-called relative *'ašer* stands between the two adjectives *ṭôb* and *yāpeh*. It is likely that this *'ašer* and the one which follows the opening *hinnēh* are co-ordinated; thus Qoheleth saw 'what was good, what was even beautiful'.

5.18(19) Qoheleth expresses the belief that the good things of life and their enjoyment are divine gifts. This is the theological stance from which he calls upon his readers to accept the gifts gladly.

'Riches' (*'ōšer*) connects this verse with the thought of v. 12(13), in which the wealthy person hoarded his possessions, but then lost them all. Wealth, if it is actually divine in origin, cannot be viewed in other than a positive way by Qoheleth. The emphasis he gives to these material things is supported in this context by the addition of a parallel term 'possessions' (*nᵉkāsîm*), of Aramaic origin (Ezra 6.8; 7.26). Not only do the gifts themselves come from above, the power (*šlt*, hiphil) to enjoy them also derives from that same source. Enjoyment of one's goods is in this verse conveyed under the idiom of 'eating from (by virtue of) them', *le'ᵉkōl mimmennû*. The fact that one's 'portion' (*ḥelqô*) and 'labour' (*'āmāl*) are cited together under the rubric of God's gift, assures us that they both are positive elements. The phrase *mattat 'ᵉlōhîm hî'* is repeated from 3.13.

5.19(20) As this verse consists of two motive clauses, the question of its relationship to the preceding statement arises. Gordis (1968: 256) argues that the first clause relates back to v. 17(18), and the second to v. 18(19). This thesis has merit as the phrase 'days of his life' (*yᵉmê-ḥayyāw*) occurs also in v. 17(18), while the verb 'enjoy' (*śmḥ*) is found in v. 18(19).

What then might be the relationship between v. 17(18) and v. 19(20)a? If 'he will not remember much (= for long) the days of his life', then v. 19(20)a adds urgency to the call to enjoy life while it is available. (See also Gianto, 1992: 528-32)

The second *kî* clause picks up the enjoyment theme from v. 18(19). Much ink has been spilled discussing the meaning of 'keep one occupied' (*ma'ᵃneh,* hiphil ptc.), the problem being that the root *'nh* has a variety of meanings: 'answer', 'afflict', 'occupy' (see BDB, *ad loc.*). It is perhaps best to read 'occupy' in light of its use elsewhere in Qoheleth with this same sense (cf. 1.3; 3.10). It is the deity who provides the power with which to enjoy life, and this contrasts with the former discussion about the inability of material things *of themselves* to satisfy. When one appreciates them as divine in origin and responds to them appropriately, then some measure of satisfaction from them is possible. One possible implication if the verb *'ānāh* here means 'answer' rather than 'occupy' is that God as it were distracts people with a joy such that they do not face (*zkr*) the real issues of life (see also Lohfink, 1990: 625-35).

This section marks the close of another major segment of Qoheleth's discourse. The 'Nothing is better'-sayings in 2.24; 3.12, 22 provide Qoheleth's response to the programmatic *yitrôn* question (cf. 1.13; 3.9). In 5.17-19(18-20) a similar thesis is put, though without the *'ēn yitrôn* form, and it represents the reply to the question of *yitrôn* in 5.15-16(16-17). This question in turn is grounded in the eclectic material presented in chs. 4-5. Although variety is the major feature of material in these two chapters, the basic discussion still relates to one's potential *yitrôn* in a world filled with oppression, pain, disappointment, folly, and where materialism fails to satisfy deeper human needs. Therefore, we are to view all the material in chs. 4-5 as providing the basis for the final conclusion or advice presented in 5.17-19(18-20). This follows closely the pattern noted earlier in chs. 2 and 3.

Regardless of the type of problem encountered in life in this enigmatic and painful world, we have only one wise response: to grasp life as a divine gift, and to seek within it the divine portion which is available.

Chapter 6

Is it Worth Being Wealthy?

The evil which Qoheleth spied in 5.12(13), namely potential dangers associated with being wealthy, is a theme which recurs in ch. 6. Despite the fact that the programmatic question in 5.15(16) and the response in vv. 17-19(18-20) appeared to terminate that part of the discussion, we find Qoheleth returning to the theme for further reflection.

The problem is stated in vv. 1-2, and this prompts reflection from two vantage points. The first is in vv. 3-5: an apparently successful individual—the criterion of success is his many offspring—finds that he knows no satisfaction (v. 3). Qoheleth argues that such an individual cannot be reckoned to be as fortunate as the still-born child. His reason for such a conclusion comes in vv. 4-5. A second perspective is offered by the situation outlined in v. 6: longevity as a measure of success. Once again, no satisfaction is derived from that (v. 7). As for the structure of the unit, we may portray it as a Question (vv. 1-2) + Reflection A (vv. 3-5) + Reflection B (v. 6).

The programmatic question whose appearance we have been tracing recurs in v. 8, and a 'Better'-proverb follows (v. 9) as the means of concluding this section.

A change of theme marks the transition at v. 10, where we detect vocabulary and concepts not found in the preceding section. Resorting to the use of the question-form, Qoheleth builds up to a statement about the limitations to our ability to comprehend life in this present world. Even more elusive is the possibility of determining what life will be like in the future.

6.1–2 No Pleasure in Wealth

6.1 Qoheleth, as observer, finds yet another painful human situation (*rā'āh*) crying out for analysis (cf. 5.12[13]). Not only is this situation a grievous one, it is also wide in extent and common throughout society (*rabbāh hî' 'al-hā'ādām*). *Rab* in Qoheleth denotes extent, rather than something onerous as in RSV's 'it lies heavy upon men'.

6.2 What 'evil' could this be? It is the case of a person with abundant material wealth but who lacks the power and ability to derive pleasure from it. Several points are made. The first is that, as in 5.18(19), God is the one who provides wealth and possessions (*'ōšer ûnᵉkāsîm*). In addition, this wealthy person has received *kābôd*, a term generally conveying honoured status, but also carrying the meaning 'abundance' or 'riches'. The latter meaning is the one which perhaps best fits the intention here. The choice of the three terms (*'ōšer, nᵉkāsîm*, and *kābôd*), used to describe Solomon in 2 Chron. 1.11-12, is to be noted though the more obvious parallel to this verse comes from Qoheleth's description of his own success in 2.1-8. His blessing and good fortune were so complete that there was no lack (*'ēnennû ḥāsēr*). All his heart desired (*'āwāh*, hiphil) was his. However in contrast to 2.1-10 and 5.18(19), this person was totally deficient in the ability to enjoy the divine gift of these goods (*lō' yašliṭennû hā'ᵉlōhîm le'ᵉkōl mimmennû*). The rare verb *šlt* is a late word meaning 'to master', in the sense of being able to control one's environment. The expression here, apart from the fact that it is cast in the negative, is only marginally different from that of 5.18(19). Yet we should note that here in ch. 6, Qoheleth makes more specific the fact that the power to enjoy one's wealth likewise originates with God. The references in vv. 1-2 to God's gift of wealth, and the power to enjoy the same, reflect the theological understanding of this sage: all things and enjoyment of them stem from God. In a manner similar to Amos (9.4), Qoheleth also believes that good and ill have only one possible source. Whatever theological difficulties such a view creates, we still must recognize that for most of the OT the all-encompassing nature of divine authority and power remains as its undergirding theological concept.

As in 5.18(19), we note that the 'enjoyment' theme is carried by the verb 'eat' (cf. also Prov. 13.25; Ps. 81.16). Salters has pointed out the appropriateness of this verb if *kābôd* bears the meaning 'abundance'. What the rich man cannot eat or enjoy falls to the hand of the 'stranger' (*'îš nokrî*). This latter is a term occurring elsewhere only in Deut. 17.15. *Nokrî* regularly is employed to describe one who is an alien, one from a different tribe or family; thus occasionally it means 'foreigner' (cf. Exod. 21.8). Here it is simplest to render it as 'someone else'. The *kî* with which the clause opens has an adversative function, 'on the contrary', following the negative. It is precisely the condition noted here that provides the nub of the issue Qoheleth takes up: wealth becomes a source of pleasure for a person other than the one whose wealth it is, and perhaps even for a foreigner. This possibility is not only an enigma, it is in Qoheleth's words 'an evil disease' (*ḥolî rā'*). This latter is a very forceful expression, probably a variation on the phrase *rā'āh ḥōlî* in 5.12(13).

In raising the question of the absence of satisfaction from what one possesses, Qoheleth is touching a raw nerve. Some within the wisdom tradition, as reflected in statements such as Prov. 13.21, 25 as well as those in the deuteronomic stream (e.g. Deut. 8.10), held firmly to the notion that material success, tangible possessions, evidenced divine blessing which was the consequence of living in a manner pleasing to God. They took literally the view that God blessed in material ways those who obeyed him, and by logical extension determined that one who had much of this world's goods must be the one who pleased God. It was therefore axiomatic that by adhering to the sage's advice a person would not only discover wisdom, but would also know material benefits and the satisfaction and pleasure they could bring. What Qoheleth is doing is to place a large question mark alongside such thinking. He does so by suggesting that a wealthy person may not derive any joy from possessions, and to that extent the wealthy person is like the fool who does not know how to find enjoyment. In other words, like Job, Qoheleth points up an anomaly in human experience which in theological terms is an embarrassment to the traditional view.

6.3–5 Children and Longevity are of Questionable Worth

In this section, the honour of the person concerned consists in producing large numbers of children and in living a long life. This scenario is the first of two relating to the theme of 6.1-2.

6.3 Qoheleth poses the question of one who produces 100 children during a long and fruitful life. The reiterated *rab,* 'much', indicates the extent of the blessings falling to this person. The two phrases describing long life are identical in meaning if not in form; thus they provide emphasis. However, despite receiving the traditional blessings (*ṭôbāh*) of descendants and longevity (cf. Gen. 1.28; Deut. 7.13), the person concerned misses out on any satisfaction. The use of imperfect verb forms suggests that this is a typical or hypothetical case. Additionally, this individual, when he eventually deceases, is not accorded a burial *(g^e^bûrāh),* a most unusual oversight and one seemingly without reason. Presumably the mention of the lack of burial is to indicate that this was the final humiliation. However, we also need to bear in mind that there is a strong element of hyperbole in this scenario: 100 children and lack of burial are exaggerations used to make the scenario more vivid. Seow (1997: 211) argues that the noun *g^e^bûrāh* refers to a place for burial rather than to the act of burial. Although there may be inscriptional evidence in support of this argument, the focus in v. 5 upon the importance of 'rest' would seem to support the view that here the noun does in fact refer to the act of burial.

Gordis proposed an emendation to read *lû'*, 'even though', in place of *lô'*, the negative particle, in the phrase *gam g^e^bûrāh lô' hāy^e^tāh lô.* His translation would then run, 'even if he were to have an (elaborate) funeral'. However, there is no adequate reason for such a change, and additionally the introductory *w^e^gam* indicates that here we are dealing with another negative to be added to the lack of satisfaction. Scott's solution (1965) is to relocate *g^e^bûrāh... lô* at the end of v. 4, making it refer to the still-born child. This alteration cannot be substantiated from textual evidence.

If the above is the descriptive portion of the scenario, then the final clause of the verse offers a conclusion drawn from it. To Qoheleth a still-birth (*nēpel,* cf. Job 3.16) is better than being a very fruitful parent with a long life if throughout that time one does not know satisfaction. Qoheleth may at this juncture be adapting imagery from Isa. 14.18-20. It is the *quality* of life to which Qoheleth is referring, not its duration. If one is denied the opportunity to enjoy one's life, then one is better off never entering the world at all (cf. 4.2). In this hyperbolic statement Qoheleth makes the point that material things have their place in our lives, but if, as so often happens, they cannot bring pleasure, then they are of very limited worth.

6.4-5 The argument on which the above evaluation rests comes in two parts, v. 4 and v. 5. The still-born child, having come in what Qoheleth describes as *hebel,* that is, for a brief moment, leaves in darkness. It neither sees nor is seen, and thus its 'name' (*š^e^mô*) or identity is hidden from view (*y^e^kusseh*). It has no experience of life under the sun, passing directly to the grave. Its total lack of awareness of how brief and enigmatic life can be is to its advantage, and thus Qoheleth rates it as more fortunate than one who amasses much wealth but is denied satisfaction from it.

The concluding phrase speaks of the still-born at 'rest' *(naḥat)*. The choice of the term 'rest' in this context is consistent with the view of 4.2 that in death one is released from a world marked by oppression and other evils. Gordis feels that 'rest' is an inappropriate rendering of the Hebrew *naḥat*, preferring 'satisfaction'. He bases this translation on the Mishnaic use (see 1968: 259). However, elsewhere (4.6; 5.11 [12]; 9.17 etc.) the root meaning 'rest' seems in order, and is consistent with Job 3.17, with which our passage here seems to be related. Whatever the precise nature of the state to which the stillborn has passed, Qoheleth's evaluation holds: it is better off than a rich person denied satisfaction from what he or she has accumulated.

The final clause, 'to this more than to this' (*lāzeh mizzeh*) refers to the two elements in a comparison. Krüger (2004: 117) links the phrase with the sun, rendering the phrase as 'The sun has more peace than he'. However, the more logical view is that the first demonstrative *zeh* points to the still-born just mentioned, and the second *zeh* to the wealthy individual, the other subject of reflection.

6.6–9 What is the Benefit of Longevity?

A second scenario is now offered for consideration. The vocabulary shared with 6.4-5 (*hāyāh, ḥāyāh, ṭôbāh, šānîm*) shows that it stands in close relationship with those verses. Yet there are other terms not found in that sub-section: for example, *'āmāl*, 'work', and *hālak*, 'walk', together with the question form in v. 8. Like 6.3, this section also opens with a supposition, 'even if ...' (*'illû*) and terminates with a 'Better'-proverb and a variant on the *hebel*-phrase (v. 9).

6.6 The long-living person with all his wealth and influence spoken of in 6.3 is not the same as the person referred to here. This conclusion rests on two points. The first is the statement that here he 'sees' or enjoys no good thing or blessing (*wᵉṭôbāh lô' rā'āh*); the second point is that the structure of the section has v. 6 as a further illustration of the issue in vv. 1-2. The person in mind in v. 6 is yet another long-living person. In this case he lives for more than 2000 years! For effect, Qoheleth uses an even greater exaggeration than the previous one. The introductory *'illû*, a late word otherwise used only in Esth. 7.4, means 'let us suppose that...', supporting the thesis that we have to do with a second example of the problem under review. Though living a virtual eternity, this unfortunate soul finds no blessing in it. We note again the ambiguity which Qoheleth forces his readers to confront.

In Deut. 1.11 the term *'elep pe'ammîm* is bracketed with the concept of blessing. Qoheleth takes this association, multiplies by two the idiom for unbounded blessing, but then denies that any blessing is available. Under these circumstances, what should have been a blessing, a long life, is actually an interminable sentence, an unmitigated curse. The question for Qoheleth, and thus for his readers, is not how long one lives, but whether or not one finds meaning and satisfaction in life. Regardless of how long life endures, all must face the reality of death, and it could well be that the sooner one reaches that final moment, the better—that is the point of the example about the still-born. The question with which this section closes (*halô' 'el-māqôm 'eḥād hakkōl hôlēk*) is merely a variation on the statement in 3.20.

6.7 From the two scenarios above Qoheleth draws a conclusion. It is generally assumed that this verse represents a proverbial saying quoted by Qoheleth (Barton: 135; Fox [1999: 244]). Human labour (*'āmāl*) knows only one end: it is to feed oneself (cf. Prov. 16.26). In 5.10(11) Qoheleth commented that as one accumulated more goods one's rate of consumption rose for no net gain (cf. 6.3). Modem economic theory has advanced little beyond this!

Ackroyd (*ASTI* 5, 1967: 85) and Dahood (*Biblica* 49, 1968: 368) understand the suffix on *pihû*, 'his mouth', as the mouth of Sheol welcoming humanity and all its achievements. The final clause also refers to the appetite of Sheol as that which cannot be sated (cf. Prov. 27.20), meaning of course that all must die. If our v. 7 is a quotation of a proverbial saying, then it is almost certain that Sheol is not in mind; rather, as the surface meaning suggests, it refers only to human labour, as 5.10(11). Furthermore, the phrase *lô' timmālē'* in 1.8 identifies the ear in the physical or anatomical sense. This suggests that 'mouth' and 'soul' are most probably intended as figures of human physical needs.

Qoheleth is in this passage making clear that a materialist definition of blessing is basically flawed. No amount of material goods can guarantee a sense of personal satisfaction. Thus Qoheleth moves back to ask once more his fundamental question about *yitrôn*.

6.8 The initial *kî* is to be viewed as an asseverative, 'indeed'. On this interpretation, v. 8 provides Qoheleth's reflection, in interrogative form, arising from the material presented in vv. 1-7 above.

Qoheleth once again ponders the matter of 'advantage' (*yôtēr*). Here and in v. 11 *yôtēr* is a qal participle, and may have a nuance different from the nominal form *yitrôn*. In 2.15 it carries an adverbial sense. Human industry, generally speaking, provides material reward. It is against this background that Qoheleth asks whether this would remain true for both the wise and foolish alike. As v. 8 closely follows the standard form of the programmatic question *mah yitrôn lā'ādām* (1.3; 2.22; 3.9), 1 would incline to the view that *yôtēr* is here the equivalent of *yitrôn*.

In 2.12-17 Qoheleth has pointed out that the wise and fool stand united at certain moments; for example, they both die. Therefore, to ask whether the wise has some *yôtēr* is to ask whether there is not some point at which the wise has something 'left over' which is not available to the fool. Clearly, Qoheleth is not thinking of material distinctions, for even the poor (*'onî*) may obtain it (v. 8b). This is also indicated in 6.1-7. Wise and fool both share the reality of death (v. 6), so we are even more aware of the possibility that Qoheleth is continuing his search for an answer to life which moves beyond the limits of this present world. He looks for some ultimate advantage to the wise which transcends death, thus placing them ahead of fools.

In 6.8b the repeated *mah* recalls the initial *mah yôtēr*. It is an abbreviation for that earlier form, indicating that both questions run parallel. On this basis we are to see the 'wise' in v. 8a and the 'poor' in v. 8b as equated (see Bryce, 1972). Though lacking possessions, the poor 'know how to walk' (*yôdē'a lah^{a}lôk*) among the living. Poverty is no hindrance to learning how to conduct oneself in all circumstances. But does such a person have the possibility of *yôtēr*? If Qoheleth is looking away from material definition and towards that which transcends this material world, then we can see how he can make an affirmative response: yes, *yitrôn* is available to the poor as well.

6.9 Like all aphorisms, this concluding saying (v. 9a) depends on context for a close definition of its meaning. Four of its central terms *ṭôb, rā'āh, hālak,* and *nepeš* occur in 6.1-8. It asserts that 'sight of the eyes' (*mar'ēh 'ēnayim*) or what one perceives, is preferable to what the RSV describes as 'the wandering of desires' (*h^{a}lak nepeš*). Qoheleth has used the term *nepeš* in vv. 3, 7 to express that part of one's being which may be the locus for satisfaction. *Hālak* in vv. 4, 6 speaks of progress through life, suggesting that *h^a^lak nepeš* has to do with our search for meaning and satisfaction in life. However, Crenshaw (1987: 129) and Whybray (1989: 109) have both pointed out that the verb *hlk* often refers to death and thus the phrase can also mean that a person progresses through life to death.

The interpreter now faces a dilemma. This resides in the demonstrative *zeh,* 'this' in v. 9b. Exactly what is it that qualifies as *hebel*? Should we determine that 'this' recalls the quotation *in toto,* then the conclusion that the values contained in the quotation is an enigma can be understood. In previous remarks (5.10[11]), Qoheleth has shared his views about material possessions. Satisfaction comes only as one's *nepeš* finds its purpose. If, as the quotation suggests, the tangible world provides the utmost reward, then Qoheleth wants to express a strong, negative vote. He can do this by affirming that 'this' (evaluation) is beyond comprehension. Whenever Qoheleth uses the *hebel*-phrase, he does so to point up an anomalous situation. On this basis, 'this' actually refers to the entire proverb as quoted. Thus, satisfaction derived from life's journey is more to be treasured than the tangible rewards we might enjoy along the way.

Contrary to the interpretation just given, most commentators determine that 'this' in v. 9b refers only to the second component of the saying, that the 'wandering of desires' is a vain and useless undertaking.

6.10-12 On Human Limitations

The *hebel*-phrase with which v. 9 concludes, a general shift in the topic under review, and the return of the programmatic question in 6.11, indicate that vv. 10-12 introduce a new section, though not totally independent of the foregoing.

Generally this section picks up an earlier theme from 1.9 and 3.15, while 6.12 corresponds to 3.21 and its mention of our possible knowledge of the future.

One feature of the unit before us is the reiterated use of the interrogatives *mah*, 'what,' and *mî*, 'who'.

6.10 The opening words echo 3.15. The initial *mah* is the distributive 'whatever' (cf. v. 12); it does not have the normal interrogative sense. All existent matter, says Qoheleth, 'has been named already' (*niqrā' š^e^mô*). The expression 'giving the name to' something may well be of Babylonian origin, in which case it refers to the coming into existence of some object (Isa. 40.26). Possible association with Gen. 2.19 may also be suggested.

The second phrase *nôdā' 'ašer-hû' 'ādām,* is syntactically difficult as it stands and so has presented problems for the exegete resulting is a variety of solutions. MT should be translated 'it is known that he is man'. However, some wish to separate 'man' from the previous phrase and link it with what follows (see Whitley: 61). Although this is a seemingly intractable problem, the major challenge lies with determining what connection it has with v. 10a. In Barton's view, the connection is made by giving the term *nôdā'* the meaning 'foreknowledge', thence 'foreordain' (p. 136; see also Lauha: 119). From other examples of the initial phrase in 1.9 and 3.15 it is possible to conclude that the phrase describes an immutable fact about the world: there is nothing new. That is to say, things are as they are, as they have been, and as they always will be. This thesis has already been put forward in 1.4-11, and is rooted in the notion that God is the creator and sustainer of all life. Within that framework, one other fact which is beyond dispute (*nôdā'*) is that an individual cannot contend (*dîn*) with someone much more powerful than oneself. Lauha's suggestion, that this one might be 'a heavenly despot', is unnecessary. Nor need one posit a doctrine of predestination, even in incipient form. The verse itself merely states that human potential works within very clear limitations. One cannot expect to be victorious if one's rival is much more powerful—that is axiomatic. The purpose of the saying is to remind the reader of human limitations; thus, 'it is a known fact (*nôdā'*) that one is only human'. The noun *'ādām* has been seen as a reference to Adam because of the mention of 'naming' rather than as a generic term for humanity (Whybray, 1989: 110).

Two verbs here require comment. The first is the infinitive construct *lādîn.* The root meaning, 'judge', seems not entirely applicable here, so a derived meaning, 'contend with', is suggested (see BDB: 192; *TDOT,* III: 188). On this reading we have a unique use of the verb, drawing it close to the regular meaning of the verb *ryb.* The second textual matter relates to the Ketib *šettaqqîp.* Rather than a verb, the context dictates an adjective. Thus, with or without the definite article, *taqqîp,* 'strong', makes perfectly good sense. Thus we can render the text, '... one who is stronger' than him. Whether this is a reference to the deity, as some have believed, is doubtful, the saying itself being too general to allow dogmatism.

6.11 The initial *kî*, 'because', binds what follows to the previous verse as the basis for its thesis. From this relationship we draw clues for our interpretation. The contention between the two adversaries in v. 10 is essentially a verbal one (*dîn*). This makes intelligible the phrase 'many words' (*d^a^bārîm harbeh*). The result of this bellicose confrontation is that it increases (*marbîm*, hiph. ptc.) one's sense of frustration (*hebel*), for it brings the weaker party no closer to explaining why things are the way they are. In the light of this verbal encounter and its unsatisfactory outcome, Qoheleth once again asks about a person's 'advantage'. Here we meet the briefest form in which the question appears.

6.12 The two parts of the verse are each introduced by the question word *mî*, 'who'. The first asks 'who knows' (cf. 3.12) what is good for one during one's short earthly pilgrimage. The second wonders, 'who will inform' a person of events after the latter's demise, that is, of world events following a person's death, not necessarily what happens to one after one's own death. It is also possible that it asks who might explain to a person what their individual destiny is. Implicit in the rhetorical questions is the belief that *nobody* knows, or that at least only God knows. Qoheleth himself does not pursue an answer; he rests content merely with raising the issue.

If we accept that there is a sequential relationship between v. 11 and v. 12, then the question of *yôtēr* in v. 11 is expanded in v. 12. This aids our definition of *yôtēr*, namely that it has to do with the quality of life now as well as in the future. On the one hand, there is the value (*ṭôb*) of this enigmatic life whatever its duration, and on the other, there is the matter of the future. Unfortunately, the existential present as well as the future are both beyond human comprehension. The significance of the term 'shadow' (*ṣēl*) as descriptive of life needs to be grasped: life is brief, passing, but nevertheless real. The rhetorical questions permit Qoheleth to highlight once more human impotence when it comes to the grand question of life both present and future.

The verbal form *ya'^a^śēm* (RSV 'pass') may carry the rabbinic thought of the root *'śh*, namely 'spend time'. This would make it the only OT example of such a usage. The third-person masculine plural suffix on the verb refers either to the plural 'days' or to *ḥayyîm* 'life'. The so-called relative *'^a^šer* parallels the introductory *kî*.

The concluding pericope (6.10-12) once again reminds the reader that the human situation is such that we are unable to discover all we might want to know about it. Our frailty, the limitations under which we labour as we seek to make sense of our world, these are facts from which we cannot escape. Qoheleth at the end of chs. 7 and 8, moves to a dogmatic denial that even the sage can fully comprehend life's meaning. So the question of *yitrôn* persists, and before responding again in 8.7, ch. 7 intervenes to take us on another mental journey. Let us follow.

Chapter 7

Good, Better, Best...

A sudden change in form and content marks ch. 7 off from the preceding. Qoheleth presents a collection of sayings most of which exhibit a parallel structure, either synonymous or antithetical. The key word around which these sayings gather is 'good' (*ṭôb*). The 'Better'-proverb which Qoheleth uses so frequently is found in concentration within this collection, in vv. 1-12. Other rhetorical features such as assonance in v. 5 (*šîr, šāma', 'îš*) and v. 6 (*sîr, kᵉsîl, sîrîm*), and *rûaḥ, nûaḥ* in vv. 8-9, further identify this opening section's special character. Emphasis upon the wise and their behaviour is achieved by the use of contrast with the fool.

Although many scholars (e.g. Lauha: 129; Whybray, Seow, Fox, for example) would see vv. 13-14 as belonging with the previous section and providing its conclusion, the grounds for so including them are not obvious. Actually the focus in the two verses moves to relate to the work of God hidden from human understanding. This links with the closing verse of 8.17. The gulf fixed between good and evil in vv. 13-14 has more in common with the theme of 7.15 and the advice predicated on it in vv. 16-17. A 'Better'-proverb summarizes the section in v. 18.

As we move to vv. 19-24 we encounter what appear to be three independent sayings, but it is clear that v. 19 represents an idea similar to that in v. 12, and the notions of 'righteousness' (*ṣdq*) and 'good' in v. 20 relate to the ideas expressed in vv. 15-16. Verses 21 and 22, however, are only with difficulty linked with the preceding, while vv. 23-24 provide a bridge to what follows.

Then Qoheleth in vv. 23-29 speaks of 'testing' (*nsh*) what he has seen (cf. 1.13; 2.12), the work of God, in a final section which is bound closely with vv. 13-14 by their shared keywords—'see, consider' (*rā'āh*) and 'can(not) find' ([*lō'*] *māṣā'*)—as well as by the notion of the deeds of God (*'āśāh hā'ᵉlōhîm*). In this final section we find once again the theme of 'searching for' (*bqš*) and '(not) finding' ([*lō'*] *mṣ'*) the meaning of what God does.

A brief analysis like this establishes that the chapter falls into two basic divisions—vv. 1-12 and vv. 13-29—though within those sections we note several smaller sub-divisions which carry the argument.

There stands also the wider question of the relationship of this chapter as a whole to the context. We have already noted that ch. 6 closed with some questions, including a reiteration of the programmatic question driving Qoheleth's quest. The theme in 6.12 that man cannot know the future recurs in 7.14, and so provides a context for the gathered aphorisms of 7.1-12. But more significant is the fact that the responses to the questions in 6.12 are not presented in detail until 8.7. Then the kind of advice Qoheleth regularly presents that is predicated on that response, that is, the call to enjoyment, we find in 8.15. Recalling Qoheleth's basic movement from question through answer to advice, we can place ch. 7 between the discussion at the end of ch. 6 and flowing through to the final summation and advice of 8.15. Under the general thesis of wisdom and its limitations, Qoheleth continues to pursue an answer to the question of a person's *yitrôn*. It is this wider relationship we seek to bear in mind as we consider the chapter in detail.

7.1-12 Priorities and Values

The opening section of the chapter is constructed around a series of 'Better'-sayings. At first glance it might appear that this unit lacks formal structure (Whybray, 1989: 118), but closer examination reveals material loosely organized but nevertheless cohesive (Murphy, 1992: 62).

Having established the principle of death's priority over birth in v. lb, Qoheleth moves on to a related concept about the 'house of mourning' *(bēt-'ēbel)* and its contrasting 'house of feasting' *(bēt-mišteh)*. This duo reappears in v. 4 in an application of the principle in v. lb to the wise and the foolish. From a literary viewpoint these two 'houses' provide the inclusion binding vv. 2 and 4 together. The contrast between the wise and the fool dominates the thought of vv. 5-10. It is v. 4 which provides the pivot for the unit. The importance of vv. 1-4 for this entire chapter cannot be overestimated; they introduce the subject of death as that which must be pondered for its instructional, and thus theological, significance to the living. The living must, if they are to be accounted wise, devote their minds to discovering what death means. Verses 5-10 indicate that the fool does not do this.

The discussion proceeds to include v. 10, after which vv. 11-12 draw on the 'Better'-form to express a conclusion. It is here that the two concepts of wisdom and *yitrôn* are brought together.

7.1 Qoheleth gives us two balanced clauses. Both are 'Better'-sayings though the second lacks the operative word 'good'. Of these two sayings, the first is almost certainly a popular aphorism (cf. Prov. 22.1). It features a chiasmus (a:b:b':a') and assonance (*šēm, šemen*), with the thesis that a good reputation (*ṭôb šēm*) is better than 'good oil' (*šemen ṭôb*). On the assumption that v. lb is an aphorism, it is possible to concede that liberties have been taken with syntax for the sake of style. Thus, the initial *ṭôb,* which theoretically is a predicative use, could be rendered as an attributive—'a good name' (so RSV). The term *šēm* is not simply any name, but one's good reputation. The 'good oil', whether perfume or medicine, would be of high quality and expensive; nevertheless it is of less value than a good reputation. A highly prized material object does not have the same worth as personal integrity and character.

The purpose of the quotation is to serve as a type. Alongside it Qoheleth places two other values for our comparison. Just as a good name is preferred, so, argues Qoheleth, is the 'day of death' more important than the 'day of birth'. This is not a new idea, for Qoheleth has already spoken in this manner in 4.2 and 6.3. Here, however, Qoheleth argues the case with more force by setting it on a level equivalent with that of an accepted set of values. How then do we interpret the phrase? Is it, as some would have us believe (e.g. Gordis, 1968: 267; Lauha: 124), a comment on the meaninglessness of human life? Certainly life has its problems, but is it for this reason that Qoheleth argues that death is preferable? For Lohfink it is evidence of Qoheleth's powerful irony. Qoheleth will make the point in v. 4 that the mark of the sage is that he reflects on the fact of death as much as he does on life. The reason is that death and life are intertwined, and mutually defining. If we can accept that in the word *yitrôn* our author is probing after some more satisfactory solution to the problem of injustice in human society, then we can appreciate why Qoheleth will agree that death is better. It is preferable because it may open the way into a future where injustice as a problem is finally and perhaps happily resolved. Qoheleth is certainly not a pessimist when he says that death is preferable, but unless there is some *yitrôn,* some meaningful future both now and beyond death, then the evaluation he presents in v. 1b cannot be sustained. More recently Krüger (p. 136) has suggested that Qoheleth is saying that 'people should forego enjoyment in their "earthly" life in order to experience true happiness in the "beyond"'. However, Qoheleth's regular calls to enjoyment would argue against such a conclusion.

The term *hiwwālᵉdô,* 'his birth', is the niphal infinitive construct with suffix. The use of an infinitive in this manner as a verbal noun is often found after prepositions (see Gen. 2.17; 29.7; Qoh. 3.4; GK: 363).

7.2 Having argued that death is preferable to birth, Qoheleth explains further what specifically is in mind. The 'Better'-proverb of v. 2 is clearly one of Qoheleth's own manufacture because it enshrines the values of the preceding v. lb. The two halves of the verse balance perfectly. Better is it to go to the 'house of mourning' (*bēt-'ēbel*) than to the 'house of feasting' (*bēt-mišteh*). It is evident that Qoheleth means one would join a group of mourners in preference to being part of a celebration no matter for what purpose (cf. Jer. 16.5, 8). Here, then, Qoheleth is not suggesting that one's own death is better than one's birth, though that may have been true in 4.1-3; rather, here he is contending that the sage can learn from participating in another's joy or sorrow.

There is a root *šth* used to describe drinking bouts (Isa. 5.11-12; Job 1.5; Esth. 2.18), so our term *mišteh* here is related. In v. 4 a synonym, *śimḥāh*, appears, indicating another aspect of pleasure and the 'good life'. Actually, both these root concepts are present in Qoheleth's 'there is nothing better than...'-sayings in 2.24; 3.13; 5.17(18); 8.15, making it obvious that Qoheleth has no intention of denying the validity of all life's pleasures; nor is he adopting a pessimistic view of life. The comparative form allows him to say, 'yet I will show you a better way', a way which will add significance to all of life.

In the second half of v. 2 we read Qoheleth's reasoning. The 'house of mourning' symbolizes the fact of death, the end (*sôp*) of earthly existence, and the destination of all (3.19). The living, for whom all Qoheleth's advice is intended, are advised to ponder what this means. His own problem is to find some way of coming to terms with death, especially when it comes to the oppressed and poor who so frequently die without witnessing justice (4.1-3), or when it strikes the wealthy who have never found enjoyment in their material accomplishments (6.1-6). If there are so many in society who are unable to 'enjoy' life as God provides it, then the sage is confronting a problem of monumental proportions—God's very justice is at stake.

Pondering the meaning of things is expressed by his phrase *nātan 'el lēb*, literally 'to give (or apply) one's heart/mind' to something. We note the use of the word *lēb* with the sense 'mind' or 'intellectual faculties' in this chapter in vv. 3, 4, 7, 21. It highlights for us the search for meaning which is the sage's trade. He is given the responsibility to detect the meaning of even so-called ordinary events which might otherwise pass without notice (cf. Prov. 24.30-34).

7.3 Consistent with the thesis of vv. lb, 2, the 'Better'-proverb in v. 3 places 'sorrow' (*ka'as*) above 'laughter' (*śᵉḥōq*). Actually *ka'as* also denotes 'vexation', leading some to translate it in that way here (it has that meaning apparently in v. 9). However, this latter meaning seems inappropriate in the present context. The laughter envisioned is presumably a general term for empty hilarity (cf. Prov. 14.13), as distinct from the profound enjoyment (*śmḥ*) which Qoheleth advocates throughout.

A motive clause occupies the second half of the verse, Qoheleth arguing that 'sadness' (*rōa' pānîm*) improves one's mind. It is evident that *rōa'* does not have an ethical meaning when applied to facial expression, but it connotes that which causes the face to express sadness. The translation 'improves (the mind)' derives from the hiphil imperfect *yîṭab*. Again we note the thought that the sage uses every opportunity to ponder the meaning of events, especially in this case, the fact of death. Thus vv. 3b and 2c are essentially identical in meaning. There is here no identification of sadness with wisdom (contra Gordis, 1968: 268). Qoheleth believes that a distinguishing feature of the sage is that he appreciates the educational value of a crisis, whether it befall another or oneself.

7.4 Closing this first sub-section is the inclusion *bēt-'ēbel* and *bēt-śimḥāh*. Flowing naturally from what we have seen above is the thought that the sage will be associated with those who are in mourning, for death is a necessary subject of reflection. The fool, on the other hand, thinking only of pleasure and enjoyment, has detached his mind from associations with death. A refusal to think about death is thus proof of one's folly. This, of course, is a severe criticism, but one should add that Qoheleth is most probably critiquing those so-called sages whose advice or philosophy is worked out only in the context of life's lighter moments. Inevitably this approach results in advice which can say nothing constructive when life's darker side turns its face. The definition of a true sage is one who also tries to take full account of the tragic. This view is supported by Qoheleth's own autobiography. In chs. 1-2 he chronicled his great success, but found there no answer to the *yitrôn* he sought, because it cannot be found only in success and material benefits, in this world. So throughout this book Qoheleth will dwell on the distaff side of human experience, for only in considering all dimensions can one expect to reach an answer, if indeed there is an answer.

Having introduced the wise and the fool, and the mind's focus, we can appreciate v. 4 as an introduction to vv. 5-10, which discuss their relative merits. Note also its formal identity with 10.2.

7.5 Yet another 'Better'-proverb is Qoheleth's medium for contrasting the sage's 'rebuke' (*ga'ᵃrat*) with the fool's 'song' (*šîr*). To 'hear and heed' (*šāma'*) the wise man's comments is the advice given, and it is especially valid when the advice is of a critical nature. The word *ga'ᵃrat* conveys the idea of 'constructive criticism', whose purpose is to correct a behaviour pattern that is morally questionable, or detrimental (cf. Prov. 13.1; 17.10). The careful use of singular and plural nouns in this advice is also worth noting: one sage's advice counts more than the sung praises, the flattering words, of numerous fools.

The assonance in v. 5b (and in v. 6a) is carried by a series of 's'-sounds, a stylistic device for ridiculing the fools' words.

7.6 Qoheleth's advice in v. 5 has its basis in v. 6. The pleasant sounds of the fool's song are likened to the crackling of thorns (*sîrîm*) as they fire the cooking pot (*sîr*). The play on words is another expression of the poet's imaginative mind and aids in memorialising the saying. The slender stalks of the thorn bush produce limited heat, perhaps sufficient to warm the pot, and in the process generate much noise, noise which is irrelevant to the task of cooking. Qoheleth develops this theme of 'noise', likening it to the fool's laughter (*śᵉḥōq hakkᵉsîl).* There is obviously some connection between this theme and the earlier one of the house of feasting (vv. 2, 4). Laughter, of course, is not a bad thing, but insofar as Qoheleth's mind is focused on the instructional value of experiences, of sorrow and rebuke, it takes on a negative cast for the moment. So, like the noise of sticks burning, praise or flattery from a fool has no instructional value. His words have not passed through the filter of his mind.

This situation is another which can be classified as *hebel*. Why? Song and laughter can be enjoyable and beneficial. It is the fact that it stems from the lips of a fool that denies it value.

7.7 A second *kî*, 'because', clause relates to the sage, just as the previous verse spoke of the fool. It introduces the basis for the conclusion noted in v.6.

This verse is yet another conundrum for the interpreter, one which is made more so by the Qumran text of Qoheleth (see Muilenburg, 1954: 26-27). The problem has two dimensions: one is the meaning of the text itself; the other, the relationship of the verse with what has preceded.

We begin with the text itself. The term 'oppression' (*'ōšeq*) occurs, indicating that Qoheleth once more returns to this matter (4.1; 5.7[8]). To introduce it again in the present context seems unwarranted, and textual emendation has been suggested to account for it. But for this there is no corroborating evidence other than the fact that there seems to be a gap in the Qumran text at this point. Gordis (1968: 270), following Seidel, interprets it to mean 'bribe' on the basis that this is discussed in the following clause. However, there is no compelling reason to see *'ōšeq* as having anything other than its regular meaning. The verb in the first half of the verse, *y^ehōlēl*, is also difficult. It is presumably a po'el imperfect from the root *hll* (III) (see also 2.2; Isa. 44.25; Job 12.17). For Barton it is the pol'el form of *hll* (I, II) meaning 'boast, shout'. Its origin is unclear. To assign it a meaning is a problem. Cazelles (*TDOT*, III: 411) regards it as a picture of irrational behaviour, and suggests the translation, 'makes powerless'. This would correlate well with *'ābad* in the latter half of the verse. The most frequent use of the root *hll* in Qoheleth is in the nominal form *hôlēlût,* 'folly'. In the absence of other evidence we should seek a translation which bears that in mind. Thus: 'oppression makes a sage foolish'.

Even if we grant this translation, it is obvious we have yet to determine what the author means. How does oppression have this effect? Is it the existence of oppression that makes folly of the sage's advice? Is it that some sages engaged in oppression, thus undermining their role and the advice they offered? Or is it, as Murphy suggests (1992: 64) that the wise are victims of extortion and thus may be tempted to pay a bribe. I suggest the following interpretation: In a world where the oppressor seems to breeze through life with few difficulties (4.1-3) there is great tension for the one who would be wise or would teach wisdom.

Much of what the sage represents is called into question by a world which is less than ideal. Thus the instruction of the wise seems of little worth—people will prefer the flattering sounds of the fool. More's the pity (v. 6b)!

The second half of our verse opens with the verb 'destroy' (*'ābad*) in the forceful piel imperfect. Difficulties meet the interpreter here also because the verb is in the masculine form, whereas the subject is the feminine *mattānāh,* 'gift'. Irregular though this be, it is a frequent phenomenon in Biblical Hebrew when the verb is followed by a subject which is inanimate (see R. Williams, 1974: 228 [b]). The Qumran fragment contains this text (see Muilenburg, 1954: 27) and here reads *wy'wh* in place of *wy'bd,* and this could well be the correct text. The root *'wh,* 'bend, twist', is close to the meaning of *hll* in the first stichos. This understanding of the text would allow that the purpose of the gift is to 'pervert' the mind (cf. Prov. 12.8; Job 33.27; Jer. 3.21) and thus the 'gift' is intended as a bribe.

As for the absence of the definite article from *lēb,* we note a similar feature in 3.15 (cf. also 2 Sam. 4.11; 1 Kgs 12.31; Salters, 1976: 419). Here, as elsewhere, *lēb* means the 'intellect' or 'mind'.

Verse 7 contains two parallel thoughts: oppression in society makes apparent folly of the sage's advice, in the same way that a bribe destroys the ability of donor and receiver to act appropriately in the circumstances. Both scenarios cite practical problems which confront the sage, and threaten to undermine the validity of his advice.

As for the second question raised above, namely the relationship of this verse with its context, we note that ties at the level of vocabulary between v. 7 and the preceding are absent. This fact has caused some to suggest a rearrangement of the text, with v. 7 following v. 12 (Hertzberg *et al.*). Some, like Delitzsch, believed that a phrase has fallen from the original, and that a statement similar to that in Prov. 16.8 could be supplied to complete it. This kind of surgery has no textual support, although there are some strange gaps in the Qumran MS. The relationship between v. 7 and its immediate context, however, can be explained as follows: in vv. 1-4, 5-6, the wise person is given priority over the fool. Although the advice of the wise should be heeded (v. 5), many are dissuaded from following that advice. Problems abound. For example, bribes and corruption work against popular acceptance of the sage's comments, so that although the fool's advice is largely empty sound, many are prepared to follow it (cf. also 8. 10-11). This is another of those situations which arouse a deep sense of frustration (*hebel*) in the mind of Qoheleth.

7.8-10 From a structural viewpoint, these verses display an interesting chiasmus. Two 'Better'-proverbs form v. 8. Their first elements represent the preferred items, and are identified with correct or wise conduct; conversely, their second elements are what we would classify as foolish. The second component in v. 8a corresponds to the keyword in v. 10a, and the second element in v. 8b is that which is implicit in v. 9a. Both vv. 9a and 10a are warnings to avoid foolish behaviour. Motive clauses in vv. 9b and 10b complete the unit, and stress that it is unwise to ignore the attached warnings.

7.8 In v. 1 Qoheleth provided a set of values insisting that death was better than birth. The first of the two 'Better'-sayings in v. 8a follows that pattern. It states that the 'conclusion' (*'aḥ^{a}rît*) of a 'matter' or 'word' (*dābār*) carries more significance than its inception (*rē'šîtô*). This was true of Job's situation (8.7; 42.12; cf. also 1 Kgs 20.11). In Prov. 23.18 and 24.14 the word *'aḥ^{a}rît* signifies an individual's future, and parallels the word 'hope'. The fool is without such a future (Prov. 24.20). *'Aḥ^{a}rît* may also denote the conclusion of a series. Such a general comment as we find in this verse requires a context for its definition, otherwise we can do no other than translate it in a way which preserves its universality.

The second 'Better'-proverb (v. 8b) suggests that 'patience in spirit' (*'erek-rûaḥ*) should take precedence over 'pride' (*g^{e}bah-rûaḥ*). This latter is used of the haughty and proud in Prov. 16.18 (see Hentschke, *TDOT*, II: 359).

Each of these proverbs asserts a general truth, and it is not necessary to search for some relationship between them. We might say that Qoheleth has placed them alongside each other, then added two warnings against falling into the errors there represented.

7.9 The keyword *rûaḥ* from v. 8b recurs in v. 9a following the call not to be hasty (*'al t^{e}bahēl*). This latter warning has been issued in another context in 5.1(2), and although not a frequent verb, it will reappear in 8.3. In every instance it is associated with the action of fools. What is to be avoided is an expression of anger (*k's*). In v. 3 above this root had its other meaning, 'sorrow' (cf. 11.10). Fox's point about this apparent difference in meaning is that *ka'as* refers to different kinds of anger or irritation, with v.3 referring to the irritation one feels at another person's failings, while in v.9 it refers to anger at one's own misfortunes (1999: 254).

By adding a motive clause, Qoheleth associates the proscribed behaviour with fools (*k*ᵉ*sîlîm*), in whose 'deepest recesses' (*ḥēq*) anger 'resides' (*nûaḥ*). Deep-seated and passionate feelings are said to lie in one's *ḥēq* (Job 19.27; Psa 89.50; Andre, *TDOT*, IV: 356-58). The choice of the verb *nûaḥ*, though found elsewhere in similar contexts (e.g. Prov. 14.33), probably has another attraction—it sounds like the keyword *rûaḥ*.

7.10 A second warning is directed against those who would ask about the former days (*hayyāmîm hāri'šōnîm*). This latter is the keyword which links with v. 8a to complete the chiasmus. That the past could have been better than the present or might exceed any future is a notion which Qoheleth has disputed throughout under the rubric that 'the past is the future' (cf. 1.9-10; 3.15; 6.10). There are reasons, no doubt, why one would be tempted to think of the past as an ideal from which we have declined. Human beings have a way of putting from the mind some of the discomforts and unpleasantness of the past, thus idealizing it. Reality, however, is not consistent with this selective memory, and perhaps for this reason Qoheleth counsels one not to be so foolish as to imagine that in the past there was an absence of problems commensurate with those of the present. If this is Qoheleth's meaning, we must infer it from the wider context of the unitary nature of human experience.

Qoheleth's stated reason for issuing this warning is that a wise person would never think of asking whether the past was better than the present. From wisdom's vantage point (*mēḥokmāh*), the question holds no meaning, though the fool is unaware of this.

Thus both warnings are issued in the hope that foolish behaviour might be avoided. Each warning gives the appearance of complementing the values of the preceding 'Better'-proverbs. Further, quoting them is perhaps for no other reason than to provide the setting, via their keywords, for those warnings. On the other hand, Murphy quotes with approval Lohfink's contention that this is a criticism of conventional wisdom as represented by vv. 8-9, criticizing the sage who 'cultivated the teaching of the past' (1992: 65). This approach requires interpreting 'days' as figurative for 'the tradition', a view that appears too narrow, or, as Whybray opines, 'too subtle'.

7.11-12 As in most sub-units in 7.1-12 a 'Better'-saying is attended by a motive clause bolstering or justifying the values it advocates. The theme of this final sub-section is that of the priority of wisdom. It is not insignificant that the term *yôtēr*/*yitrôn* is found at this point as a further reminder that Qoheleth's main purpose is to answer the question of *yitrôn* and its relationship to wisdom.

A structure is evident in these two verses: both clauses in v. 11 speak directly to the two elements in the motive clause in v. 12. Thus v. 12a is explanatory of v. 11a, and v. 12b expands the meaning of v. 11b.

7.11 An interesting comparison is made in this verse with the suggestion that wisdom is good, it is 'like' (*'im*) an inheritance (cf. Lauha: 128). There are those who have understood the preposition *'im* to mean 'together with' (see e.g. Barton, Gordis, Rankin etc. also RSV). Two factors argue against this and for the view that here *'im* marks a simile. One is that the motive clause (v. 12) equates wisdom and money; the second is that in other instances, such as 2.16, the preposition denotes likeness. On this view, then, Qoheleth makes the point that wisdom is a good thing in the same way as an inheritance (*naḥ*[a]*lāh*) is.

Is it possible to ascertain why Qoheleth offered this kind of comparison? An inheritance, be it money or especially property, is something expected at a future date, either at or even before the father's death (cf. Luke 15.11-12). Wisdom is similar; it, too, may offer a better and secure future.

Verse 11 continues with a phrase we may translate as, 'And there is an advantage (*yôtēr*) for the living, to those who see the sun' (*rô'ēh haššemeš*). In this manner Qoheleth forges a link between wisdom in this present and hope of a future (*yôtēr*). We note the participial form *yôtēr* in this verse, and the close association Qoheleth draws between *yitrôn* and the wise, for only they can hope to obtain it (v. 12).

7.12 If we were to ask in what specific manner wisdom could be likened to an inheritance, we find in v. 12 that wisdom and 'money' (*kesep*)—the latter we presume is equivalent to 'inheritance' in v. 11—both provide 'shade' or 'protection' In view of the limited value Qoheleth places on money and things material (cf. 2.1-11), it follows that wisdom and money *per se* are not being compared, but rather their function. Under the metaphor of 'shade', wisdom and an inheritance both are tied to a future, both are in some sense guarantees of a better future, and to that extent have a protective role. Seow, however, sees this as part of Qoheleth's 'subversive strategy' (1997: 249) because neither wisdom nor possessions can offer anything reliable. However, we would argue here that Qoheleth draws on the inheritance concept for illustrative purpose, believing that wisdom does offer some hope of dealing more adequately with the question of death and beyond.

The use of the preposition *b*[e] in *b*[e]*ṣēl* has occasioned comment. One would have expected *k*[e], 'as, like', as closer to the intention of the text. Support from other MSS for emending to *k*[e] is absent, though they interpret the sense of the text as *k*[e]*ṣēl*.... *k*[e]*ṣēl*. It seems likely that the MT is original, in which case *b*[e] is the so-called *Beth essentiae* (GK: 119 i), or of identity (Williams, para. 249[x]).

Having established the manner in which wisdom and inheritance are alike, v. 12b returns to the concept of *yitrôn*. All living can enjoy the 'advantage', the knowledge that wisdom gives life (*t*[e]*ḥayyeh*) to those who possess it (*b*[e]*'ālehāh*). Here, *yitrôn* is defined in terms of the protection and life-giving powers of wisdom. The 'life' it offers must be understood in terms wider than mere present existence, as having a quality or depth greater than simply living each day, for this latter is enjoyed by the fool also.

This entire unit (vv. 1-12) is artfully arranged about a series of 'Better'-sayings, some from the tradition and some the product of Qoheleth's own fertile mind. Throughout they advocate wise conduct and spell out numerous concrete examples of what that conduct is. The high point of this section is in the tying of *yitrôn* to wisdom, and in defining it as that which gives life. In this way we see again how Qoheleth is using the term as a tool for probing after that which transcends the limits of this present enigmatic life. He believes *yitrôn* is available to the wise only, and is hinting at some distinction between wise and fool, between righteous and evil, beyond death.

On the wider scene, this chapter begins to move the reader from the programmatic question (1.3) repeated in 6.12 towards the answer he will offer in the following chapter, especially in 8.15. The next sub-section, 7.13-14, takes us a further step along that road.

7.13-29 Consider What God Does

The search for wisdom goes on in God's world, so Qoheleth calls on his readers to join him again in 'considering' events and situations transpiring there. The call to 'consider' (*rᵉʾēh*) provides the inclusion which delimits this portion of the chapter, and at the same time anticipates ch. 8. Further attention will be given to the evils of society and the implication of this situation for the sage.

This latter half of the chapter falls into an opening sub-section (vv. 13-14) which sets the theme for the following discussion. We note its keywords: *rāʾāh, rāʿāh, ṭôb, ʿāśāh ʾᵉlōhîm, (lōʾ) māṣāʾ*. Following the initial imperative, Qoheleth states that he has actually looked into (*rāʾîtî*) everything (vv. 15-18). Warnings are issued in vv. 16-17 on the basis of the observations, and then advice is tendered (v. 18). Several apparently disconnected sayings appear in vv. 19-22, though they all are statements about wise conduct. The wisdom exemplified there leads Qoheleth to report on his own search for wisdom (vv. 23-24). Essentially that search has failed to provide comprehensive results and so, in a manner reminiscent of 2.12, he turns away from the pursuit of wisdom (v. 25a) in a flight towards folly (v. 25b). His final assessment is issued in vv. 26-29.

In our reading of the preceding portion of ch. 7, we noticed the significance of death as the focus of the sage's reflection. In this section we shall follow Qoheleth as he ponders further the subject of death, especially premature or untimely death, for this constitutes a special difficulty for the believing sage. There is no simple nor final answer to this problem, but despite this intellectual setback, Qoheleth persists in holding onto his faith in the value of wisdom.

7.13 Observation and reflection are of the essence of the sage's methodology, and the verb *rāʾāh* is Qoheleth's term for this (cf. 1.14, 17; 3.10; 8.17 etc.). In the imperative form here, Qoheleth calls for deep consideration of 'the deeds of God' (*maʿᵃśēh-hāʾᵉlôhîm*). As in 3.11, 14, and 8.17, the belief that God is active in the life of his creation is a pillar of Qoheleth's theology.

The second half of the verse begins with the conjunction *kî*. In appearance, the clause so introduced is a motive clause, but such a view seems inappropriate in the context. On the other hand, if *kî* were viewed as an asseverative, 'indeed', it would draw attention to the question being put: Who is able to straighten out (*lᵉtaqqēn*) what he has made crooked (*ʿwh*)? The question clearly has its origin in an aphorism (cf. 1.15). The piel verb *tiqqēn* (also in 12.9) appears frequently in Mishnaic Hebrew, though in the entire OT it occurs only three times, all in Qoheleth. *Tiqqēn* stands in contrast with the piel *'iwwāh,* which portrays something twisted or bent. As we have seen, in principle, general aphorisms require a context for their interpretation. In this instance, the implication seems to be that what is 'bent' describes the work of God (cf. Job 19.6; 27.1), and by extension, it is humanity which is frustrated in attempts to set it straight. The bald statement does not give the sense that this is unfortunate, immoral, or unjust. It merely speaks of a reality. It says two things to us: the first, that things are as they are and we are powerless to change them; the second, that from the human perspective, those things we view do appear to be twisted. This latter problem arises, no doubt, because we cannot see the whole, but it is fully consistent with Qoheleth's perception that life is so replete with enigmas, with situations which we cannot possibly explain or comprehend, that it looks 'out of shape'. It is this reality, broken or twisted, on which we must reflect.

7.14 The human experience is divided by Israel's sages quite simply into two general categories: 'good' (*ṭôbāh*) and 'ill' (*rā'āh*). Such division may be deemed simplistic, but that is how the wisdom movement dealt with the matters before it. Times of prosperity are to be 'enjoyed' (*hᵃyēh bᵉṭôb;* cf. 2.1) for that is the only wise response. In times of calamity, on the other hand, one can only ponder (*rᵉ'ēh*). From what was a general call in v. 13a, Qoheleth has narrowed the focus so that it falls on the darker side of human experience (cf. 7.2, 4), for that is the area of concern in what follows.

What God has done is described as 'the one as well as the other' (RSV). The Hebrew term *zeh* in the phrase *zeh lᵉ 'ummat-zeh,* means 'one... and the other' or 'both'. The unusual preposition *lᵉ'ummat* which links them indicates close proximity (cf. 1 Chron. 24.31). The demonstratives *zeh* refer back to the 'good' and 'ill' of v. 14a. As far as Qoheleth's theology is concerned, he stands very close to the view expressed by Amos in 3.6; 9.4: he believes in a God who is ultimately responsible for *all* that transpires on earth, good and ill alike.

God is charged in the third clause with deliberately making it difficult for people to discover what he does, even after their much reflection. That the deity 'frustrates' the endeavours of the sage is the thrust of the phrase *'al dibrat še,* 'so that', equivalent to another preposition indicating purpose, *lᵉma'an 'ᵃšer.* A verb which will dominate the following discussion, *māṣā',* appears here in the negative. It makes the point that even the sage has no guarantee of success in his attempt to discover the final meaning of life. More specifically, what he can in no way discover is the future, what transpires beyond this life.

In earlier statements (cf. 1.9-10; 3.15; 6.10 etc.), Qoheleth had indicated that, on the basis of experience, it is possible to conclude that there is some pattern to life. His way of expressing this is to state that past, present and future all follow the same course. There is no way Qoheleth can establish that this pattern extends beyond death, as there is no well of experience of 'life' at that level upon which to draw. Knowledge of the past and present, and the empirical method on which the sage depends, do not enable one to make projections about the future beyond death, though this dilemma does not diminish his own desire to probe that question.

The Hebrew phrase rendered 'find...after' has been identified as an idiomatic form meaning something like 'find fault with' (see Murphy 1992: 61 quoting Whitley, 1979: 66). This would mean then that humans have no way of filing a complaint against God for the way things are in this life. Such an understanding would certainly accord well with v. 12, but even if this were so it would require interpreting the suffix 'him' to point away from the antecedent, *'ādām*, back to God. The majority view that 'after him' refers to what lies beyond the present seems yet to be the more acceptable view.

7.15-18 A Moral Dilemma

Following an already established pattern of observation and reflection (e.g. 3.16-22), Qoheleth cites another case of life in this world which requires consideration (v. 15). To it he attaches two warning clauses (vv. 16-17), then draws a conclusion (v. 18) couched in the form of a modified 'Better'-saying.

The cohesiveness of this unit lies in the observation-reflection model, the keywords 'righteousness' (*ṣdq*) and 'injustice' (*rš'*), the notion of untimely death implicit in vv. 15b, 17, and the inclusion 'all' (*'et-hakkōl, 'et-kullām*) in vv. 15, 18. There are numerous issues for the interpreter in this section, and each must be considered carefully.

7.15 For the sake of emphasis, Qoheleth places the object *'et-hakkōl*, 'all', before the verb. The parameters of its meaning, as in 2.14, are the two contrasting lifestyles, the good (*ṭôb, ṣaddîq*) and the evil (*rā'āh, rāša'*). We can therefore translate *kōl* more appropriately as 'both'. This means that Qoheleth has observed two permanent features of the human scene. Nor are these mere casual observations, for he has spent his life pondering these things. He has reached the conclusion that this life, here described as *y*ᵉ*mē-heblî,* was not devoid of meaning or empty, as some have suggested; it was simply that it produced more questions than answers. Barton's translation, 'my short life', supported by Whybray, Crenshaw and others, is without warrant since there is no suggestion that in this context *hebel* focuses on the length of life, whether short or long. Since Qoheleth is presenting yet another case-study from his own experience, the phrase *y*ᵉ*mē-heblî* characterizes his life as one marked by frustration at life's multitude of unanswerable questions.

Pondering the situation of the righteous and the evil, he observes that the righteous 'perishes' (*'obēd*) despite being righteous, while the evil one 'prolongs' (*ma'*ᵃ*rîk*, cf. 8.12) life although he persists in doing wrong. The use of two participial forms expresses the good and evil lifestyles, a continuous pattern of living rather than the occasional good or evil act. The preposition *b*ᵉ on *b*ᵉ*ṣidqô* and *b*ᵉ*rā'ātô* is an adversative usage, 'in spite of', rather than temporal or instrumental (cf. Num. 14.11; Isa. 9.11). Two contrasting lifestyles are linked with fates which, from a traditional deuteronomic viewpoint, ought not to be associated.

What does Qoheleth mean when he says that the righteous 'perish'? Clearly, he means to contrast this with the long life of the evil person, so his meaning is that the righteous die an early and untimely death. It is the wicked who appear to enjoy long life, traditionally the prerogative and reward of the good. In ch. 6 Qoheleth has presented the view that the quality of life is more important than its duration. However, in this section, he addresses the question of longevity as it touches the good and the evil person, in order to discuss another problem facing the tradition.

Israel's legal tradition (Deut. 4.40; Exod. 20.12) took the view that the good live longer. There was support for this view from wthin the tradition of the sages (cf. Prov. 3.1-2; 4.10; 21.21). Conversely, the wicked were assured of an early death (Pss. 1; 8.14; 73.18; Prov. 7.24-27). Qoheleth takes issue with this tradition, observing that goodness cannot guarantee longevity; in fact, longevity could well be proof of one's evil. At this point, the interpreter must avoid the mistake of assuming that we are dealing with a general principle. Qoheleth merely observes that this phenomenon occurs, that it occurs sufficiently often, and that the tradition is at a loss to explain why. This danger we shall endeavour to keep in mind as we interpret the following admonitions.

7.16-17 Whybray has set out clearly for us the internal order in these two verses (1978: 192). Such use of parallelism is an acknowledged device of Qoheleth (cf. 1.8; 3.21; 9.1-6; 10.16-17). Each verse consists of a pair of warnings followed by an interrogative clause beginning with *lammāh,* 'why'. When Qoheleth employs parallel sayings elsewhere, the two clauses indicate two possible responses to the situation observed (cf. 3.17, 18). The personal view of Qoheleth is not to be identified with either of those views, but rather with the one which is then added, often in the form of a 'Better'-saying. From this vantage point, there is a note of irony in these two verses. However, there has been a tradition that views these two verses as advocating something immoral, what Whybray has called the 'golden mean' in human behaviour, that one should not be too wise or good, nor too evil, but act simply on the basis of what is expedient. (See also Choi, 2002: 374, who sees the 'golden mean' as a universal cultural phenomenon).

Applying this pattern to our present unit we find that in v. 15 Qoheleth has reminded readers that the righteous often fall prey to an early death. This is a distressing but undeniable fact in an enigmatic world. Thus some would react to the call to learn wisdom (goodness) by saying 'do not claim exceptional righteousness or ardently pursue wisdom'. To do so would be to invite an early death: 'why should you invite destruction upon yourself' (*lammāh tiššômēm*). This is one possible reaction to the observation Qoheleth records in v. 15. As Seow points out (1997: 253) the admonition is against boasting of one's righteousness or wisdom.

A second response warning against boasting of one's evil is given in v. 17. According to the scenario in v. 15, because some enjoy long lives despite their evil ways, one might be tempted to think that the pursuit of evil will open the door to longevity (cf. 8.10-12). Such a devotion to folly, from Qoheleth's point of view, would be equally hazardous, for untimely death would most probably result then also. This would be the traditional perception of a corrupt life and its inevitable rewards. Therefore, the second possible reaction is that one ought not to give oneself to evil (*'al tirša' harbēh*) or to folly (*'al t^{e}hî sākāl*) either. The view that a corrupt life will lead to an early death more closely approximates to the traditional view, but it is important to recognize the anomaly. Qoheleth does not claim that either pursuit will actually increase the possibility of a premature death or guarantee longevity; rather, early death can strike anyone at any time. In a world where the sudden and untimely death of a righteous person is possible, while the scoundrel may escape to live long, the claim to be exceedingly just and wise, or the uninhibited pursuit of evil, may well have the same end result: early death.

It is not until v. 18 that, according to Qoheleth's pattern of presentation, we actually encounter his *personal* view of the situation in v. 15. However, before turning to that, we note some textual matters which have determined the above interpretation.

In v. 16a a warning is issued against becoming a *ṣaddîq*. *Ṣaddîq,* as in v. 15, is a noun, descriptive of a certain kind of person, the just one. The *harbēh* which follows this term as an adverb, 'exceedingly', normally qualifies an associated verb rather than a noun. It therefore qualifies *hāyāh,* 'become'. Whybray has argued that *harbēh* does not refer to an individual who is '*too* righteous', but it speaks of the manner in which the just pursue righteousness. In other words, in the context of a warning, it calls one to guard against the urge to self-righteousness. The attendant *titḥakkām yôtēr,* 'do not overdo making yourself wise', supports this view. However, as Seow has indicated, the forms here refer more to pretension than to pretence.

The final verb in v. 16, *tiššômēm,* is perhaps a variant on the hithpoel form *titšômēm*. Its meaning in places such as Isa. 63.5 and Ps. 143.4 is 'be horrified', which is not quite appropriate in this present context. Rather, its other sense, 'destroy oneself,' is to be preferred.

In v. 17c we meet the phrase *bᵉlō' 'ittekā*. The initial preposition *bᵉ* would suggest a temporal meaning, 'when', and the translation then would run, 'when it is not your time'. In ch. 3 God determines the critical moments of all events on earth, death being one of them (3.2). Implicit in the phrase here is the notion that one who sets out deliberately to grasp folly is actually attempting to overturn the divine order.

7.18 In customary fashion, a 'Better'-proverb concludes this section, and it brings with it Qoheleth's own personal view. Its two imperatives are complementary, using the balanced concepts of grasping and of not letting go. Qoheleth's point is that one should 'grasp this' (*te'ᵃḥōz bāzeh*) while not withholding one's hand from 'this' (*mizzeh*). It is a simple statement using a positive and an antithetical negative form for mutual reinforcement. But what does it mean? Each *zeh,* 'this', refers to the items in vv. 16, 17 respectively. In this manner, Qoheleth advocates avoidance of pretensions to wisdom, as well as of indulgence in corruption. Despite the fact that the righteous and wise may face premature death, following the sage's advice and living a just life is preferable. It is always good to reject folly and evil regardless of how long one might live. Again, duration is not the issue, only quality of life. Qoheleth's position is a fascinating one. He agrees with the two notions in vv. 16 and 17, but not for the reasons they advance. Their concern was premature death, whereas Qoheleth is arguing from the perspective of awe of the divine (v. 18c). As Murphy notes (1992: 70) this 'bottom line' cannot offer security but is the only attitude to adopt regardless of one's fate.

The meaning of v. 18c has troubled commentators, though syntactically it is not disputed that it provides the basis for the advice which precedes. The phrase *y^a^rē'-'^e^lōhîm* is 'one who fears God' (cf. Prov. 1.7), which, in this setting is a synonym for the sage, so the purpose of the verse in broad span is to advocate wise conduct. Such conduct has its reward. It is portrayed as *yēṣē' 'et-kullām.* The root meaning of *yṣ'* is to 'depart, leave'. Gordis suggests (1968: 277-78) that it means 'doing one's duty', on the basis of the Mishnaic usage. To do one's duty by both then means that both good and evil will be pursued with moderation. This typical interpretation is unfortunate as Qoheleth does not advocate a *via media.* He does, however, call upon his readers to take both warnings seriously: they should shun pretensions to righteousness and also keep free from evil. He is firmly on the side of justice and wisdom at whatever cost, even that of an early demise. Surely it is Qoheleth's *yitrôn* concept as something transcending the limitations of this life and experience which makes this attitude possible.

7.19-24 Who Then Can be Wise?

This sub-unit is divided into two parts: (a) vv. 19-22 consisting of two independent quotations coupled with a warning (vv. 21-22), and (b) vv. 23-24, with a personal statement from Qoheleth addressing the matter of the pursuit of wisdom.

With regard to the quotations, we observe that the first (v. 19) speaks for wisdom and its power, and the second (v. 20) points to the fact that not even the just person is totally without fault. Hence the quotations have a counter-balancing effect.

The warning (vv. 21-22) urges prudence in evaluating another's speech.

In the second part (vv. 23-24), the reflective portion, Qoheleth returns to an autobiographical style to share his feelings about the pursuit of wisdom.

The main keyword for the unit is the root *ḥkm*, 'wisdom, be wise'. It also provides the link with the following section.

7.19 Wisdom (*ḥokmāh*) furnishes the wise person (*ḥākām*) with strength. The verb *tā'ōz* derives from the root *'zz*, 'be strong', here perhaps best given the transitive meaning, 'make strong' (cf. Ps. 68.29; Prov. 8.28). However, Seow has argued that it could also mean 'cherished' or 'held to be dear'. The power of wisdom is sufficient to enable the sage to confront successfully ten rulers (*šallîṭîm*) who have the advantage of the defensive walls of a city (cf. 9.13-16; Prov. 21.22; 24.5). That the figure 'ten' should appear in the illustration could be due to the fact that certain large cities in Israel under the hellenistic pattern of government were administered by a ten-man council. The real point, however, is simply to contrast one with many.

Textual evidence from the Qumran fragment of Qoheleth indicates that *tā'ōz* should read *t'zr,* from *'zr,* 'help'. This reading was known to the LXX, and may well be the more original reading. If so, the meaning differs little, and the message that wisdom endows one sage with more power than ten rulers who presumably lack wisdom, is clear. Again note the 'one sage is better than several others'-theme (cf. 7.5).

7.20 An asseverative *kî*, 'indeed', opens this second independent saying. It argues that there is no just person (*ṣaddîq*) on earth who regularly does good. The imperfect verb form conveys this sense of regularity or constancy. The claim that there is no sage who is without sin is far from being linked with the doctrine of 'original sin', a concept of which the OT knows nothing. Nor is it to assert that there are no righteous persons on earth. That would fly in the face of v. 15. Qoheleth is insisting that among the wise or righteous, there is none who does right on every occasion. Even the righteous will occasionally fail, for perfection is not possible in a broken world. It is this fact which might bear on the anomaly in v. 15.

Whereas in v. 19 Qoheleth has made the case for wisdom's advantage, v. 20 is a concession which recognizes that even the *ṣaddîq* has certain shortcomings. They may be few, but they are there nonetheless. This fact neither invalidates the quest for righteousness or wisdom, nor detracts from its real value when attained. However, occasional failure is a fact of life in this world. This interplay between wisdom's power and limitations we shall meet again in 9.17-10.20.

7.21-22 The warnings and supporting argument in these two verses bring with them a new situation and attendant vocabulary, making it an easy task to identify them as separate from vv. 19-20.

Do we have here a concrete example of the principles enunciated in vv. 19-20 as Lauha (p. 135), Zimmerli (p. 211), and others would argue? If these verses were to exemplify the power and limits of wisdom, that view would be acceptable. Yet the warning in v. 21 is independent of that theme, suggesting rather that it is prudent not to investigate too closely (*'al-tittēn lēb l*^{e}, cf. 1.13) what others are saying. The imperfect *y*^{e}*dabbērû* presumably has frequentative intent, so that the warning is not to take to heart the many matters (*d*^{a}*bārîm*) about which people gossip. Under what circumstances might such advice be meaningful and helpful? The second part of the verse uses *'*^{a}*šer lō'*, 'lest', to express the hazard to be avoided—that one might overhear something one was not supposed to know. Two translations are possible for the phrase *lō' tišma' 'et-'abd*^{e}*kā m*^{e}*qall*^{e}*lekā*: the first is, 'lest you hear your servant revile you'. The other is, 'lest you hear that your servant is reviling you'. The latter is probably the more correct—the servant (or 'subordinate' [Seow]) is speaking against the employer. We are left to suppose that should the master hear such things, he would be required to take action. So the statement appears to suggest that there are some things it is best to be in ignorance of, or as Murphy suggests, be ready to forgive.

The underlying reason for this stance is that the master is aware (*yāda' libbekā*) that he himself frequently (*p*^{e}*'āmîm rabbôt*) indulged in similar activities. The *'*^{a}*šer* in v. 22 functions differently from that in v. 21. Here it introduces the content of the knowing: thus, '... that you too cursed others'. Where does the significance of the statement lie? Is it simply to indicate that criticism of others is a common trait? Everyone knows servants complain about their superiors, so Qoheleth's comment is that it is wise not to take it too seriously.

7.23-24 Returning to personal reflection is the most obvious feature of these two verses. Initially we need to determine the scope of the term 'all this' (*kol-zōh*). We shall presume that it describes the material presented in vv. 19-22. In those verses

Qoheleth quoted two complementary examples of wisdom's power and the sage's 'feet of clay'. A third statement, another example of practical wisdom, also recognized human failings. This, the value of wisdom and justice within an imperfect world, is what Qoheleth 'tested' (*nissîtî*). His research was grounded in accepted wisdom methodology (*baḥokmāh*), as it was in 1.13 and 2.3, 9. The determination with which the task was undertaken can be felt in the strong expression, 'I said, I will be wise' (*'eḥkkāmāh*). This latter verbal form is unique in the OT. The end result of the test was the demonstration that the wisdom he sought was unattainable (*r^eḥôqāh mimmennî*), or perhaps more precisely in this general context, that there was no explanation forthcoming for the phenomenon of early death. Within its context, Qoheleth asserts not that wisdom of any kind is utterly beyond human reach, but that a wisdom which transcends all limits, which can lift the sage above the boundaries of human thought and experience, is unattainable. Be that as it may, it does not in the least detract from wisdom's inherent role, nor from his own determination to live by, and to promote the cause of, wisdom.

To express how inaccessible pure wisdom is, in v. 24 we read that wisdom is 'deep' (*'āmōq*). This adds to the previous description of wisdom as *rāḥōq*, 'distant'. The phrase *mah šehāyāh*, as in 1.9 and 6.10, really means 'whatever exists' or 'whatever happens', that is comprehension of everything. As Zimmerli puts it, 'der Grund der Dinge' is so far from us that it is like the deepest deep. This duplicated expression functions as a superlative. For intrinsic reasons, no human can attain or find true wisdom. Additionally, Qoheleth resorts to one of his favoured forms, the rhetorical question, to make an unequivocal negative statement. There is here also a play on words, with the two adjectives *rāḥōq* and *'āmōq* being chosen for their similarity of sound.

The rhetorical question with which this bridge-verse closes, serves as a link to the following material by means of the keyword *māṣā'*, 'find'.

7.25-29 Pure Wisdom Cannot be Found

As vv. 19-24 related to the testing of wisdom and justice, vv. 25-28 treat of the matter of evil. Keywords here are *biqqēš* (vv. 25, 28, 29), (*lō'*) *māṣā'* (vv. 26, 27, 28, 29), and *ḥešbôn* (vv. 25, 27, 29). The opening call to 'consider' (*r^e'ēh*) in v. 13 enters again in this section (vv. 27, 29) as the inclusion; it is bound together with the theme of 'God's work' (vv. 13, 29).

7.25 A change of direction is the main emphasis of the verb *sbb,* which Qoheleth selects here to indicate that his research was moving into new territory. Thus, he says he gave up wanting to know wisdom in order to devote himself to the study of evil and folly. We presume that this is in reaction to his conclusion that the pursuit of pure wisdom was from the outset a false trail.

The frequently used term *lēb,* 'mind', normally has the accusative particle attached (cf. 2.20). Here it is missing, though there is some MS evidence to suggest that we should read *b*ᵉ*libbî,* the preposition denoting instrumentality.

What Qoheleth has for the moment agreed to put aside is the search for 'wisdom and the sum of things' (*ḥokmāh w*ᵉ*ḥešbôn),* and in lieu to channel his efforts towards knowing the 'evil of folly' (*reša' kesel*) and its partner 'the folly of madness' (*hassiklût hôlēlût*). This is a procedure Qoheleth noted earlier in his autobiographical section, 2.12ff.

In the first clause, determining to change the direction of his research, Qoheleth employs the form *lāda'at* to signal his purpose, that is, 'in order to know'. And here we can assume that the verb 'know' has the wider semantic value of 'experience'. That original purpose was not simply to know, but also to search out (*lātūr*) and to seek (*baqqēš*), these latter defining the verb 'know'. The bringing together of three cognate verbs emphasizes the rigour with which this study was undertaken before being put to the side. In its place he adopts the standpoint of evil and folly. This would require him to seek pleasure for its own sake, and to forgo reflection on the issues which human experience threw up, in this case the time of death and its relationship to one's lifestyle. He will tell of his experience in v. 26.

Ḥešbôn is a late Hebrew term deriving from a root meaning 'to devise, deduce'. As it appears here alongside *ḥokmāh* we assume it conveys a synonymous idea, 'understanding'. Its special nuance is of knowledge reached by a process of deduction (v. 29). In this section, it is the key term used to indicate human knowledge.

An unusual term, *kesel,* is cited here to denote folly; this is its only appearance in Qoheleth. The word regularly used for folly is from the root *skl,* as in the latter part of this verse. The remaining terms conjoined to *kesel* have already been used in 1.17. From v. 17 above we understand that *rš',* 'evil', and *kesel, siklût,* 'folly', are to be associated. What specific kind of evil or folly did he investigate? For the answer, we return to the thought of vv. 15-17:

the enigma of longevity for the evil one and premature death for the righteous.

7.26 Results of his investigation into evil are announced. In lieu of the more regular perfect verb form, Qoheleth introduces his findings with the participial construction *môṣē' ʼanî*. The problem for the interpreter lies not with this expression as such, but with the meaning of the passage as a whole, for Qoheleth on the surface seems to take a negative view of women. Fox opines that 'this passage remains irreparably misogynistic' despite attempts to water down its apparent meaning. Almost every commentator, with the exception of Haupt, is agreed that despite 9.10, Qoheleth does not trust the female, or certain types of women (Crenshaw). What this attitude has to do with the testing of evil and folly is not clear. However, it prompts the question whether the term *'iššāh,* 'woman', is cryptic, a metaphor for folly, evil or adultery as in Prov. 2.16-19. 5.1-23. If the answer were affirmative, it would accord well with vv. 15ff., though there would seem to be a problem for v. 28 below. However, that Qoheleth is contrasting male and female personalities in this passage is not obvious, the term *'ādām* being a generic one which includes both male and female. Our difficulties are many.

As we focus more closely on v. 26, we note initially the problem of the accusative particle *'et* prefixed to *hā'iššāh,* as it appears not to be the direct object of the participle *môṣē',* 'find'. The clause in which 'the woman' appears is nominal (*mar mimmāwet hā'iššāh*), and the sign of the accusative out of place. The statement should read, 'The woman who... is more bitter than death'. There is a difficulty with this view as the adjective *mar* is masculine, but we will persist with it because the use of a masculine form may well be due to its preceding the noun *māwet,* 'death'. Her heart (*lēb*) is likened to 'nets' (*meṣôdîm*) and 'fetters' (*ḥarāmîm*), these latter being parallel terms. Her hands are equated with the idea of entrapment (*'asûrîm,* 'bonds'). In ch. 9 this same idea of being snared is used with specific reference to untimely death. In view of the problems noted above, we must ask whether 'woman' is to be understood literally or whether it functions as a figure. Seow (1997: 271) argues for a figurative sense, namely as a reference to 'Folly', while Krüger (2002, p. 145) suggests it is 'wisdom'. However, we wish to argue here that it is a figure for premature death, the issue with which this section began (vv. 1-4, 15). If we accept this metaphorical sense for 'the woman' then the verse comes to mean, 'an untimely death is more bitter than death itself', according perfectly with the thesis of the second half of the verse.

Untimely death does not strike those with whom God is pleased (*ṭôb lipnē hā'ᵉlōhîm*), but it does snare the sinner (*ḥôṭē'*, cf. v. 18). This is a possible interpretation for v. 26b which notes that the God-pleaser will escape from her (*yimmālēṭ mimmennāh*). The feminine singular suffix on the preposition *min* presumably relates to the 'woman', that is, to premature death. Such a statement fits closely with the tradition (Prov. 9.18; 12.28 etc.). Testing of evil and folly produced for Qoheleth the same results as those observed in 7.15, for many evil persons were seen to be prey to premature death. If this verse is viewed as an independent word of Qoheleth's findings, and the introduction to v. 27 would give that distinct impression, then v. 26 is to be seen as a word from Qoheleth in support of the traditional view of divine justice and reward. Of course there are many instances, as Qoheleth has already indicated above, where the righteous does not fall to sudden and untimely death, even though one might occasionally commit sin. In balancing vv. 15-18 and v. 26 Qoheleth forcibly states that it is folly to claim that every evil person will in this life meet justice, just as it is unwise to argue that the righteous will always be rewarded. There is partial truth in the tradition, but life is also replete with painful exceptions, so that no dogma will adequately explain the human enigma.

7.27-28a The final summary comes in two parts, vv. 27-28 and v. 29, both of which open with the inclusion, 'consider this' (*rᵉ'ēh zeh*). Qoheleth now calls others, his students, to consider (*rᵉ'ēh*) what he discovered as a consequence of his study. Bringing together varied pieces of information (*'aḥat lᵉ'aḥat*), he supposed that it was possible to construct a total picture, a conclusion (*ḥešbôn*). The 'one to one' phrase speaks of thoroughness, attention to detail, as well as of diligence in covering the spectrum of experiences. It is, we might presume, another definition of what in v. 23 was described as wisdom methodology, that careful consideration of many examples and situations from which conclusions then could be drawn and substantiated (see also 12.9-10).

Our verse here speaks of purpose; that is implied in the infinitive construct *limṣô'*, 'in order to find'. Qoheleth seeks a reasoned conclusion, or *ḥešbôn*.

The initial *r*ᵉ*'ēh zeh* takes us back to v. 13 with which the section opened, and to the call for honest examination of the work of God in the world. The *-h* suffix on the verb *'āmᵉrāh* is no doubt a copyist's error; it should be the article prefixed to *qōheleth.* What is distinctive about this verse is the third person reference to Qoheleth. Apart from 1.2 and 12.8 there are no other examples of such an editorial note within the book. What significance might be attached to this form is uncertain, though Galling has suggested that it intends to mark Qoheleth's private opinion.

Verse 28 is not to be separated from v. 27; the introductory *'ᵃšer* relates directly to the 'conclusion' (*ḥešbôn*) at the end of v. 27 (contra Murphy). That conclusion he sought (*'ôd biqšāh napšî)* was not to be found, for there was sufficient conflicting evidence to establish that *'aḥat lᵉ'aḥat,* 'one plus one', does not always equal 'two'. What was proven was that, like wisdom itself, an answer to the riddle was unattainable. If this interpretation proves accurate, then v. 26 supports the tradition that the God-pleaser will find suitable reward while the sinner will be justly punished. In the latter case, that means untimely death. In juxtaposition, vv. 27-28a present the thesis that life will not always 'add up' in the way we might anticipate. Both statements are true of the human condition some of the time; neither is true on every occasion. Methodologically and essentially, the sage is prevented from discovering all that God does.

7.28b We are here face to face with another of those tantalizing parts of this book, where the interpreter must admit a measure of uncertainty about its meaning. We have a simple statement to the effect that Qoheleth found 'one man among a thousand' (*'ādām 'eḥād mē'elep māṣā'tî*), but had no luck at all when it came to finding women among them (*'iššāh bᵉkol 'ēlleh lō' māṣātî*). Commentators generally assume that this lone male figure was good and wise, a God-pleaser who escaped the wiles of the female. No woman did he find in that category. The first assumption is just that, for the text tells us nothing about the kind of person the male was. If we grant that he was wise and moral, then we are asked to assume that no woman was aware of the other female's ruse, and so were all snared. It would be a peculiar situation if such were the case. Furthermore, that only one male in a thousand escaped the wily woman is in no sense a commendation of the male at the expense of the female. To posit, as is usual, that Qoheleth took a negative attitude to women, is absolutely unjustified. Murphy agrees that Qoheleth here 'rejects a saying that is demeaning to women' (1992: 77).

A review of commentaries demonstrates clearly that the verse is decidedly difficult to interpret. It begins with a generic term *'ādām* which embraces both male and female. Gordis points out that when the generic is followed by the specific term 'woman', then the generic is a restricted term meaning 'male'. This is acceptable in principle.

What Qoheleth discovered was *'eḥād mē'elep,* that is 'one from a thousand'. If he is adding one to one to find a total (v. 27; cf. v. 25), then the phrase 'one from a thousand' is possibly another mathematical analogy for the process of deduction from a given. What he failed to find was a woman 'in all these' *(bekol 'ēlleh).* 'These' in this setting cannot mean all the people surveyed if we accept that *'ādām* means males only.

The nature or character of the solitary male which the survey discovered is not addressed. Nor is it clear that Qoheleth was searching for the same kind of woman as the male he sought. Is the male he did manage to find one who escaped, or one who was snared by the 'woman'? The text is unclear because of its generalized expression and unclear relationship with its context. If he was the one snared by the woman—which is a possible interpretation—and there were no women so trapped, then the entire picture is reversed with regard to the relative status of male and female.

If 'woman' is figurative for premature death, as was suggested in our interpretation of v. 26, then 'man' probably represents longevity. However, this equation is difficult to sustain. It would imply that Qoheleth found only one example of longevity (man) among the thousand considered, and no example of premature death. The significance of such a conclusion is baffling to say the least, and would certainly not lead to the conclusion in v. 26 that premature death was the more bitter.

Despite the many difficulties which this verse raises, there does seem to be a principle within, namely that Qoheleth set out in search of something, but it eluded him. What he did find was so miniscule that it must surely be of limited value. Such a thought is in full agreement with the general thesis in chs. 7-8 that what humanity can discover is minimal.

7.29 The final call to 'consider' terminates this chapter. It is preceded by an unusual usage of *lebad* from the root *bdd* meaning 'alone' or 'only', emphasizing that this was the sole discovery he made. This accords with the previous verse and the statement that very little was found. However, he did reach one conclusion: that in all of God's creation human beings were all 'upright' (*yāšār*). A decision has to be made about the specific nuance of the word *yāšār,* because it can be applied to a variety of different contexts. It may refer to a moral rectitude (Job 4.7), a pleasing trait (Deut. 12.25), or to righteousness (Deut. 32.4). However, *yāšār* can also mean 'straight' as opposed to that which is crooked, and so our minds turn back to v. 13 above and we ask whether there is some relationship between them. God has made humankind straight, not bent and twisted; everyone has the potential to develop in the right way, that is, toward righteousness and wisdom. Although the creation story is perhaps not in mind here, we can note that the OT has a very optimistic view of humanity in essence. There is no trace of the doctrine of 'original sin' such as developed in the NT by Paul and especially by some of the Reformers.

Depending on our evaluation of the function of the *waw* preceding the second half of this verse, our interpretation will be significantly affected. If the *waw* is the adversative 'but' (Barton, Gordis, Lauha, Zimmerli etc., and the RSV reflects this view), then the second half of the verse presents the perfect human falling away from that state by a search for 'many devices' (*ḥiššbônôt rabbîm*). The implication is that the search distorts the original plan. However, if the *waw* is an ordinary conjunction 'and', then its meaning is that humanity, having been made upright, has gone on from that point to search out many ways to explain things. That these human attempts to find out are aberrations, or forbidden, is not a thought present in the text. *Ḥiššbônôt* are not base schemes of the human mind, a departure from its 'upright' state; they are attempts to deduce meaning (cf. v. 25). This leads then to the conclusion that Qoheleth takes a positive view of humanity and of the struggles to comprehend existence. Even though his own and others' results are not as complete as he might like, the effort expended is both necessary and worthwhile.

This final section of ch. 7 pictures a sage who methodically sets out to comprehend wisdom and evil/folly, both sides of the human experience. Little that was conclusive seemed to result. However, he is still committed to the essential rectitude of humankind, and the need to continue the struggle to make some sense out of life. The purpose here is to call the reader to fresh meditation on the mystery of God's dealings, and to point decisively to the fact that the good things of life, its material benefits, its joyous experiences, are to be thankfully enjoyed as in 2.24; 3.12 etc. However, as this section indicates, the focus for reflection is also on the darker side of human experience and its many anomalies. Specifically, the problem is of death and its premature arrival for some. Despite the acknowledged power and value of wisdom, even the sage finds that fully comprehensive conclusions or insights elude him. From this we move to ch. 8, which quite logically brings the question, 'Who then is like the wise man?'

Chapter 8

The Unknown Future

The thesis with which we have been working is that the programmatic question in 6.11-12 repeated from 1.3 will find its next response in 8.7, which in turn will prepare the reader for the call to enjoy life in 8.15. This thesis provides us with the framework within which to interpret the material of both chs. 7-8. We find in ch. 8, especially in vv. 1-9, many points that are shared with ch. 7. From this we conclude that death is still the issue lying in the background, and against which we should seek to understand ch. 8. The related theme, the possibility of discovering final answers to the problems of life, given this universal phenomenon of death, is the pressing issue in the foreground.

Chapter 8 divides into three parts: 8.1-9, which continues the theme of the inability to know the future (cf. 7.23-24); 8.10-14, in which is discussed the matter of God's judgment and justice in this broken world; and 8.15-17 with which the chapter climaxes, issuing the call to enjoyment and the summary of Qoheleth's attempt to 'get wisdom'. It closes off the discussion which began in ch. 7.

The major keywords of ch. 7 recur throughout ch. 8.

8.1-9 Who Then Is Wise?

The first half of ch. 8 appears not to have a readily discernible structure, though the practical wisdom of the sage as that which can save, is a theme which interweaves with the theme of his inability to penetrate the mind of God. This latter has special reference to the hiddenness of the future. In the light of v. 9, the material in vv. 1-8 is to be viewed as representing some of the kinds of things the sage can and cannot know.

8.1 The opening question enquires about one 'who is like the sage' (cf. 6.11-12). An infrequently used uncontracted form *k^e^heḥākām* stands in lieu of *keḥākām*. Fox and Seow prefer to follow the LXX rendering, meaning that the MT *mî k^eheḥākām* should be divided differently to read *mî kōh ḥākām*, 'who is so wise'. Fortunately for the reader, Qoheleth adds a parallel question which focuses the intention of the first and general question: he asks who is so wise that he is able to know the meaning of things (*pešer dābār*). The Qumran community, among others, had their own private commentaries on Scripture. Each was known as a *pešer*, an interpretation of a given text. This term, which can refer to a solution to a problem, makes its appearance very late in pre-Christian times, and is not found in any other text in OT Hebrew. The *pešer* relates closely to the work of the sage, as the sage was the one charged with reflecting on situations and events to discern their significance, with confronting problems met, and then hopefully with deriving therefrom useful instruction. It was in following that instruction, accumulated over generations, that one could learn to cope with life. So the two questions in v. 1 are supplementary.

Rhetorical questions are at times a way of making a negative statement (cf. 7.13b). However, in this instance, it defies logic to interpret Qoheleth's first question as a statement that nobody is like the wise man. The latter half of the verse also requires that we adopt a positive response to the two questions in 8.1ab. Qoheleth is asking, 'who is the one best resembling the sage?' 'Who knows how to interpret things?' The questions are really exclamations and their purpose is to cause the reader to ponder these questions. Such an approach permits us then to make sense of v. lb, where Qoheleth answers his own question by saying that, 'you can tell (who is wise) by looking'. The wise person has a 'glow' about him (*tā'îr pānāw*), a resource welling up from within (cf. Num. 6.25; Job 29.24), which transforms and softens his appearance (*w^e'oz pānāw y^ešunne'*). The harshness or coarseness (*'ōz*) of one's appearance, one's impudence when confronting authority, will be altered (*y^ešunne'*) under the influence of sound learning and wisdom (cf. Job 14.20).

8.2 The use of the personal pronoun 'I' at the head of this verse and in an imperative context, seems to be a difficulty (see RSV margin). Two possible explanations present themselves: the first is to emend *'^anî,* 'I,' to read *'et,* indicating the verbal object. This solution, though followed by some of the versions, would require the definite article as a prefix on *melek,* 'king'. However, there are instances in which the definite article may be omitted from a noun yet for the noun to retain its markedness (e.g. Gen.

14.19 etc.). The second suggestion is that the verb *'āmartî,* 'said', has fallen from the head of the verse (cf. 2.1, 15; 3.18 etc.). Gordis (1968: 288) and many others would dispute this latter, but some recognize a Rabbinic expression in which the personal pronoun *'ᵃnî* itself functions with the meaning, 'I said'. Fox demurs from this suggestion, as he does the suggestion that it can mean 'I do'. Most translations seem to ignore it. Fox would prefer to solve the issue by regarding the pronoun as the pronominal suffix on *yᵉšannᵉ'ennû,* 'changes it'.

What the king says is rendered as the king's 'mouth' (*pî-melek*), as in Gen. 45.21. Qoheleth advises that the royal word is to be obeyed, for the reason stated in the following clause. A late expression, *'al dibrat* (used only here and in 3.18, 8.2 and Ps. 110.4), means 'for the sake of' or 'with regard to'. Although Fox disputes the sense 'because of', others including Murphy and Crenshaw see it as providing the motive for the advice that follows. Seow on the other hand prefers to read it as an emphatic or explicative 'in the manner of'. The grounds for complying with the royal edict is that a 'divine oath' (*šᵉbū'at-'ᵉlōhîm*) has been given. On account of God's oath sworn to the king (so Hertzberg: 164), as for example in Ps. 89.19-21, the prudent thing is to recognize the authority resident in his person and conform to his requests. This reads the phrase 'sacred oath' (RSV) as a subjective genitive. However it could also be an objective genitive. Thus, other scholars (e.g. Rankin, Barton, *et al.*) suggest that obedience is a recognition of the popular loyalty sworn to the monarch by the community at his accession. Either interpretation is acceptable, the first on the basis of a Davidic theology of kingship, which is presumably that to which the sage adheres. The second view would be grounded in a practical expression of the loyalty promised by the community in the enthronement liturgy. Qoheleth's point is that wise persons will be aware of the need to respond to a royal edict, because they will recognize the circumstances under which it was issued (cf. Prov. 16.14-15). It is possible that the purpose of the advice here is to do as the king says, something which will save the person at court, even if the royal advice is not particularly wise.

8.3 Further instances of wise conduct are recorded. The note of caution already met in 5.1 and 7.9 is found again here with the form *'al tibbāhēl,* 'don't be rash'. Rashness is one of the more obvious marks of the fool (Prov. 21.5). Qoheleth's advice here is to avoid precipitately leaving the royal presence (cf. also Prov.

23.1-2). Of course, one needs to know the circumstances against which this advice is issued. The second half of the verse helps us fix the meaning. The verse consists of two balanced statements in parallel. The second part contains the phrase *dābār raʿ,* literally 'an evil word/ matter', which RSV renders as 'an unpleasant matter'. The context, however, makes no suggestions as to whether this could be something problematic for the king or for those at the royal court. Waldman (1979: 407-8) has gathered supporting evidence from Akkadian and Amarna material to demonstrate that this phrase may refer to conspiracy against the king. The verb in this clause, *ʿmd,* can mean 'persist' as well as 'join', giving the following possible translation: 'Do not abandon the king precipitately, and do not join any rebellion against him'. The specific warning, whether more general in the sense of 'anything problematic', or specific in the sense of 'some seditious act', is intended to call for wise conduct. So, to refer back to the question posed in v. 1, we may respond that one who is mindful of the power imbalance between king and subject and acts in accordance with the warning issued in v. 3 is wise.

As to the reason one should follow these two complementary warnings, v. 3c tells us that everything he desires (*kol ʾašer yaḥpoṣ*), he does. The subject of these verbs can only be 'the king', so the verse as a whole calls for conduct which recognizes that royal authority is absolute. Consistent with this is the idea that the king should be both feared and obeyed, for he is divinely elect. In this sense the motive clause in v. 3c also speaks to the advice in v. 2.

8.4 A further reason for doing as a king bids is now given. The initial *baʾašer* functions like *kî,* 'because', in v. 3c.

What was described as a king's 'mouth' (*pî-melek*) in v. 2, is the equivalent of his 'word' (*dbar-melek*) in v. 4. That word is characterized as *šilṭôn,* as 'rule, power'. The root *šlt* has already been used in 2.19, 5.18[19] and 6.2, but in the nominal form *šiltôn* it occurs only here and in v. 8. Though nominal in form, functionally it is an adjective: the royal word is powerful.

To highlight the power and authority of the king's word, Qoheleth asks, 'who would question, in a critical way, what the king does?' As a rhetorical question, the implication is that no sensible person, no sage (v. 1), would oppose royalty (cf. Isa. 45.9). Kings not only have the power to do as they will (v. 3b), but that power places their actions above questioning by their subjects (cf. Prov. 16.14-15).

8.5 Thus far the focus of this section has been directed towards the one who would be called wise, and examples of wise conduct are given in the context of admonitions about appropriate behaviour in the royal court. Heeding the royal command is one criterion of wisdom, because due weight is given to the king's divinely sanctioned position and to his authority. These various examples are all responding to the leading question of v. 1.

In v. 5 this theme continues. The verse itself demonstrates a chiastic structure (A,B,C: C',B',A'), a structure which regards the 'one who keeps the (king's?) orders' (*šômēr-miṣwāh*) and the 'mind of the sage' (*lēb-ḥākām*) as co-equivalent. We presume the participle *šômēr* describes one who follows the call in v. 2, and thus one who will refuse to be party to opposition (*dābār ra'*, cf. v. 3). In Prov 19.16 it refers more generally to the instruction given by a teacher. More positively, such a person will be aware of (*yāda'*) what the RSV renders as 'the time and way' (*'ēt ûmišpāṭ*). Chapter 3 drew attention to the divine ordering of every aspect of human life in the poem constructed around the term *'ēt*. Qoheleth now reaches back to those thoughts to define who is wise. The correlate of *'ēt*, the term *mišpāṭ*, does not appear in ch. 3. Conceivably the term *mišpāṭ* (RSV, 'way') balances the concept of 'commandment' (*miṣwāh*) in v. 5a. However, the meaning of *'ēt* and *mišpāṭ* require further exploration.

The moments of time (*'ēt*) are discernible to the sage (3.lff.) and their function within the divine plan is clear. *'Ēt* is therefore a term connoting order and purpose within the mind of God. One further point: the 'time'-poem opens in 3.2 with the twin ideas of 'birth' and 'death'. In the 'Better'-poem of 7.1ff. we again find the theme of 'death' and 'birth'. Chapter 7 has taken up the issue of untimely death, and we shall meet the subject again in 8.8. It therefore is not inconceivable that v. 5b, though apparently general in its basic form, has a more restricted meaning here because of this context. Thus, *'ēt* refers both generally to time and specifically to the 'time of death'.

In the legal tradition, the noun *mišpāṭ* simply means 'judgment', and then by extension may depict its execution, or application to specific cases (Exo. 21.31). Its various usages all group around the idea that a person, or his/her conduct, is being evaluated against the demands of the law. With this in mind, we may suggest that in the present context of v. 5b, the term *mišpāṭ* is best rendered as 'evaluation' or even 'assessment'. It would not be straining the sense inordinately to see it as the equivalent of the word *pešer* in v. 1. A sage knows both the times and their import. This saying appears to promise success to the wise since they know the times and ways. However, there is a question as to whether this is something with which Qoheleth agrees or whether it is merely a foil to what is to follow.

8.6 Timing and significance are two elements in every matter (*ḥēpeṣ*, cf. 3.1). Of course, the precise significance of any matter has to be discovered, but the sage is the one to face that challenge; there he sets his mind (v. 5b).

While every event has its 'time', in vv. 1-9 reference is to death, and specifically to untimely death. It cannot be too distant from Qoheleth's meaning if we suggest that in v. 6a he is speaking of this matter. That such death is a calamity or an incomprehensible disaster, is supported by the final part of v. 6. Many are the trials which afflict mankind (*rā'at-hā'ādām*). Gordis (1968: 289) seems alone in viewing *rā'āh* as moral evil.

It is not entirely certain whether the 'matters' (*ḥēpeṣ*) of which Qoheleth speaks are restricted to those whims or fancies of the king (v. 3). However, its likelihood is great in view of the use of *dābār ra'* and *ḥēpeṣ* conjoined by *kî*, 'because', a feature which occurs in both v. 3 and vv. 5-6. This would lead to the suggestion that the *rā'āh*, 'calamity', of v. 6b is akin to the rebellious act in vv. 3, 5. The saying, however, is sufficiently general to allow for a view that in this final clause Qoheleth is countering the notion that the sage is in a difficult, and for him a deeply troubling, position because one cannot know what lies ahead.

This verse and the following are marked by four examples of clauses introduced by the particle *kî*. The function and meaning of this particle is obviously important to one's interpretation of the text. For Crenshaw each use of the particle serves a different function (1987: 151): the first is asseverative, 'indeed'; the second adversative, 'but'; the third expresses a result, 'for'; and the final one indicates reason or cause, 'because'. Murphy also adopts this position. Seow on the other hand argues that each example of *kî* marks the object of the verb 'know' at the end of verse 5 and so he renders each as '(knows) that...'. Thus for Seow there are four matters that Qoheleth himself claims are knowable: that for every matter there is a time and judgment; that the evil of humanity is their burden; that nobody knows the future; and that nobody can tell the future.

8.7 Verse 7 is one of the markers for the framework of 6.12—8.15, indicating as it does the response to the question (6.12) based on the various observations made in 7.1—8.6. For this reason we should interpret the verse in that wider context rather than as exclusively referring to the king. Not only is it connected to 6.12 but also to 8.1, responding to the question about who knows what meaning things or events have.

We have come to expect that on the issue of knowing the future Qoheleth will affirm that nobody knows (*'ēnennû yôdē'a*) what it holds for us. 'Who indeed can tell people what the future holds?' is a repetition of the second question in 6.12, and as a rhetorical question asserts that none can tell. The initial *kî*, 'indeed', reinforces this conclusion.

As in 7.14, that future about which vital information is elusive must be a reference in part to one's future on earth, but more so to the future beyond death. We have seen that Qoheleth, projecting forward on the basis of universal experience, concludes that in general terms, the future will be as the past (1.9-10 etc.), though he is here speaking in strictly earthly terms. What he can never discover by the observation-reflection method is the future of the human spirit (*rûaḥ*) beyond the grave (cf. 3.21), for it is a matter about which no evidence exists. Nor is there any way of testing one's thesis about it. The 'times' and their 'meaning' are in Qoheleth's purview, but by dint of circumstances the search for meaning cannot extend to life beyond the grave, even if there should be any (3.19-21). We found that in 7.19-24 there was also a reference to the efficacy of wisdom, that much is indeed knowable, but conjoined with this fact and providing its counter-balance is another, and less optimistic, view, namely the essential bounds to human knowledge. Death gives rise to one such barrier; we cannot see beyond it, nor analyse any possible form of existence there. It will be evident that this present interpretation differs markedly from those who associate 'what will be' (*ka'ašer yihyeh*) with the actions of the king in vv. 2, 4.

8.8 The pervasiveness of death as a theme underlying this chapter is evident in this verse, offering further proof that Qoheleth's deepest concern is with the fate of the wise after death.

Verse 8 consists of four clauses, the first three of which are introduced by *'ēn*, 'there is not', as was v. 7. Qoheleth contends that there is no person (*'ēn 'ādām*) with power (*šallîṭ*) over the breath of life or the wind (*rûaḥ*) to the extent that they are able to restrain it. As a possible adjective (see BDB), *šallîṭ* describes one who 'has power over' another (v. 9). The infinitive construct *k^e^lô'* expresses a withholding or restraining action. So the phrase relates to one's ability or power to hold on to life or to frustrate death. It is also reminiscent of the concept 'shepherding the wind', that fruitless pursuit spoken of in 2.11, 17 etc.

The second clause represents a parallel thought: there is none with power (*šilṭôn*) over the moment of death (*yôm-hammāwet*). Thus v. 8ab agrees with the view expressed in 3.1 that the 'times' are in God's hand to determine. There is also a sense in which the aphorism of 7.13 speaks to this issue, as does the general theme of ch. 7, the theme of untimely death. No effort of ours will prolong our lives; we are powerless to postpone the moment (*'ēt*) of our demise.

A further constraint upon human power is recorded in v. 8c, Qoheleth indicating that there is no 'discharge' (*mišlaḥat*) from war (RSV). The rare term *mišlaḥat* occurs in Biblical Hebrew otherwise only in Ps. 78.49, where RSV renders it as 'a company of ...' It originates in Aramaic, though the root *šlḥ*, 'send', is frequently found in OT. The meaning assigned to this rare term must be tentative. Its root would suggest a possible meaning 'discharge', but if by that some formal release from military duty is in mind, then there are problems, for Deut. 20.5-8 already provided for just such a contingency. Gordis's view (1968: 291) has merit if we allow the context to define its meaning. In this case, just as we have no ultimate power over our life-breath, so too we can exercise no decisive control over a battle. We are always partly victims of circumstances and cannot flee from them. This is the sense in Scott's translation, 'there is no immunity in the battle', for all are equally exposed to danger. Seow's view (1997: 282-3) is that *mišlaḥat* refers to sending a substitute into battle and so the comment is that nobody can send a substitute when the time for one's death arrives. One other possible interpretation, dependent on the assumption that the preposition *b^e^* in *bammilḥāmāh* indicates instrument, is that 'there is no discharge or escape *by means of* war'.

Yet another decision faces the interpreter. If the two clauses v. 8ab were of parallel meaning, does this correspondence flow into v. 8cd? Our decision will affect the way we interpret the latter. Although v. 8d does not begin with *'ēn,* it does commence with a negative verb, and so is of a related form. The piel imperfect *y^e^mallēṭ,* 'escape', 'deliver', continues the theme of *šlḥ* in v. 8c. Evil, says Qoheleth, will not save 'him who is its master' (*b^e^ 'ālāw*); scoundrels will always have to face the consequences of their actions. Neither war nor evil can save or prolong life, offering further proof that human power is subject to very real limitations.

8.9 What Qoheleth has observed is 'all this', and as usual we conclude that it is a summary term for what has preceded. The statement is forceful, as there is added the phrase *nātôn 'et-libbî,* indicating the great care exercised in considering the matters before him, matters described in the customary way as 'everything under the sun' (cf. 8.17). Also in mind are the actions depicted in 7.13.

On the other hand, human interaction has to come to terms not only with the deeds of God who determines and controls the 'times', but must also cope with the behaviour of one person towards another. Rampant injustice and oppression within human society, to which even the wise may succumb on occasion (7.20), is a highly problematic issue for the sage. That is because the sage is called to defend the justice of God in a world where evidence of such justice often seems at least dubious. In this section of his reflection Qoheleth touches on both sides of the issue. He has thought at great length about the limits of the human mind, the anomaly of its powerlessness (8.8) and of its energetic strength (7.19). Although people are unable to determine their longevity, cannot control the breath of life, some do exercise power over (*šālaṭ*) their fellow beings (v. 9c), often then using that power for ill (*lᵉra' lô*). Whether that evil is the effect of such behaviour on the perpetrator of the crime, or on the object of such actions is perhaps deliberately vague. Both are affected by it adversely.

Point of time is the emphasis of '*ēt* (cf. ch. 3), so its use here as a descriptor of human history seems out of keeping. The infinitive absolute, *nātôn,* as equivalent to *nātattî,* 'I gave', is a late linguistic phenomenon.

8.10-14 Bad Examples Lead Others Astray

Once again, a deplorable situation is cited because of its educational value. It is a case of unjust members of society who are held in esteem by the community, religious authorities included. A situation in which wicked people are given a grand public funeral mocks at justice, and what is worse, directly encourages others to follow the bad example set (vv. 10-12a). Qoheleth appends two reflections on this situation in v. 12b and v. 13, and follows them with a final statement about the irony of an unjust world.

8.10 A difficult verse, we shall have to proceed carefully to find its meaning. The opening word is an unusual combination of a preposition and conjunction, *bᵉkēn,* literally "in thus". It is found elsewhere only in Esth. 4.16, and is presumed to be the result of Aramaic influence. It is a marker that turns the reader's attention to something new, in this case a section in which the observation-reflection process will face yet another challenge. The situation in question has to do with the burial (*qᵉburîm*—passive participle qal) of some corrupt persons (*rᵉšāʿîm*) in the community. The use of the plural suggests frequent occurrence. It is with the following verb, 'and they came' (*wābāʾû*) that our difficulties begin, for as it stands at present, the text is meaningless. Most of the versions witness to another text, or are attempts to make sense of the MT. If we assume that the *mem* presently attached to *qᵉburîm* rightly belongs to the following word, then, as the LXX presupposes, the reading *mūbāʾ îm* brings us close to a meaningful text. The present *qᵉburîm* would lose its final *mem* and become the noun *qeber*, 'grave'. This would mean that the evil were brought for burial. The importance of decent burial is stressed in Israelite culture, hence when one is denied it, as in the scenario in 6.3, a major problem is to hand. Here the issue is not that the wicked were buried, for that would have been expected, but rather is it the circumstances under which they were buried. That they were buried 'with pomp' (Gordis, 1968: 295) may be implied, though the text would refer the adulation, not to the burial itself, but to popular response to the examples of the life lived by these corrupt individuals.

The specific problem Qoheleth identifies lies in the association between these corrupt persons and the sacred place, perhaps the Temple. The text of v. 10b runs, 'they went from the temple' (*mimmᵃqôm qādôš yᵉhallēkû*). 'From the Temple' should read *mimmāqôm*. The appearance of a piel form *yᵉhallēkû* is unusual, though not impossible. It indicates that the funeral 'set off from' the holy place, implying that the religious authorities were involved in the funeral despite the notoriety of the deceased. This interpretation depends on the view that *māqôm qādôš* represents the Temple or other sacred place, and is not an Egyptian term for 'grave' (Loretz, 1964: 75-76), or as Gordis suggests, a euphemism for the grave. The reason for preferring 'Temple' is for the likely balance between this term and 'city' in the final clause.

The other textual difficulty arises with the MT *yištakkeḥû*, from the root *škḥ*, 'forget'. Other MSS, especially the LXX, read *yištabbeḥû*, 'and they were lauded'. This latter appears more appropriate. However, as Fox and Seow point out there is no particular difficulty in accepting that the just persons are 'neglected'. The point is clear nevertheless that corrupt persons were not only given public burial, they were also praised by those who knew them best, those who lived in the city where their evil deeds were perpetrated (*bāʿîr ʾašer kēn- ʿāśû*). At the same time it often occurred that the just person was ignored, their manner of life overlooked. It is this unacceptable situation which calls forth Qoheleth's cry: this is *hebel*! 'This should never happen!' 'It is unacceptable!'

One must not forget that these scenarios Qoheleth paints are deliberately generalized so that each is actually representative of a certain kind of problem rather than being an actual case history. The implication here is that the 'holy place' and the 'city' are not intended to specify Jerusalem and its Temple, though they would both be included in their frame of reference. As is the case with most wisdom writing, generalized terms and expressions which can cover multiple situations are preferred.

8.11 Qoheleth steps back, as it were, from the scene just painted to describe the impact it has on the community at large. At the head of the verse stands *ʾašer,* here with the sense of 'because' (cf. Jer. 16.13; Job 34.27). The phrase *ʾēn naʿaśāh,* the negated niphal perfect, is unusual and should perhaps read *naʿaśeh,* the participle. Its subject is *pitgām,* a word which came into Hebrew from Persian via Aramaic, and found elsewhere in OT Hebrew only in Esth. 1.20. It describes an edict or decree issued by the authorities. An appropriate contextual translation is 'sentence'. The sentencing of the evildoer (*maʿaśēh hārāʿāh*) is due, but for whatever reason has been delayed, and is not given speedily (*mehērāh*). The delay, and the consequent impression it creates that it might not come at all, is damaging and very demoralizing. The general nature of the verse leaves open whether the sentence should be issued by the civil authorities or by God. Likewise, that the evil person then goes on to live a long life also seems to be implied. Be that as it may, the point made is that evil, if not dealt with appropriately and summarily either from a legal or theological perspective, results in havoc.

Flowing from the above predicament are certain consequences which, in this instance, have impact upon the entire community (*b^enē-hā'ādām*). The *'al-kēn* indicates that what follows is a result clause, the minds (*lēb*) of people being filled (*mālē'*) with thoughts of pursuing the same evil course (*la'ᵃśôt rā'*). The closing infinitive construct (*la'ᵃśôt*) speaks of their purpose. The adverbial phrase *bāhem,* 'within/among them', refers to the community members.

So justice either from God or the magistrates is not seen to be done, resulting in negative and destructive effects upon society. When people are tempted to turn to evil almost certain that they will escape its dire consequences, then society is in trouble, and religion as well.

8.12 As in v. 11, so here also, the introductory *'ᵃšer* means 'because'. Thus, v. 12 we presume will also address itself to an issue raised in v. 10. However, rhetorically, it flows on from the closing expression in v. 11. The community members are attracted to a life of evil by delayed or uncertain justice. The sinner who steps into that lifestyle may find that it actually pays off. His descent further into serious evil is conveyed in the phrase 'doing evil a hundred times' (*'ōśeh ra' mᵉ'at*). *Mᵉ'at* is a construct form, suggesting that the noun it governs has fallen from the text. The most likely word to insert is *pᵉ'āmîm,* 'times'. However, Seow suggests a slight emendation to the MT giving a meaning the evil done 'by hundreds' (*ra' mē'ōt*). There seems no adequate textual reason for emending the MT to follow the LXX equivalent *mē'az*, 'from then'. Commitment to evil allegedly adds years to one's life (*ma'ᵃrîk lô*). As the reader will sense, this is a scenario only, following a theme akin to 7.15. The interesting thing is that one should attribute one's longevity to doing evil, for had the person persisted in doing right, in following wisdom, he would have lived just as long. But that is to miss the point of the tale, which is that the delay in bringing justice is perceived as encouraging others falsely and foolishly to assume that evil is the gateway to long life.

What response will Qoheleth make to this trend? Verse 12b, introduced by *kî gam*, is perhaps best seen as the adversative, 'however' (cf. 4.14; 8.16) or perhaps concessive, 'even though'. McNeile (Barton agrees) suggests, 'surely also', but the context requires an adversative sense. Two theses are advanced by Qoheleth. Both are expressed by the adjective 'good' (*ṭôb*), reminiscent of ch. 7. In v. 12b, Qoheleth says, 'It will be good ...' (*yihyeh ṭôb lᵉ*), and in v. 13 the contrary expression, 'it will not be good ...' (*wᵉṭôb lō' yihyeh lᵉ*). Our author affirms (*yōdēa' 'ᵃnî*) that those who fear God will do well, or enjoy good things, a sentiment identical with that of 7.18, 26. Fear of God is the only way to success. The nature of the success or 'good' we infer from the context is long life. By contrast, the evil one will not reach old age. Qoheleth here throws his full support behind the tradition, for under no circumstances could he advocate pursuit of evil, even if it did appear that divine justice was lacking.

8.13 The evil one will never see good things (*w^{e}ṭôb lō' yihyeh lārāšā'*). His life will still run the allotted course, his immorality can do nothing to extend his days (*lō' ya'^{a}rîk yāmîm*). The argument here is consistent with the above. There is then a high degree of truth in the tradition, be it legal (Exod. 20.12), or wisdom (Prov. 11.31; 13.14; 14.27 etc.). From this we conclude that Qoheleth basically supports the traditional view about divine justice, but this does not mean that be cannot also bring before it some serious anomalies which must be faced. Such is the purpose of the scenario in 8.10. There are times when it seems that evil ones receive the reward due the just person (7.15; 8-10), but this fact can never completely overthrow the tradition.

Shadows (*ṣēl*) as an image can convey differing ideas. One relates to brevity, and this seems to be the sense implied in 6.12. Another is the notion that the shadow, like shade, can offer protection, as in 7.12. Given Qoheleth's two usages, we have to make a choice here. If we select the first meaning, then we can translate, 'his days (which are) like a shadow, will be brief'. The second sense would give us a translation, 'he will not prolong his life as a protection'. Its meaning would be uncertain, though there are some scholars (e.g. Barton, Levy) who suggest that the idea of longevity is related to the lengthening of a shadow in the evening. Weight of evidence favours the first sense above, that is, that his days pass quickly, as a shadow.

The reason the evil person will miss out on the good things of life is introduced by *'^{a}šer*, 'because'. The explanation lies in their failure to fear God (7.18), which is folly.

8.14 It is precisely the anomaly to which he has referred (7.15) which creates the problem for the tradition. Qoheleth has made the point forcefully that he who, when faced by the situation described, would say, 'sin more', is doomed to failure. Evil is not the route to longevity. Qoheleth stands in stout defence of the traditional view, that evil will be judged. Yet the anomaly (*hebel*) is clear, and the repetition of the term *hebel* makes obvious how deeply Qoheleth feels about it (cf. Job 21.7). It is truly difficult to understand how this situation can arise. What situation is he speaking of? That the just seem on occasion to suffer the fate which ought rightly to befall the unjust, and the unjust seem to escape punishment.

Qoheleth has chosen parallelism as an effective way to draw the contrast between the experience of the evil and of the righteous. His comment that this situation is enigmatic (*hebel*), or perhaps more strongly, completely unacceptable and unjust is the inclusion which brackets the verse. This literary effort is well worth setting out for our closer appreciation:

yeš hebel	*’^{a}šer na‘^{a}śāh*	*‘al hā’āreṣ*	*’^{a}šer*
yēš ṣaddîqîm	*’^{a}šer maggîa‘*	*‘^{a}lēhem*	*k^{e}ma‘^{a}śeh-hār^{e}šā‘im*
w^{e}yēš r^{e}šā‘îm	*šemmaggîa‘*	*‘^{a}lēhem*	*k^{e}ma‘^{a}śeh-haṣṣaddîqîm*
’āmartî šegam zeh hābel.			

The claim is that some righteous individuals ‘have happen to them’ (*maggia‘ ‘^{a}lēhem*) what theoretically ought to be the consequences of evil conduct (*k^{e}ma‘^{a}śeh-hār^{e}šā‘im*). This latter term is an inclusive one embracing the actions themselves, what people do, and the outcome of those actions (cf. Isa. 32.17; Hab. 3.17). The hiphil participle *maggia‘*, from *ng‘*, ‘to reach’, carries the idea of ‘extend as far as’, thence ‘befall’ (cf. 12. 1).

Again we remind ourselves that this is not a comprehensive picture of human experience, but by putting it alongside the preceding (vv. 12b-13), Qoheleth demands that his readers come to terms with how things are in the real, and less than ideal world.

What is the unfortunate fate which befalls the just? The context of chs. 7-8 leaves little doubt, and 8.12b-13 insists, that the just often die prematurely. By contrast, scoundrels all too frequently escape their proper fate and live long, some even enjoying a ‘state funeral’ (v. 10). This presents Qoheleth with yet another situation without resolution. How can it happen? It does, and that is all one can say. His utter dismay is caught in the reiterated *hebel* phrase.

8.15 The Call to Enjoyment

We have now arrived at the climactic verse for this chapter. Functionally, and from a structural view, this verse closes off the discussion which began with the questions in 6.11-12, then passed through various investigations leading to the response in

8.7. Verse 15 presents Qoheleth's advice on how to live in this enigmatic world in light of the issues presented in chs. 7-8. As advice it follows the pattern already established in 2.24, 3.12, and 5.17(18). Furthermore, this verse represents the last time that the *'ēn ṭôb,* or 'There is nothing better', saying is used. This carries a significance for the structure of the book which we shall discuss shortly.

On the basis of material considered in chs. 7-8, Qoheleth commends 'enjoyment'. The initial verb *šibbaḥtî* is the piel form of the rare verb *šbḥ,* 'praise'. Apart from several uses in the Psalms (63.4; 117.1; 147.12), the verb is found elsewhere only in 4.2. It comes with the sense of 'recommend'. The content of the word 'enjoyment' is defined by the second part of the verse.

The formal features of the *'ēn ṭôb*-form have already been discussed (see 2.24). Only one thing remains to us in this uncertain life: to eat, drink, and enjoy oneself (for comments on these verbs see 2.24). Those activities define what Qoheleth means by 'enjoyment'. Is there not some conflict here with the ideas expressed in 7.4? On the surface it would seem as though that were so. However, we noted in 7.2, 4 that Qoheleth is not averse to pleasure-seeking, except when one ignores the fact that life has another and darker side. This latter must be as significant an element in one's world-view as is pleasure. Only the fool ignores life's 'minor' key. So for Qoheleth to advocate enjoyment of the pleasures which life can afford is fully consistent with his view that such pleasures are integral parts of God's gift of life. What distinguishes the sage from the fool is the level of reflection involved in one's approach to life. Merely to seek pleasure, without due consideration of death or of life as divine gift, is typical of the fool. To enjoy life because it is recognized as God's gift is a sign of wisdom and theological maturity.

That one's attitude towards pain or pleasure is the crux, is further demonstrated by the appended clause. When Qoheleth states that 'it will go well with him (*yilwennû*) in his work (*baʿămālô*)' he means that even in toil, pleasure is available. The verb 'accompany' (*lwh*) occurs only in this instance in the qal form; other uses are all niphal (cf. Gen. 29.34 etc.). Eating and drinking are fundamental requirements to sustain life; they are not ends in themselves as they were in the example quoted in 7.4 (see also 10.16-17). Qoheleth is not advocating any form of hedonism. Additionally, we note, as in 2.24 etc., that our author draws together 'pleasure' and 'work', so that they are inextricably related. Both life and its pleasures are God-given, and this understanding is vitally important in defining Qoheleth's theological stance. He sees all things as having their origin with God. This interpretation is rather different from that proposed by Fox who has argued that Qoheleth commends pleasure 'as a distraction from the painful awareness of realities that he has just described' (1999: 287). Fox's view is based on his understanding of the term *'āmāl* as 'the burdens of life', and his apparent failure to see that physical work (*'āmāl*) and pleasure are both divine gifts.

8.16-17 Human Beings Cannot Find Out What God Does

Discussion of divine activity which marked chs. 7-8 is now brought to a close. Here we begin a summary statement whose message is simple: nobody, not even the sage, can discern all that God does. Whybray's view that these two verses are an editorial addition placed here to offer 'a more systematic presentation of Qoheleth's thought' is not necessary since the focus verb '(not) find out' (*mṣ'*) and other expressions link the passage directly with the thoughts expressed throughout 6.10-12 and 7.1-29 (so also Krüger).

8.16 Certain expressions in v. 16 return our thoughts to 1.13, and especially to 7.2, 3 and 14. The determination with which Qoheleth pursued the enquiry (*nātattî 'et libbî l^{e}*) is a feature of all his investigations to date, and is acknowledged in the Epilogue (12.9). He has devoted himself to 'see, ponder, and understand'. The two verbs *yāda'* and *rā'āh* are interchangeable (see 2.12; 7.25 etc.) and describe the work of the sage in particular, for they probe issues for their significance and meaning. Here that purpose is exemplified in the use of infinitive constructs, *lāda'at* and *lir'ôt*. The object of the search is *ḥokmāh,* 'wisdom' and *'inyān,* 'business'. The latter term, found only in Qoheleth, has Aramaic roots, portraying in a general sense all human activity. This means that the verse draws attention to the things that people do on earth, including oppression, evil deeds, and injustice. It is to these kinds of actions that Qoheleth gives his attention. As to the results of his efforts, we find him honestly admitting that they were not very fruitful, a difficulty mentioned already in 7.23-29.

In this verse the final clause has presented interpreters with considerable difficulties. The RSV suggests: 'neither day nor night one's eyes see sleep'. Presumably, people are so preoccupied with their business that they never have the chance to sleep or rest properly. The 'he' or 'it' which is the subject of the clause, has to be supplied. So Barton renders it, 'he sees no sleep' (so also Lauha: 160; Glasser: 139). Gordis' rather free translation, 'though a man sleep neither by day nor night, he cannot discover...', depends on making the subject of v. 16b the same as that of v. 17. If, however, the subject of *'ēnennû rō'eh,* 'there is no seeing', is Qoheleth himself, then the meaning changes. Fox suggests emending the third person to first person to make clear that Qoheleth is the subject. He sought frantically, forgoing sleep in his driving pursuit of an answer, but still did not find it. Yet another attempt at dealing with the problem is Seow who sees the clause 'even though...with their eyes' as disrupting the flow of thought and so suggests it has been misplaced from v.17. Its sense however, he suggests, is to emphasize Qoheleth's complete dedication to the task of finding out, of examining all that happens in this mysterious world. My own examination of the text suggests another possibility. Qoheleth says, by day and night 'sleep was in his eyes' *(šēnāh b*^e^*'ēnāw),* therefore he was unable to see (*'ēnennû rō'eh*). If the *b*^e^ preposition has a locative meaning, 'in', rather than instrumental 'with', then we avoid the redundancy of the expression 'seeing *with* one's eyes'. If Qoheleth himself is the subject, then he is saying that he failed to see or comprehend as he had hoped. The reason for this frustration was that, day and night, it made no difference, there was always 'sleep' in his eyes. The polar terms 'day' and 'night' indicate constancy, and the term 'sleep' (*šēnāh*) is metaphorical for a blindness to facts as in Prov. 20.13 and Job 14.12. Thus, Qoheleth confesses that he was so obtuse, so blind, that he could not see the answer.

8.17 Qoheleth's second focus for reflection was the work of God *('et-kol-ma*^a^*'śeh hā*^e^*'lōhîm),* as distinct from human activity which he considered in v. 16. This verse is the obvious response to 7.13-14, and it parallels v. 9, supporting our argument for the unity of chs. 7-8. Its theme affirms that we cannot discern (*lō' māṣā'*) what God does. The idea is mentioned three times in the verse for emphasis. That we are unable to discover what God does (*lō' yûkal hā'ādām limṣô'*) is the constraint central not only to chs. 7-8 but also to be found in 3.11.

The second half of the verse opens with a late phrase *b*^e^*šel* *'*^a^*šer,* 'on account of'. Aramaic influence is the best explanation of its origin (it occurs in Jon. 1.7, 12). Here the phrase returns our thought to the 'deeds of God' in the opening clause. Qoheleth suggests that people 'work to search out' (*ya'^{a}mōl... l^{e}baqqēš*), stressing the goal-oriented nature of the work. The intention is to uncover meaning in what are perceived to be the actions of God, but the results of such a search are discouraging: they cannot find out (*lō' yimṣā'*). Moreover, the use of an imperfect verb suggests that they will *never* find the answer.

If one were to say, as some sages might have been tempted to do, that one has actually unlocked all life's secrets, Qoheleth's response would be one of cynicism—he repeats his conviction that no human can ever find out all that God does. In this way, all claims to profound knowledge of God's activity are disputed. (The infinitive construct *lāda'at* is the object of the verb *'āmar,* 'say'.) In response to the question of 8.1, 'who is like the sage ... ?' Qoheleth's retort would be, 'only one who recognizes how little can be discerned of the ways of God'.

So we reach not only the end of one chapter and section of the book, we also come to a decisive point in the essay as a whole. Beginning from the initial and programmatic question in 1.3, Qoheleth has, by a series of observations and reflections, reached the opinion that the wise does have *yitrôn,* something which is not available to the fool. Within all that is enigmatic and inexplicable, Qoheleth still stands firmly committed to the inherent value of wisdom, and he advocates its pursuit as the only way by which *yitrôn* might be attained. In practical terms, he counsels enjoyment, the thankful acceptance from God of those basic needs of food and drink and purposeful work by which life is sustained and from which it derives its meaning. It is a theological statement, rooted in the assurance that all comes from God. The only way to cope with life in the kind of world which meets us daily is to accept it happily as originating with God. Never will one uncover answers for all questions, nor is a meaningful life dependent upon finding these elusive answers.

The wide variety of materials and information lying in these eight chapters all ultimately pertain to the programmatic question with which Qoheleth began in 1.3, and to his advice to enjoy what God gives. From this point on there are significant changes in the literary form of the book, and to that we now turn.

Chapter 9

The Primacy of Wisdom

A change of some significance comes over the book at ch. 9. In terms of the thesis we have been pursuing, chs. 1-8 have sought an answer to the fundamental question of *yitrôn* (1.3 etc.). Qoheleth's basic response to this has been to opine that there is no *yitrôn* on earth (2.11 etc.), and that it is best for us to take the things which God provides and enjoy life (2.24 etc.). Death, and in particular untimely death, has been a special focus for this issue of one's *yitrôn*. In chs. 1-8 various kinds of material, autobiographical (1.12—3.21), poetic (1.4-11; 3.2-8; 7.1-13), and illustrations from human experience (e.g. 4.1-12, 13-16 etc.) have all led up to the calls to enjoyment which culminated in the final call in 8.15. This was then followed by a summary statement in 8.16-17 of the human limits to understanding all of life.

As we move into ch. 9, we detect a transition from the former investigative approach to one of discourse (see Ogden, 1982: 158-169). The focus continues to fall upon the value of wisdom to life under threat of death.

This chapter divides into four basic sub-sections: vv. 1-6, 7-10, 11-12, 13-16. We shall postpone consideration of 9.17-18 until the following chapter for reasons which will be explained there.

9.1-6 Once Again, the Problem of One Fate

This first sub-section returns to the theme of one fate (*miqreh*) for all, an issue raised initially in chs. 2-3. We meet the theme in 9.2, 3b. Whether that fate is an expression of 'love' or 'hate' is the question addressed. The phrase *gam 'ahᵃbāh gam śin'āh* in vv. 1 and 6 furnishes the major inclusion for the sub-section (cf. 3.8). The most significant keywords are 'death' and 'life' (vv. 3, 4, 5), along with the frequently used negative particle *'ēn,* 'there is not'. Additionally we note the phrase, 'all that is done under the sun' (*bᵉkōl 'ᵃšer naʿᵃśāh taḥat haššemeš*) in vv. 3, 6.

We look now more closely at the many associations between chs. 2-3 and 9.1-6, and at the latter's significance for the book as a whole.

9.1 The verse opens with an asseverative *kî*, 'Now then', ... 'Indeed'. It is an important marker as the author draws attention to what is to follow.

On two occasions in this verse the phrase *'et kol-zeh,* 'all this', appears as object to the verbs of investigation. Here the direction implicit in the demonstrative *zeh* is forward rather than backward as Qoheleth marks the issues to which he now turns. The recurrent phrase, 'I laid this to heart' *(nātattî 'el libbî),* which we have seen in 1.13, 17; 7,2; 8.16, indicates again the seriousness with which Qoheleth approaches the investigation, and is confirmed by the parallel expression, *lābûr,* 'to examine'. This is Qoheleth's sole use of the term *lābûr,* and on the basis of 1.13; 2.3; 7.25, Graetz and others have suggested that we emend the text to read *lātûr.* It is conceivable that this was the original reading, but we are already familiar with Qoheleth's extreme flexibility with reiterated forms and phrases, to the point that variation is to be expected. We have little warrant for emendation for the sake of conformity.

The observation made leads to a thesis (v. lb), that the 'righteous' and the 'wise'—they are synonymous—together with their 'works' (*haṣṣaddîqîm wᵉhaḥᵃkāmîm waʿᵃbādēhem*) are all ultimately in God's hands and control. The latter term, *ʿᵃbādēhem,* occurs only this once in Biblical Hebrew and is apparently of Aramaic origin. Its emphasis is almost certainly upon the end-product of the sage's efforts, rather than on the expending of effort in labour. Qoheleth believes that not only the sage or just person *per se*, but also all that they do, is within divine control, both with regard to their actions as well as their outcomes. The underlying thought is similar to that in ch. 3, where God determines and disposes the 'times'.

Qoheleth's specific focus is now clear: it is the future outcome of the sage's present activities, and the fact that that future is unknowable (v. lc). This sets up a tension with the thought of v. lb, that all is in God's hands. Such an affirmation is an obvious faith-statement, for on the basis of the research Qoheleth has undertaken, he has concluded that we cannot know the workings of the divine mind. Even to claim that the future lies in God's hands, reflects faith rather than knowledge. This being Qoheleth's present emphasis, the text need not be emended to read *hebel* at the head of v. 2 in lieu of the present *hakkōl* with which v. 1 concludes. Qoheleth determines then that people have no way of discerning all that is before them (*hakkōl lipnēhem*). There is some ambiguity in the meaning of 'before them.' It could be temporal or locational (Lauha). However, our choice is the temporal sense, 'before them' being future in time.

In speaking of what mysteries the future might hold, Qoheleth reuses two polar terms from 3.8 to portray opposing possibilities. These are 'love' (*'ahᵃbāh*) and 'hate' (*śin'āh*); cf. Prov. 15.17. We assume that these two terms refer to either a bright or a gloomy future, 'love' speaking of God's graciousness, and 'hate' representing a future that is to be feared. These two terms are inclusions for the opening subunit and they summarize Qoheleth's concern that human beings cannot be certain whether God's actions are rooted in or express themselves in terms of 'love' or 'hate', of approval or disdain. However, despite this being the majority view of the sense here, there is the possibility that it refers to human love and hate. Indeed, Seow (1997: 298) argues persuasively that it is this latter and that the two terms are related to 'their works', meaning that human emotions as well as actions all rest upon the divine will.

Anticipating vv. 2-3 for the moment, the future about which Qoheleth expresses concern (*hakkōl lipnēhem*) is not only this-worldly, it embraces the future beyond death as well. The discussion in this section ties closely with the *yitrôn* concept, and with Qoheleth's probing of the possibility that there may be some meaningful existence beyond the grave.

9.2 The LXX understands the first three words of the MT to be part of v. 1, and for the opening *hakkōl,* 'all', reads *hebel,* 'enigma'. The three uses of *kōl* in such close proximity does suggest haplography, but each can be justified and the expression with which v. 2 opens makes good sense as it stands. It is also important to the thesis of the verse, and so we should retain the MT.

As Gordis points out (1968: 300), the initial *hakkōl kaʼᵃšer lakkōl* means 'all things are like all things', a statement of principle or constancy. Here it would imply that the situation described is the same for everyone. It is then made concrete in the examples which follow. The unity envisaged consists in a shared fate (*miqreh 'eḥād*), and its universality is indicated in the following sets of polar terms. Such polarized terms (e.g. 'love' and 'hate' in vv. 1, 6, and the twenty-eight paired items in the 'time'-poem of 3.2-8) are basic conceptualizing tools within wisdom thought. All humanity was classified simply as wise or fool, good or evil, etc. (on 'polar' structures, see Loader, 1979). Apart from identifying types of individuals, when used in tandem, these terms can have an inclusive function, incorporating all who fall between the two extremes.

The common fate *(miqreh 'eḥād)*, the topic of conversation in 2.14 and 3.19, is none other than death. Just as in 2.13-14, there are contrasting statements to embrace all manner of humanity, in 9.2 the series of contrasts is a literary device emphasizing death's universality. The categories used are 'righteous' and 'evil', 'clean' and 'unclean' 'the sacrificer' and 'the one who has nothing to sacrifice', 'good' and 'sinner', 'one who takes an oath' and 'one who fears an oath'. Variety of expression is evident in the presentation as the first pairs are linked to *miqreh,* 'fate', by the possessive *l*^{e}, 'belonging to'; sacrificing and vowing are expressed as full clauses rather than simple nominal forms. Whether such variety is to counteract monotony (so Gordis) is difficult to determine as Qoheleth does not find that necessary in 3.2-8. The preponderance of religious or liturgical elements is to be noted. Cleanliness (*ṭāhôr*), sacrificing (*zōbēaḥ*), making vows (*šāba'*) are specific liturgically relevant terms, while 'good' and 'sinner' both have religious connotations, though with a wider moral reference as well.

In ch. 5 Qoheleth has set liturgical matters within his purview. Faith and the religious life can be evaluated from the standpoint of wisdom. However, here in ch. 9 Qoheleth recognizes that whether one is devout or not, an active member of the religious community or outside it, all face the same final prospect of physical death. Since morals and religiosity seem to have no bearing on God's handing out 'love' or 'hate', this statement is a serious challenge to the pious to work towards a resolution of that mystery. It reminds us again that Qoheleth is dealing with a theological issue, the justice of a situation in which both pious and wicked meet the same end.

In the paired contrasts of this verse, *ṭôb*, 'good', appears twice, once as an independent concept and once as the first element of a pair. This oddity raises a textual question. Some MSS (e.g. Syriac and Vulgate) supply *lāra',* 'to the evil', after the first *ṭôb* to complete the duo; other MSS omit the first *ṭôb* altogether. It is a situation which makes resolution of the textual problem rather subjective, but in view of the reference to 'the good' later in the list, it is possible that the first and solitary *ṭôb* represents a later intrusion into the text.

9.3 Qoheleth pronounces judgment on the scenario of v. 2. He believes that 'one fate for all' (*miqreh 'eḥād lakkōl*) is an evil or calamitous situation (*ra'*). Fox notes that some early commentators have viewed the expression *zeh ra' bᵉkol 'ᵃšer naᶜᵃśāh* as a superlative expression, *the* worst thing that could happen. However, there is no reason of syntax to argue that the expression here has a superlative meaning, that this is *the most* evil situation (cf. 5.12(13); 6.1). It is conceivable that *ra'* here depicts moral evil, for the idea that death should come to all without regard to one's character, religious commitment, or behaviour in general, does raise a moral question: is God truly just? However, the convention in Qoheleth is to describe calamity as *ra'*, and in the absence of other evidence here we are drawn to adopt that translation. The phrase 'all that is done under the sun', here and in v. 6, reminds of the comprehensiveness of Qoheleth's survey. The form *naᶜᵃśāh* is the niphal participle, which perhaps ought to be emended to the finite verb *naᶜᵃśeh* (cf. v. 6). Once again Qoheleth points out that death strikes 'all' (*bᵉkōl*), a reference back to those specified in v. 2. The problem with death here, as in chs. 2-3, is that it fails to make an adequate evaluation of people before 'attacking' them; it is the fact that there is only one fate (*miqreh 'eḥād*) which is the root cause of the problem. Death would be more easily comprehended, and perhaps accepted, if it could be seen to make some allowance for the moral character of the individual.

If it were certain that *ra'* in v. 3 spoke of moral evil, then we might feel inclined to accept that as its meaning in v. 3b. However, it is best here to retain the idea of 'calamity' and understand Qoheleth to mean the apparent inconsistencies in the human situation. The phrase *lēb bᵉnē hā'ādām mālē' ra'*, which generally translates as something like 'the human heart is full of evil', is not a proof text for 'original sin'. Quite to the contrary, Qoheleth argues that people's experiences fill their mind (*lēb*) with painful thoughts (*ra'*) and 'madness' (*hôlēlôt*). If we reflect on 8.10ff again, we can appreciate Qoheleth's meaning. Experiences from within a broken world can drive one to an irrational choice of an evil/foolish lifestyle. One is daily surrounded by insoluble problems which are both common to all, and present throughout our lives (*bᵉḥayyēhem*). At the end of all this (*'aḥᵃrāw*), one finally departs to join the dead (*'el hammētîm*). Though *'aḥ'ᵃrāw* carries the singular suffix, 'it', the collective sense is present. Crenshaw, like most other commentators, recognizes the brevity of the final three words of the verse, 'then off to the dead!'. They do make sense despite that brevity, so Seow's argument that they are without meaning and have been transposed from verse 4 is unconvincing.

In vv. 3, 4, and 5, the most frequently used words are *ḥayyîm*, 'life, living', and *mēt*, 'dead, death' (cf. 2.16; 3.2, 19), reminding us again that the focus for all Qoheleth's investigations is life under the shadow of death. It is exactly that common end which furnishes a different perspective on the problems which life throws up. If injustice, oppression, folly and the like, are issues unresolved during one's lifetime, then God's justice comes into question. Alternatively, and this is the direction in which Qoheleth's own thought is moving, there must be some future beyond death where final resolution of life's inequities may be possible.

9.4 The initial *kî*, 'for', is perhaps more akin to the asseverative, as v. 4 does not offer a motive or result clause related to the preceding; rather, it emphasizes the inclusive sense of the pronoun *mî*, here with the meaning 'whoever' (cf. 6.12), in conjunction with the so-called relative *'ᵃšer*.

Our first problem in v. 4 arises with the verb *yᵉbuḥar*. The root *bḥr* denotes choice, and as such seems appropriate (though see Crenshaw, 1978: 209; Whybray, 1989: 142). Textual evidence from the LXX and related texts leads to the suggestion that we should read *yᵉḥubbar*, the pual imperfect of *ḥbr*, 'be joined'. Even with this emendation, however, we still are left with an unusual phrase if we do as the RSV does and render it as 'whoever is joined to the living'. In these several verses the emphasis lies with the contrast between the living and the dead. As Qoheleth describes one who is part of the community of the living (*kōl haḥayyîm*), the introductory phrase, 'whoever is joined to...', becomes redundant; he simply means 'the living'. The emendation does nothing to clarify the meaning of the verb. On the other hand, the form *yᵉbuḥar* can be viewed as meaning that nobody is exempt from death (see Murphy, 1992: 91).

The living have 'hope' (*biṭṭāḥôn*). This rare word, derived from the root *bṭḥ*, 'trust', otherwise occurs only in 2 Kgs 18.19 and Isa. 36.4. What semantic value it has is not easily determined. In view of vv. 2-3 and the emphasis on one fate for all, the 'hope' which we share is our common end. Qoheleth's meaning thus appears to be deeply ironic: one's hope is to die. Yet another possible interpretation might be suggested, namely that *biṭṭāḥôn* describes what one may rely on (see Fox and Seow), something that is certain (similar to the noun *beṭaḥ).* This would mean that Qoheleth is asserting that human beings know only one certain thing, that they are en route to death. This does not require the thesis that Qoheleth is being ironic; simply that he speaks openly and honestly of one's inevitable movement from birth to death as the only certainty we can have.

What is generally accepted as an aphorism appears in the second half of the verse, claiming that 'a live dog (*keleb ḥay*) is better than the dead lion (*ha'aryēh hammēt*)'. The introductory *kî* intimates that its purpose is to argue in support of the preceding statement. Although v. 4b appears to be a 'Better'-proverb, it is unusual to have the *ṭôb*-element of that form following the pronoun as copula. It regularly stands at the head of the saying. Furthermore, although the concept of death can be found in the major extant OT wisdom writings (e.g. Prov. 10.21; 21.25), it is actually a rarity. In fact, the adjective *mēt* is entirely absent from Proverbs. This fact raises some doubt that the 'live dog-dead lion' illustration is actually a quoted saying. Although one cannot always safely argue from silence and assume that because there is no record of a similar saying in Proverbs, therefore Israel had no such saying, yet it remains doubtful that here we are confronting a traditional saying. The probability must be that this is one coined by Qoheleth, similar to that in 7.1b, 2 etc., and that it was written for this specific context.

The contrast between the dog (*keleb*) *and* lion (*'aryēh*) poses some interesting questions. Qoheleth gives precedence to the symbol of contempt, the dog (cf. Deut. 23.18-19), because of the associated qualifying term, 'living' (*ḥay*). Conversely, the adjective *mēt,* 'dead', describes the formerly fierce lion. By this use of qualifying terms, the 'king of beasts' is assigned the inferior position. However, as we explore this saying further, we recall that the living know that life is inexorably heading for that final point. Although Qoheleth at times considers life better than death, here he does so under the image of a contemptible animal. The choice is deliberate, highlighting the tension between life and death. Qoheleth is not an obscurantist, claiming that life outweighs death; rather, he devises a clever saying which enshrines the painful tension between life and death (cf. 4.2). And never let it be forgotten that even the dog that is still alive is also heading for the same end as the lion! If there is irony in this saying, it lies deeper than the surface sense that 'hope' is death. What is ironic is the tension between life as both 'good' and 'contemptible' (= the dog), and death as 'royal' and an awful fate (= the lion).

9.5 Life is a mix of good and bad because (*kî*) the living (*haḥayyîm*) are aware (*yôdeʿîm*) that they are progressing towards death (*yāmutû*). Death, which traditionally was not joyously anticipated, does have another dimension, as was pointed out in 4.3 and 6.3-4. Death provided one with release from life's pain. Though deceased like the lion, one is at least now at rest, and that must be a bonus (cf. 4.2). However, to acknowledge the inevitability of death introduces yet another bitter fact. Death comes indiscriminately. Death itself is only part of the problem; the other is the fact that it is unable to distinguish between good and evil persons, wise and fool, or between humanity and the animals. All fall to it, and at its bidding.

The dead are portrayed in this verse as 'not knowing anything' (*'ēnām yôdeʿîm me'ûmāh*). At least the living have their intellectual faculties intact. But what do they know? They know they will die! The dead have moved beyond that point, and for them death must be a bonus rather than being the dreaded fate the living supposed it to be (cf. Ps. 115.17; Job 14.10-12).

Material reward (*śākār*), like knowledge of death, no longer concerns the dead. The final clause is conjoined to the preceding by *kî*, making it an explanatory clause. Thus the reason no 'reward' is possible is that all memory of the dead has now been forgotten (*niškaḥ zikrām*). Such a circumstance hardly accounts for the lack of 'reward', as no amount of remembrance will produce a material reward for the dead. Therefore, it is best to view the *kî* as an asseverative, 'indeed', in which case the point made is that the dead are no longer remembered (cf. 1.11; 2.16). The Israelite's basic longing that he/she might live on as part of the family memory, the collective mind, lay as a shattered dream.

There is another literary feature here, similar to those in 7.1 and 6: the assonance *śkr*, 'reward', and *zkr*, 'memory'. Both terms are used to identify what the dead lose.

9.6 The initial *gam*, 'also', brings this verse alongside the preceding; specifically, it ties the verse to the final phrase of v. 5. Three nouns, each portraying an emotion, are linked with the conjunction *gam*. Thus, 'love' (*'ahabātām*), 'hate' (*śin'ātām*), and 'envy' (*qin'ātām*)—we note the rhyming of these terms—are spoken of as having already ceased to be (*k^{e}bar 'ābādāh*). To each of these nouns is attached the third masculine plural suffix, 'them'. Our immediate task is to identify 'them'. With the final word in v. 5 (*zikrām*) as our starting point, we can suggest that 'them' is none other than the dead (*hammētîm*). The association between the final clause of v. 5 and v. 6 may be argued on the basis of these suffixes, as well as their similarity of thought, especially as expressed in the verbs *niškaḥ*, 'forgotten' (v. 5) and *'ābādāh*, 'destroyed' (v. 6). If this approach is sustainable, then we next ask about the meaning of the terms 'their love', 'their hate', etc. Is the suffixed pronoun in each case subjective—should we translate '*their* love' in which 'their' is the dead person? Or is the suffix an object, in which case we should read, 'love/hate/envy *of them*'? The thesis that there is a relationship between *zikrām* in v. 5 and the suffixes of v. 6, calls for the latter interpretation. It is not, then, the emotions of the dead which have ceased, though that must be true; it is rather the emotional response of the living towards those who are now deceased. This means that v. 6 carries a message very close to that of v. 5, demonstrating that the dead are isolated in every possible way from relationship with the living.

Not only are the dead denied any 'reward' (*śākār*, v. 5), they also have lost their 'portion' (*w^{e}ḥēleq 'ēn lāhem 'ôd*). The formal similarity between the two statements suggests that the two terms overlap semantically. *Ḥēleq* in 2.10 speaks of the pleasure and material benefits which flow from toil (cf. 4.9). As death is a permanent state, so is the separation from earth's benefits permanent (*l^e'ôlām*). The final clause of v. 6 takes us back to the same expression found in v. 3, reminding us again of the common fate, death, which casts its shadow over life and the living.

9.7-10 Enjoy Life

If 9.1-6 portray the sage's predicament, we note Qoheleth returning in v. 7 to the theme of coping with life in this contentious present. As in 2.24 etc., he advocates enjoyment.

The most striking literary feature of this section is the sudden appearance of a series of imperatives bearing on enjoyment. The verbs 'eat', 'drink', 'enjoy', 'see', 'do', which typify the 'there is nothing better'-forms in Qoheleth (e.g. 2.24; 3.13; 5.17[18]; 8. 15), are all present in this section. The pursuit of pleasure, as Qoheleth defines it, is enjoined for the reason that it is a divine gift (*ḥlq*). What is new in this section, however, is the move from advice to imperative; it gives the enjoyment theme in this case a more authoritative cast.

The inclusion upon which this section is built are the verbs *hlk* and '*śh* in vv. 7, 10. Additionally, a three-fold pattern is detected in the multiple use of an imperative, followed by a motive clause headed by *kî* (v. 7a, v. 7b; vv. 8-9, v. 9c; v. 10a, v. 10b).

A universal note is struck by the sentiments of this section. The Meissner fragment of the Old Babylonian *Gilgamesh Epic,* and the Egyptian 'Song of the Harpist' both treat this theme, with the former being especially close to the tone of Qoheleth's presentation. While common ground exists between these three texts, they are also sufficiently distinct for it to be obvious that each is a meditation within its own context on a universal concern (cf. Loretz, 1964: 116-22; de Savignac: 318-23).

9.7 The passage opens with the imperative *lēk,* 'come, go' and as well as heading the three imperatives of the verse, it also provides one of the two inclusions for the sub-section (cf. v. 10). The second imperative, 'eat' (*'ekōl*), which in the earlier calls to enjoyment always was placed first, is balanced by the call to 'drink' (*šatēh*). To both these imperatives adverbial phrases are attached (*beśimḥāh* and *belēb ṭôb*), again bearing ideas from the earlier expressions of the enjoyment theme. The object of the first verb is 'bread/food' *(laḥmekā),* corresponding to 'wine' (*yēnekā*) in the second clause. Both bread and wine are symbolic of what is necessary to sustain physical life.

The premise for the above call is that God has 'already approved' (*kebar rāṣāh*) what one does. Pleasure and approval are certainly implicit in the use of the verb *rāṣāh* in Prov. 16.7, and it offers a parallel to 'love' in Prov. 3.12. However, a bald statement which appears to give prior divine assent to whatever we have decided to do needs a measure of interpretation. Qoheleth does not mean that God will happily sanction *anything* we determine to do. From the fuller context, it is clear that Qoheleth locates enjoyment within the divine will; God wills that we enjoy his basic provisions, for he is the one who provides them (cf. 2.24 etc.). It offers what Fox has called *post facto* approval of pleasure. Given that premise, says Qoheleth, then go ahead and do as God would want. Such a response is the wise one, an expression of our own recognition that what we have is from God.

9.8 The imperative in v. 8 calls for us always (*bekol-'et*) to dress in white (*lbn*). The intention is clearly that we should wear clothing of this colour as often as possible, though not literally as a regular uniform. White, the colour associated with death in some cultures, is in the OT symbolic of joy. In Babylonian and Egyptian tradition, white robes are festal garments, so this metaphor is simply a parallel call to enjoyment. Whenever there is an opportunity to celebrate, do so, urges Qoheleth. It is possible to find in Qoheleth's other material that he looks askance at pleasure-seeking; see 7.2, 4. That is true only up to a point. Qoheleth's actual thesis is that if one's mind is given only to the pursuit of pleasure, then one is abusing its purpose. At times, celebration and joy are perfectly in order, for they accord with the divine will. This is one of the strongest points which Qoheleth can make: we are to enjoy the life God gives, despite the many painful issues with which life confronts us. In 9.8a Qoheleth would have the reader identify those moments when pleasure is appropriate, and a mark of the sage is that he/she will know what those moments are (cf. 8.5).

The accompanying example in v. 8b uses the tradition of anointing one's head with oil, *šemen* (cf. Ps. 23.5). The practice of anointing served various functions in the ancient Near East (see Szikszai, 'anoint', *IDB*), one of which was associated with the expression of joy (Ps. 45.7). In these two parallel examples of white clothing and anointing, Qoheleth expresses the longing that opportunities for enjoyment of God's blessing will not be lacking (*'al yeḥsār*), and that one will be wise enough to discern those moments.

9.9 Yet another dimension of the enjoyment theme resides in the call to enjoy life (*rᵉ'ēh ḥayyîm*) with one's 'wife', i.e. '(the) woman you love' (*'iššāh ʾᵃšer 'āhabtā*). The flexibility of the root *r'h* in Qoheleth has been seen already. Here it calls the student to *consider* life, as in 7.13. It is far more profound than merely observing life. In 2.1 and 3.13 where its meaning is of the same order as here, the notion of seeking or looking for pleasure in what one does is marked by the addition of the adjective *ṭôb,* 'good'. Although in this present case the *ṭôb is* omitted, yet the sense of seeking pleasure can be detected.

As Qoheleth presents it, the invitation to enjoyment appears paradoxical because of his view of human experience; he urges enjoyment in a life-setting remarkable for its frustrations and unanswered questions. This deliberate contrast is fully consistent with the imagery used in 9.4. Qoheleth pictures life, in his characteristic way, as *kol-yᵉmē-ḥayyē-heblekā,* 'all your enigmatic life', where the nominal form *heblekā* functions adjectivally (cf. Psa. 2.6 *har-qodšî,* 'my holy mountain'). The possibility that here the term *hebel* implies a short life is often posed, but for Qoheleth life's length is never the deeper issue; rather, it is the very nature of human existence that concerns him.

In v. 9b the so-called relative *'ašer* appears to connect with the immediately preceding *yemē-heblekā*. However, it is more likely that its proper antecedent is the 'woman' and not 'your enigmatic life'. Accepting this view of the syntax, we discover that 'woman' is qualified by two relative clauses each introduced by *'ašer*. If, as the MS evidence suggests, we retain the reiterated *kol-yemē-heblekā* at the end of v. 9b, then these two relative clauses are almost certainly in parallel. This conclusion then means that the woman/wife is both beloved, and a divine gift. Qoheleth's imperative addressed to his male students is that they seek the love of a woman and appreciate her as a divine gift (cf. 4.9-11; Gen. 2.22-24). It is another concrete example of the general principle which runs through Qoheleth's work, that the sage knows how, under God, to enjoy life in this world of ironies.

The motive clause attached to this verse refers to one's 'portion' (*ḥelqekā*), a term otherwise reserved for material benefits derived from one's work, together with the pleasure and sense of achievement they afford (cf. 2.10; 3.22; 5.17[18]). 'Portion' is something the dead no longer may enjoy (v. 6), but while one is travelling this earth, it is available from one's toil (*ba'amālekā*). Preference should be given then to the MT *hû',* 'that', and the motive clause as justifying the call to enjoyment with which the verse opens rather than following the versions whose emendation to *hî'* would link the portion more specifically to 'woman'.

9.10 The final imperative, though general in expression, is to be seen in the context of the call to enjoyment. It constitutes a challenge to do what is appropriate by way of seeking pleasure. It would hardly be acceptable to quote v. 10a as licence for unmitigated hedonism, for that is far from what Qoheleth has in mind. As a sage he knows well the place as well as the limits of pleasure-seeking, and we must accept this constraint in our interpretation.

Whatever you are able to do—literally, 'whatever your hand finds to do' (*kōl 'ašer timṣā' yādekā la'aśôt*) as in 1 Sam. 10.7—should be done with enthusiasm. The phrase *bekōḥakā,* 'with your strength', confirms Qoheleth's positive and hearty approach to life. There is no trace of pessimism or despondency. The call in this verse is rooted in the thought that life is lived in the shadow of death, and so one must adopt an attitude to this present which is cognizant of that fact. Four things are assumed to be no longer available after death (cf. v. 6). There will be nothing to do (*'ēn ma'ᵃśeh*); there will be no more philosophizing (*ḥešbôn*—cf. 7.25, 27, 29); knowledge (*da'at*) will cease; so also will wisdom (*ḥokmāh*). Of these four, three are obviously intellectual pursuits typical of the sage. Thus we have a sage's perspective on the nature of one's shadowy existence in Sheol. The other and first-mentioned activity which will cease, *ma'ᵃśeh,* is a general term for all activity, though in this context probably summarizes all the work of the sage. What this kind of saying makes clear is that Qoheleth's definition of 'pleasure' has its starting point in the realm of *intellectual* activity; it prevents us misunderstanding him as some crass hedonist.

The certainty of death and the one destination, Sheol, are ideas presented earlier in vv. 1-6, though framed differently. Whether Qoheleth means by 'Sheol' the netherworld, or simply death (so Lauhà: 170), the direction of his thinking is obvious; our terminus in death impinges on life in this present. The true sage lives with this fact before him. So again we can comprehend why in 7.14 Qoheleth feels the need to remind his readers how important death is to a definition of life and to the framing of one's lifestyle.

The participle *hōlēk,* 'going', is the second component of the inclusion, along with *ma'ᵃśeh.* Together they close off this section.

In 9.1-10 we note Qoheleth returning to some of the key themes from chs. 1-8, and in particular harking back to the advice that we enjoy life. This, of course, is the point with which his advice climaxes throughout. As we move into 9.1-10 we mark a transition from investigative reporting to the more forceful language of the imperative. Also, Qoheleth builds on the notion that life is best understood when viewed from the perspective of universal death. Beyond the grave it is assumed that the good things which God provides during one's lifetime, especially wisdom, will cease. Murphy calls this description of Sheol 'a classic'. This the sage knows, and so he accommodates to that awareness.

9.11-12 Death Knows No Schedule

The remainder of ch. 9 consists of two observations. Here in vv. 11-12 the first one takes our minds back to the theme of death's unpredictable timetable. The sub-unit is marked off by its introductory *šabtî wᵉrā'ōh*, 'again 1 saw', as in 4.1. Its keyword is *'ēt*, 'time', specifically referring to the time of death. The connections with ch. 3 are abundant and clear, not only through the *'ēt* concept, but also by the use of the verb *qrh* 'befall' (cf. 3.19). Additionally, the similarity of humanity's fate to that of the animals in 3.19-21, is in 9.12 paralleled by examples from the natural world of fish and birds.

There are other factors than the above which exemplify the relationship between vv. 11-12 and what has preceded. Most obvious is the inclusion *'ēn/lō' yēda' hā'ādām* (9.1, 12). A second factor is the use of *rā'āh* in 9.3, 12, qualifying human fate.

9.11 Having urged enjoyment (vv. 7-10) because of Sheol as the looming fate, Qoheleth turns attention to death's unpredictable appearance in the world. In v. 11 he draws analogies from the field of human endeavour (cf. Amos 2.14-16), insistent that at the core of human life there lies an element of uncertainty. Balancing the certitude of death (v. 5) is the almost fickle and unpredictable timing of its entrance.

To express this principle, Qoheleth puts together a sentence formed of three essential elements: (1) the introductory note of his observation (v. 11a); (2) the testimony of life's vagaries (v. 11b-f); (3) a motive clause (v. 11g). The central element is somewhat complex, consisting of five parallel phrases built around the theme of the unexpected outcome of events or situations. The purpose is to establish the truth that life is characterized by the unexpected.

In the introductory portion we note the use of *šabtî*, 'I turned', used elsewhere only in 4.1. Its nuance is similar to that of *pānîtî* (2.12). Reasons for emending the infinitive absolute *rā'ōh* are unconvincing, especially as the extant form is an alternative to the regular perfect (see Williams, para. 210). What was observed is indicated by the particle *kî*, 'that'.

The series of five clauses in v. 11b-f may be schematically presented to help us appreciate its literary impact. Its form is (a) a negative particle; (b) the preposition *lᵉ* with masculine plural noun; (c) a noun expressing the outcome or reward. Thus:

lō' l^{e}qallîm	*hammērôṣ*	not to the quick, the race
w^{e}lō' luggibbôrîm	*hammilḥāmāh*	and not to the mighty, the battle
w^{e}gam lō' laḥ^{a}kāmîm	*leḥem*	and also not to the wise, bread
w^{e}gam 1ō' lann^{e}bônîm	*'ōšer*	and also not to the clever, riches
w^{e}gam lō' layyōd^{e}'îm	*ḥēn*	and also not to the knowledgeable, favour

The first two clauses represent physical abilities, speed and power. Under normal circumstances the fastest runner should win the race (though here 'the quick' may refer to the messengers who carried official news and messages). Likewise the powerful would normally be expected to win victory in battle. However, Qoheleth's examples cogently point out that things do not always work out as one would expect. Even without citing the factors necessary to overturn the expected outcome, Qoheleth's point is clear.

The last three examples—the wise, clever, and knowledgeable ones—provide examples specifically from the wisdom circle. Contrary to what the deuteronomic tradition taught, or Prov. 13.15 etc., one can never be absolutely certain that material or other benefits and success will accrue to the sage. The final potential benefit, 'grace' (*ḥēn*), is essentially a relationship which works to one's advantage (cf. Prov. 3.3, 34; 4.9 etc.). The message of this verse is terse and to the point: life has its own way of working out. This fact is yet another aspect of the wider issue of the limitations to human knowledge, our inability to forecast the outcome of any event. The one who is truly wise always must make allowance for the 'chance' factor.

What is particularly fascinating about the state of affairs which Qoheleth describes is that he argues from a *theological* premise, namely that it is God who determines the outcome of the 'times' (cf. ch. 3). To the 'time' concept, Qoheleth adds a term *pega'*, normally rendered as 'chance'. It is an unusual term only used on one other occasion in the OT, in 1 Kgs 5.18(4). In this present context it appears to be semantically close to the way in which Qoheleth has made use of the concept of *'ēt*, those moments in time that lie in God's hand. Therefore, only by the most unusual argumentation can Gordis conclude that the tenor of the thesis here is negative, though in theory the term can have both positive and negative applications. The verb in this final clause, *yiqreh,* derives from the same root as *miqreh,* 'fate'. It denotes events overtaking one, and so we conclude that v. 11 records a principle analogous to 3.1, 10. Both would assert that the outcome of all events rests finally with the divine will. We may project forward on the basis of our experience of the world, but unless we make some allowance for 'chance' or divine ordering which is outside our realm of order, we may often find we are mistaken.

9.12 Two parallel similes are the central literary feature of v. 12. A chiastic structure in this unit becomes evident as the *kî*-clause introduces the examples rather than following them as in v. 11. Keywords are provided by the terms *'ēt*, 'time', and *rā'āh*, 'see'.

Humanity cannot determine its 'time', a message echoing ch. 3. However, the context requires a narrower focus than this earlier discussion. It speaks principally of the time of death (cf. 8.5-6).

In v. 12bc we note the parallel expression:

kaddāgîm	*šene'ᵃḥāzîm*	*bimṣôdāh rā'āh*
wᵉkaṣṣipporîm	*ha'ᵃḥuzzôt*	*bappāh*

The operative verb *'ḥz* describes the springing of a net (*mᵉṣôdāh*) or trap (*pāḥ*) as the fish or bird is snared. Elements of suddenness and surprise are introduced to the theme of death's arrival by means of this illustration, justifying Qoheleth's argument that it is this factor more than any other which makes life a painful experience (*'ēt rā'āh*). On a syntactical note, the participle *yûkāšîm*, 'snared', in v. 12d is irregular. The qal passive participle should have the elemental vowels in reverse order; the pual participle would require an initial *mem*.

The final clause (v. 12e) is temporal introduced by *kî*, and speaks of the subject 'dropping' suddenly (*tippôl .. pit'ōm*) upon unsuspecting objects. The verb in question is a third person feminine singular, and agrees with the subject, *'ēt rā'āh*, though the noun *'ēt* occasionally may be treated as a masculine.

In this sub-unit Qoheleth discourses further on the theme of time, with special attention to the moment of death. The suddenness with which it comes is a particular concern, along with the inevitable fact that we can never predict when that moment will be. This is simply another expression of the limitation we must acknowledge in face of the divine ordering of the world (cf. 7.15; 8.14).

9.13-16 Wisdom's Power to Save

This sub-section stands apart from the preceding by virtue of its introductory formula and its closing 'Better'-proverb. Its theme, in some measure reminiscent of that in 4.13-16, is also a factor helping us to determine its limits, dealing as it does with a city's rescue by a poor sage when it faced certain defeat. The keywords *ḥkm*, 'wise', and *gdl*, 'great', focus that theme, along with the thrice-used *miskēn*, 'poor'. The repetition of the phrase 'under the sun', indicates its relationship with what has gone before (vv. 3, 6, 9, 11), a relationship further noted in the terms *m*ᵉ*ṣôdîm*, 'net, trap' (vv. 12, 14) and *gbr*, 'mighty' (vv. 11, 16).

9.13 The illustration now about to unfold may be viewed as complementary to that introduced in v. 11. This would be the emphasis provided by the opening *gam*, 'also'. In the five observations in v. 11 above, attention was drawn to the fact that the outcome of events was frequently unpredictable, and this was especially so with reference to rewards which the wise and learned might be expected to receive (v. 11def). The deuteronomic tradition had encouraged Israelites to greater obedience to the Law in the firm belief that the way in which God would honour this obedience was through material reward (cf. Deut. 7.12ff).

In 9.13 Qoheleth focuses on wisdom and its power by offering an illustration of a successful application of wisdom. Whether the case cited is an actual one or merely illustrative, its importance is nevertheless significant to Qoheleth (*g*ᵃ*dôlāh hî' 'ēlāy*; cf. Jon. 3.3).

9.14 The scenario which will illustrate wisdom's power is built upon a number of contrasts, and it is this stylized and overdrawn contrast which suggests that we are dealing with a 'parable' rather than an historical record. There is a *small* city (*'îr q*ᵉ*ṭannāh*) with few inhabitants (*'*ᵃ*nāšîm bāh m*ᵉ*'āt*), while arrayed against it is a *powerful* king (*melek gādôl*) who has the city surrounded, and has set a powerful trap or siege (*m*ᵉ*ṣôdîm g*ᵃ*dôlîm*). Significant in this description are the adjectives which carry the contrast so starkly. The invading forces have thrown siegeworks (this requires a reading *m*ᵉ*ṣûrîm* rather than MT *m*ᵉ*ṣôdîm*) around the city to permit the troops to fire their projectiles into the tiny town. The description itself makes it impossible to think of the defenders as potential victors. It brings to mind the later siege of Massada in AD 66-73, in which the besieged, though not overlooked by the invading forces, nevertheless had no way to break free and gain a military victory over the Roman armies surrounding them. However, Qoheleth has already indicated in v. 11 that on occasion the outcome of a situation or event is quite other than what one would expect; the battle does not always go to the stronger party (v. 11c). Earlier again (7.19) he had spoken of wisdom's power (cf. Prov. 24.5-6), so we are already led to anticipate the strange turn of events in v. 15.

9.15 There is within the besieged city a poor wise man (*'îš miskēn ḥākām*). The fact that he is poor bears out the observation of v. 11d-f that wisdom is not necessarily the companion of riches (cf. 4.13). This is a challenge to the kind of thinking represented in the deuteronomic tradition as we have seen; it is also found in aspects of the wisdom movement, as Prov. 15.6, 22.4, and other aphorisms testify. A rare term, *miskēn,* 'poor', is found only in vv. 15, 16 and in 4.13 in Biblical Hebrew. It connotes a person who does not come from the ruling classes, but is an ordinary member of the community.

By virtue of his wisdom (*b^{e}ḥokmāh*), the poor sage delivered (*millaṭ*) the city and its inhabitants. How he managed to save the city is not of concern to Qoheleth and given that this is a 'parable' such a question is irrelevant. He simply narrates that against insuperable odds a sage's power was such that it overcame that of massed armies. It was his wisdom which provided the 'weapon' to overcome the enemy. However, there are those (Zimmerli, Seow, Whybray for example) who argue that the verb *mlṭ* expresses the sage's potential rather than actual success. Their understanding depends on the following phrase about the sage not being remembered. However, although it may be possible for the perfect mode of the verb to express potential, the scenario presented here seems to highlight the fact that the sage actually rescued the city. The real problem being addressed is that he was never credited with that success by the rest of the community. So, rather than the community not thinking to approach the sage for advice on how to escape the siege, it would be more appropriate to see him as one subsequently ignored despite his success in rescuing them. The reason for that lack of recognition was the fact that he was a poor and insignificant member of the community. The 'parable' is more of a social comment from Qoheleth about the link between wisdom and poverty, that wisdom is not the road to lasting recognition or status.

Verse 15c indicates the fickle nature of humanity: not one person recalled this great event. What Qoheleth is claiming by this exaggerated 'parable' is that the community at large fails to appreciate the power and value of wisdom because of its 'blindspot' when it comes to social status.

Additionally, the notion that after death one's memory lives on, Qoheleth contests (cf. 4.16; 9.5). The sage can draw no comfort from the thought that beyond the grave he might continue to have a place in the communal mind. Such a theory, says Qoheleth, is a myth, for people are so fickle that even the most incredible events can be forgotten. Only another sage might recall such an event, as he keeps alive the tradition; only the sage appreciates the achievement.

9.16 This unit is closed off in traditional fashion by means of a 'Better'-saying. Its emphatic 'I said' (*'ᵃnî 'āmartî*) indicates clearly that this is Qoheleth's conclusion drawn from the 'parable' just cited. The simple conclusion is that wisdom is better than might (*ṭôbāh ḥokmāh miggᵉbûrāh*). The shift from *gdl* to *gbr,* 'might', is significant literarily, for it binds this unit to that which precedes (v. 11), indicating the intimate relationship between vv. 11-12 and vv. 13-16. Semantically there is little to choose between *gdl* and *gbr.*

The terse 'Better'-proverb argues that wisdom is powerful, more so than military might. Wisdom enables one to transcend the pain of this present life's enigmas, and, we would argue, provides *yitrôn,* the possibility of meaning and hope both now and in the future beyond death.

The second half of the verse adds a constraint whose purpose is to sustain the value of wisdom against the scenario of v. 16b. Though the poor sage's wisdom and achievements are universally undervalued, despised (*bᵉzûyāh*), and his accomplishments soon forgotten, wisdom is still of inestimable value. As an advisor, Qoheleth's teaching and counsel may be ignored (*'ēnam nišmāʿîm*), yet its worth is not thereby diminished. The use of the participial forms *bᵉzûyāh* (qal passive) and *nišmāʿîm* (niphal), has the effect of stressing the perennial nature of this rejection of wisdom by so many.

In defence of wisdom, this is a stirring piece of writing, while at the same time it offers a damning commentary on human nature. If Qoheleth is judged a pessimist, as some would argue, then we should make clear that his pessimism is directed towards the foibles of the human community, rather than against any particular view of life.

Chapter 9 has taken us back quickly to what Qoheleth conceived to be the major issue confronting the living, namely death. Certain features of death's intrusion into the world of the living, such as its universality, its finality, and the suddenness with which it appears, all create practical as well as theological problems. These problems, moreover, are insoluble from the human standpoint for two reasons: they are beyond human control; and they are not within our ability to comprehend, being hidden in the divine mind. Despite these vast problems, Qoheleth consistently maintains a resolute stand, never faltering in his defence of wisdom. In the midst of such a life as meets us and about which we can really know so little, Qoheleth's unceasing advice and call is that we should never abandon the pursuit of wisdom.

As for the query with which 9.1 began, whether our future in God's hands is 'love' or 'hate', one senses that Qoheleth would actually trust that it is 'love'. This assumption can be made because of his undergirding notion that all is in God's hands. This is a faith statement rather than one that is to be proved since life throws up so many unanswerable challenges.

Qoheleth has thus opened up his discourse by stressing once again the power and value of wisdom. A second point with regard to wisdom will be discussed in the next chapter, and to that we now move.

Chapter 10

Wisdom's Strength and Vulnerability

We begin this chapter not with 10.1, as one might suppose, but with 9.17-18. This seemingly unorthodox position needs justifying. Among those who study Qoheleth there is little consensus about where some sections end and others begin, and especially is this so with regard to this portion of the book. (For a review of this problem, see Ogden, 1980: 27-32.) We have noted above that the scenario in 9.13-16 which spoke of wisdom's power, concluded with a 'Better'-proverb in support of wisdom despite the latter's failure to attract public acclaim. In 9.17-18 we encounter two other 'Better'-proverbs, the first of which is bound to v. 16 by the terms 'words' (*dibrē*) and 'heard' (*nišmāʿîm*). This connection accounts for their editorial juxtaposition. However, from the vantage point of content and message, 9.17 proclaims the superiority of wisdom, but then that truth is balanced by recognizing (v. 18) that its power is conditional, such that wisdom is exceedingly vulnerable. These two 'Better'-sayings move in a direction different from that of v. 16, and discuss the negative effect upon the sage of even a minor indiscretion or folly. It is a theme without prior treatment in Qoheleth. Furthermore, its keywords *ḥokmāh* / *ḥākām* and *kᵉsîl* are important to the discussion in 10.1-20. Our thesis here will be that the two 'Better'-proverbs in 9.17-18 function as introductory devices for the unit which follows by establishing the twin themes to be discussed.

R. Murphy (1992: 99) has suggested that the thesis proposed here for 9.17-10.20 has been overdrawn, that this portion of the book does not exhibit the unity that I have claimed for it. Most other commentators are unable to find an overall structure, as Whybray notes (1989: 150), 'despite various attempts that have been made'. It is obvious that for this part of Qoheleth, as with so many other portions, determining where sections begin and end is still a challenge. Nevertheless, I would maintain that there is a thematic connection between 9.17-18 and 10.1-20 and so wish to continue to work with the thesis as I have outlined it above.

The sub-sections of this chapter are: 9.17-18; 10.1-4, 5-7, 8-11, 12-15, 16-20. Within the illustrative material of 10.1-20 the theme of wisdom's vulnerability in 10.1, 8-11, 20 has the effect of binding together all the material in the chapter, as does the reference to small insects or animals as illustrative of the source of danger. This theme is woven closely into the material which argues for wisdom's power, indicating that Qoheleth believes both themes reflect the reality with which every individual has to deal.

9.17-18 Setting the Theme of Wisdom and its Vulnerability

9.17 The first of the two 'Better'-proverbs in this introductory statement is created by Qoheleth out of ideas present in 9.16. However, whereas the latter had a negative cast (nobody paid attention to the wise man's words), in v. 17 the saying clearly has a positive sense. This of course conforms to the structure of the 'Better'-proverb in which the first or A-element of the comparison is the higher value. The two statements (v. 16 and vv. 17-18) in juxtaposition illustrate the literary artistry of Qoheleth. Whereas the general public took little notice of the sage's teachings (v. 16), Qoheleth affirms that there is great benefit for anyone who will heed them.

The 'teachings' or 'words' of the wise (*dibrē-ḥᵃkāmîm*) are elevated over the 'shouting of a ruler' (*zaʿᵃqat-môshēl*). These two nominal forms constitute the major elements of the comparison. The adverbial components are 'in quiet' (*bᵉnaḥat*) and 'among fools' (*bakkᵉsîlîm*). The phrase 'in quiet' should be linked to the speaking of the words rather than their being heard. Words spoken quietly (cf. 4.6) by the sage are set over against a noisy outburst by an authority figure; the co-ordination of 'noise' with 'fools' is familiar from 7.5b, but one might expect that the words of a ruler would carry some weight. However, the use of the term *zaʿᵃqāh* as the foil to *dᵉbārîm* in the prior portion carries a pejorative sense. The words of the wise are for instruction and advice, but the 'cry' of the ruler implies a plea. The object of the word *zaʿᵃqāh* may be human (1 Kgs 20.39) or divine (Neh. 9.9), but its tone is always that of a call for help from distress (see Hasel, *TDOT*, IV: 112-23). This is the only use of *zaʿᵃqāh* in Qoheleth. The comparison between sage and ruler here offers no surprises, for the instruction of the sage has more efficacy than the plea of a ruler for help, especially when the ruler is appealing to fools to save him.

In this saying we observe the middle term, the niphal participle *nišmā'im,* 'heard', as the action common to both elements of the saying. The superiority of wisdom is proclaimed. Whybray (1989: 149) agrees that the verb 'heard' carries the sense of 'are worth hearing' following the suggestion offered by Kroeber and Lauha. This is claimed to overcome the apparent problem of the MT in which 'in quiet' is associated with hearing rather than with speaking. Fox's solution (1999: 300) is to move the disjunctive forward so that we have the phrase *d^{e}bār(îm) b^{e}naḥat*. However, if we understand the verb *šm'* to mean 'listened to' or 'obeyed', it is clear that the clause as a whole implies that the words are spoken calmly, then responded to appropriately.

Crenshaw links this saying about the ruler with the ruler of the city mentioned in verses 14-15, suggesting that his cry of distress is that of a frantic ruler whose city is under siege. Seow agrees, and so sees this and the following verse 18 associated with the situation in the city, identifying the 'one sinner' (v. 18) with the 'ruler' in this verse.

9.18 Our second 'Better'-proverb is more brief than that of v. 17, since adverbial and other qualifying elements are absent. In fact this is one of the briefest forms of the proverb (cf. 7.1). In short, wisdom (*ḥokmāh*) is better than 'weapons' (*k^{e}lē-q^{e}rāb*). In its present context, juxtaposed with 9.13-16, its intention is clear, though without that setting, interpretation would be decidedly less obvious. In the phrase *k^{e}lē-q^{e}rāb* we meet the unusual word *q^{e}rāb,* 'war', in lieu of the more regular term *milḥāmāh.* Its presence may be due to Aramaic influence (cf. Psa. 55.22[21]; 144.1 etc.).

Initially, v. 18 presents thoughts similar to those of v. 17. However, there is an appended clause which plays a more significant role because it adds a qualification. One sinner (*ḥôṭe' 'eḥād*), that is to say, one fool or one foolish act, may destroy a great deal of good (*ṭôbāh harbēh*). In this case, 'good' is a description of the benefits which may accrue to one, and we may assume that 'the good' is equivalent to wisdom and its benefits. We observe again the contrast which is made more stark by the qualifying terms *'eḥād,* 'one' and *rab,* much/many'. It is akin to the *one* wise man delivering a city from *many* enemy soldiers in 9.13-16 (cf. also 7.19). A piel imperfect *y^e'abbēd* draws attention to the destructive power of sin and folly (cf. 7.7).

Verse 18, therefore, offers a qualifying observation. Wisdom is indeed powerful and beneficial, but may be rendered impotent by even a minor indiscretion. Wisdom is vulnerable. Its vulnerability is presumably predicated upon the fact that, as Qoheleth has stated in 7.20, even the sage on occasion may fall into sin and error. In this sense, 9.17-18 shares the view of 7.19-20 with its balance between the power of wisdom and the sage's potential for error. This interpretation of the verse differs from that of those commentators who link the saying directly to the previous situation in the city since those interpreters identify the 'bungler' (one sinner) with the ruler rather than with a sage who may fall into sin and thus undermine his standing as a sage. The interpretation offered here is to be found in NJPS, REB and NJB.

The two 'Better'-proverbs in 9.17-18 with their balancing truths, identify the twin themes which will be explored in 10.1-20, advancing the discourse on wisdom and its power begun in ch. 9. This functional use of introductory statements to establish the scope of the discussion to follow is a new literary device developed by Qoheleth. We shall find it also in 11.1-2 and 11.8, as each introduces the theme(s) to be pursued in the pericope to follow. Failure to appreciate this phenomenon may limit our understanding of the discussion which Qoheleth appends.

10.1-4 Dead Flies Cause Problems

Several important literary features illustrate the relationship between this sub-section and 9.17-18. They are:

inclusion-	'quiet, remain', *nwḥ* (9.17a, 10.4b twice); 'rule', *mšl* (9.17b; 10.4a); 'sin', *ḥṭ'* (9.18; 10.4c).
chiasmus	wisdom's superiority (9.17; 10.2-4); folly's power (9.18b; 10.1);
contrast	'one sinner' (*ḥôṭe' 'eḥād*) and 'much good' (*ṭôbāh harbēh*); 'deference' (*marpē'*) and 'much sin' (*ḥ*^{a}*ṭā'îm g*^{e}*dôlîm);*
keyword	'mind' (*lēb*).

10.1 The opening term is literally 'flies of death' (*z*^{e}*bûbê-māwet*). Its meaning, along with that of the verse as a whole, has occasioned much discussion (see Gordis, 1968: 313-14). The flies are either 'dying flies' (cf. 1 Sam. 20.31, *ben-māwet*, 'one destined to die'; 2 Sam. 19.29), or 'dead flies', although this latter would more regularly be expressed as *z*^{e}*bûbîm mētîm*. The point is, whether the flies are dead or in their dying moments, they cause contamination (*yab'îš*). Though the verb stands as a singular, Qoheleth frequently shows indifference to certain basic rules with regard to number (see 1.16; 2.7 etc.). The root *b'š*, 'stink, smell bad', in the Exodus narrative describes the bad odour of the fermented manna (cf. Prov. 13.5 of shameful conduct). There is an accompanying verb *yabbîa'*, from *nb'*, 'flow', or perhaps from the root *b'/bw*. In the hiphil, these verbs describe the formation of scum on the surface of a liquid. It is possible that the verb *nb'* here expresses something parallel to the root *b'š*, 'stink'. Gordis's suggestion that a nominal form is required in lieu of *nabbîa'* (unless *nabbîa'* means 'container') is not self-evident, but to omit it as the versions do is without warrant.

The oil (*šemen*) which was contaminated is qualified by the participle *rôqēaḥ*, describing one who blends aromatic compounds, hence 'perfumer' (RSV). The oil is not an ointment (cf. 7.1) so much as an aromatic perfume whose delicate essence would be destroyed by the flies which fall into it.

The first half of v. 1 states a principle: an expensive item can be quickly rendered useless or spoiled by a small insect. This principle, the vulnerability of costly things, provides the basis for an analogous statement about wisdom (v. lb). The comparative saying opens with the adjective *yāqār*, an Aramaic term for something heavy, but also denoting something precious, similar to the Hebrew root *kbd*. Thus more 'weighty' than wisdom, than honour (*mēḥokmāh mikkābôd*) is a little folly (*siklût mᵉ'aṭ*). The term *kābôd* also has associations with the concept 'heavy', so Qoheleth is clearly playing with two related concepts. Even one foolish action is sufficient to do damage to the wise. History is replete with examples of individuals who have found this to be true at the cost of their careers. Qoheleth's illustration is directly related to the saying in 9.18.

10.2 A balanced aphorism contrasts the wise man and the fool. As usual, the term *lēb* applies to the intellectual faculties, to one's mind. The adverbial phrase which is the point of contrast indicates the wise man moving in one direction, to the right (*lîmînô*), and the fool moving in the opposite one (*liśmō'lô*). This is more than a simple contrast, for it carries an evaluation as well. The sage, in moving to the right, is moving in the correct direction, for 'right' is expressive of power and strength (e.g. Gen. 48.14; Isa. 41.10). The fool is condemned for going in the wrong direction. Note that in 7.4 we have a formally identical saying.

The term *k^esîl*, 'dullard', a description of the slow-minded individual, occurs almost entirely in the Psalms and wisdom material. Here it appears in vv. 2, 12 and 15.

10.3 Although the contrast in the previous verse was expressed in a balanced clause, it is the latter half, the conduct of the fool, which becomes the focus for attention, a situation mirrored in vv. 12ff.

Qoheleth argues that 'even on the road' (*gam badderek*), while actually walking (*k^ešehassākāl hôlēk*), one's folly is obvious. All can see that 'his mind is lacking' (*libbô ḥāsēr*). So in ordinary activities—'walking' is an idiom for one's conduct, and here *derek* almost certainly is a figure of speech for one's lifestyle—lack of wisdom makes itself evident, as does one's wisdom (cf. 8.1). In the term *k^ešehassākāl* (Kethib) or *k^ešessākāl* (Qere), both of which are possible, the introductory *k^eše* is the equivalent of *ka'^ašer*, 'when'. The participle *ḥāsēr*, 'lacking,' carries a negative sense, denoting a deficiency (cf. 4.8. 9.8. Prov. 6.32).

The final clause is open to two interpretations in what appears to be a deliberately ambiguous statement. The fool says 'Concerning someone else' or 'to everyone' —*lakkōl* is capable of either meaning—that they are fools, or that he is a fool himself (*sākāl hû'*). Although the meaning of *lakkōl* is determinative, we need to consider word usage associated with it. The form *w^e'āmar* may be an independent verb, in which case the subject is *sākāl*, 'fool', in v. 3a, or (with Lauha and Hertzberg) the preceding *libbô*, 'his mind'. When speaking of himself, Qoheleth most regularly says, *'āmar b^elēb*, which would imply that in v. 3 we should give preference to the view that the fool proclaims to all that he himself is foolish. In view of the fact that the previous action words are participles (*hōlēk, ḥāsēr*), it is conceivable that *w^e'āmar* ought to be pointed *w^e'ōmēr*. Whichever interpretation we select—either the fool proclaims his own folly to others, or he regards others as fools—the actions of the fool, his attitudes, indicate that he has lost touch with reality. This is in explanation of the phrase in v. 2 about his mind tending 'towards the left', and indirectly is an argument in support of the superiority of wisdom.

10.4 Attention now focuses on the wise. Qoheleth posits a situation in which an irate ruler turns upon one of his subjects. Anger (*rûaḥ*) is said to 'rise' (*ta'^aleh*) as in Ezek. 38.18; Ps. 78.21, 31 etc., The term *môshēl,* 'ruler' or 'official', is one which links this verse with the opening comparative in 9.17. Qoheleth's advice to a young person training to be a sage, that is a counsellor to a ruler, and faced with this kind of irrational response from above, is to stand firm (*'al-tannaḥ*) in his position (*māqôm*). What precisely is intended by this advice is not easily determined, as *māqôm* refers to a physical location (e.g. 2 Sam. 11.16) as well as to one's station in life (Gen. 40.13). The jussive *'al-tannaḥ* is understood to mean 'do not leave/abandon' (cf. 7.18). In 8.3 the possibility was raised that to 'leave the king's presence' means to participate in rebellious activity. It is possible that a similar sense is intended here, in which case Qoheleth urges the student not to contemplate joining plots against the ruler.

The motive clause appended suggests that one should not leave a position because the prudent action of staying at one's post, or not joining the rebellion, will overcome 'great offences' (*ḥ^{a}ṭā'îm g^{e}dôlîm*). The offences are clearly the ruler's angry response. So conduct appropriate to the wise is to allay (*yannîaḥ*, hiphil impf) his anger. The noun *marpē'*, 'healing', 'calmness', is used in the same sense as in Jdg. 8.3; Prov. 12.18; 14.30. The sage, because of self-control and an awareness of interpersonal dynamics, as well as of his own maturity, knows how to defuse a situation (cf. 4.6). Wisdom can bring calm and restoration to a situation.

From a literary point of view, we note the contrast between one small example of wisdom counterbalancing 'much sin' (*ḥ^{a}ṭā'îm g^{e}dôlîm*), as well as the assonance *rûaḥ, nûaḥ* (cf. 7.8-9). The power of wisdom in the face of the ruler's authority (cf. 9.13-16) is again illustrative of 9.17.

10.5-7 Fools in High Places

The introductory formula 'there is an evil which I have seen under the sun', as in 5.13 and 6.1, together with the use of *šallît*, 'ruler', in lieu of *môšēl* and a new range of vocabulary, leads to the conclusion that these verses form another distinct sub-unit. Present also is an inclusion in the use of *rā'āh*, 'seen', in vv. 5, 7.

Qoheleth identifies the 'evil' (*rā'āh*) in v. 5, and then proceeds to describe the nature of the problem in vv. 6-7. It has to do with fools occupying positions of authority.

10.5 The situation presented is characterized as 'like a mistake', *kišgāgāh*, a term we have actually met once before in 5.5(6). Found frequently in a legal setting (e.g. Deut. 23.21-23; Lev. 4.22, 27 etc.), *š^{e}gāgāh* denotes a thoughtless error, the kind of behaviour associated with a fool. Crenshaw (1987: 170) regards the initial *k^e* as the asseverative particle rather than indicating a simile. Here the 'mistake' is said to 'proceed from the ruler' (*millipnē-haššallît*). This translation (cf. RSV) leaves the impression that it is an action of the ruler himself which is the problem. Such is not necessarily correct, for the text could just as well mean that folly is found in his presence, and involving his person, yet distinct from his own conduct. Indeed, the examples which follow in v. 6 would require such a view. This allows a translation such as: folly is found 'in the presence of the ruler' (cf. v. 7), or, wherever you find a leader, there you will also find stupidity present. On the word *šallît*, 'ruler', see 7.19; 8.3.

10.6 The verse is formed of two halves that draw a contrast between the fool and the rich (= the leader in society). The initial verb *nittān* is the niphal perfect, 'is put', the subject of which is uncertain. Despite this, the thrust of the verse is clear. The fool may be found in many 'high places' (*m*e*rômîm*), in positions of influence and authority (cf. Isa. 24.4). By contrast, the wealthy (*ʿ*a*šîrîm*) sit in 'lower places' (*šēpel*). In using a niphal form, 'is put', Qoheleth gives the impression that the situation described is a contrived or unnatural one.

10.7 Parallel to v. 6, this verse continues the theme of the exalted status of lower members of society.

Qoheleth notes servants (*ʿ*a*bādîm*) who ride about on horseback while there are princes (*sārîm*, cf vv. 16-17) who have to walk. Although horses were common in later Israel (cf. Neh. 7.68; Ezek. 27.14), it is highly unlikely that servants would ride them. Thus Qoheleth describes the princes walking *kaʿ*a*bādîm*, 'like servants', i.e. as servants would normally do, to emphasize the role reversal and thus the contradiction. It is obvious that Qoheleth is setting up a hypothetical case for others to reflect on. In this dichotomy between 'folly in high places' and 'slaves on horseback' on the one hand, and 'rich in low positions' and 'princes walking on the ground' on the other, the author is able to make explicit his contention that this scenario represents a calamity (*raʿ*). Qoheleth undoubtedly sees this social anomaly as a situation that is lamentable, for he supports the right of the wealthy class to rule (see Prov 30.21-23). Thus v. 5b portrays a scenario behind which lies a great social upheaval. Whether this situation is actually caused by the aristocracy themselves, or happens to them on account of other factors, is not the issue and so is not discussed. Qoheleth concerns himself only with the possible anomaly itself, that it is possible for the present order of social relations to be overthrown.

In the context of the chapter, we recognize this sub-unit as illustrative of wisdom's vulnerability (9.18).

10.8-11 Risks to the Worker

Subject matter and formal features delimit this sub-unit, which may be seen as held together by the inclusions *nāḥāš* and *nšk* in vv. 8, 11, and by the bridge-term *barzel*, 'iron', in v. 10.

In vv. 8-9 Qoheleth employs a series of four participles, each of which speaks of the use of metal implements in digging or cutting. In each clause the worker is portrayed by means of the participle, and the danger to which his work exposes him is expressed by an imperfect verb form, that form indicating that the danger is always present.

In vv. 10-11, two conditional clauses introduced by *'im*, 'if', contrast *yitrôn* (v. 10d) with lack of *yitrôn* (v. 11b).

Emphasis in this sub-unit is upon the danger to which one is exposed in one's work situation, relating it directly to the theme of 'vulnerability' in 9.18.

10.8 The one who digs pits (*ḥōpēr gūmmāṣ*) is ever at risk; he may fall into the hole being dug. The term 'hole, pit' (*gūmmāṣ*), is an Aramaic word appearing only this once in the OT, while the participle *ḥōpēr*, which Qoheleth does not use elsewhere, is a further example of the unusual vocabulary in this verse. The frequentative nuance of the imperfect verb forms connotes the ever present nature of the danger to the worker, so *yippôl* here should be rendered 'may fall' rather than 'will fall'. The imperfect verbs throughout this section are best viewed as marking possibility rather than making statements of fact.

In parallel with the first clause, the second half of the verse speaks of the potential hazard for 'the one who breaks through the wall' (*pōrēṣ gādēr*). The term *gādēr*, 'wall', often applies to a wall bordering a roadway (cf. Num. 22.24), but could refer to any wall. As to the purpose in breaking it down, Qoheleth leaves us without clues. However, this apparent oversight reminds us that the function of the statement is to highlight the danger present rather than the action of breaking the wall itself. The serpent (*nāḥāš*) is the danger, and it lies in or on the wall in question (cf. Amos 5.19), representing the constancy of the threat.

The moral character, the wisdom or folly of the person involved in the actions described in this verse, cannot be determined from the context (contra Barton: 171, and Gordis, 1969: 320). To suggest that the hazard is actualized and that it comes as punishment, goes far beyond the text and is not the point Qoheleth is trying to make. The text itself depicts only the constant and potential danger posed by a man-made hazard (cf. Prov. 26.27) or small animal to a person in the process of one's ordinary work. This interpretation carries through into the examples in v. 9. Thus Qoheleth's point is clear and consistent with his many plaintive sighs about life's anomalies.

10.9 'He who quarries stones' *(massîaʿ ʾᵃbānîm)* describes one frequently seen in the Israelite hill country where most building makes use of the abundant supply of stone. *Massîaʿ*, as a hiphil participle, actually portrays the action of 'pulling up' stones, removing them from the ground, thus of quarrying (cf. 1 Kgs 5.31[17]). It is an occupation with its own hazards, so Qoheleth draws upon another familiar task to illustrate the risk of possible injury in one's toil. It is impossible to concur with Scott's view that the stones are to be rolled over a cliff onto an enemy. The root *ʿṣb*, here in the niphal imperfect, means 'hurt, grieve' (cf. Gen. 3.16).

In the second half of the verse we read of yet another occupation, that of the carpenter or wood-cutter, the 'one who splits trees' (*bôqēaʿ ʿēṣîm*). This person is often at risk (*yissāken*) from the trees as they fall or from the logs as they are cut.

So in what are essentially four parallel clauses, Qoheleth in vv. 8-9 suggests that people face dangerous hazards in their daily occupations. No individual is exempt from the physical dangers posed by working at ordinary tasks or occupations. Most often such accidents are caused by momentary lapses in concentration, small hazards not guarded against. Each is illustrative of the thesis in 9.18 that a small amount of folly (in this case, carelessness) can undo much wisdom.

10.10 In the first of two conditional clauses the theme of work or labour continues in the reference to tools (*barzel*). The text, and thus its interpretation, is fraught with questions, so that any interpretation must be tentative.

The initial verb *qēhāh* is a piel form, the only use in Biblical Hebrew, and has the meaning 'be blunt'. Its protasis consists of the phrase, 'if the cutting implement (*barzel*) is blunt', though the second clause appears to be a conjoined expression that explains the first rather than its apodosis. That second clause (v. 10b) is formed by the demonstrative *hûʾ*, a reference back to the iron tool, or to a new and impersonal subject, 'one'. There follows the negative particle *lōʾ*, though some versions read *lô*, 'to him/it'.

The MT is probably best accepted. If the preceding demonstrative *hû'* points to the implement, then the term *pānîm* describes a portion of that tool. Problems arise in this case because the use of *pānîm* in such a context is unknown elsewhere. A sharp metal tool may have a 'mouth' (*peh*), its edge, as in the case of the sword which 'devours' its enemies. To speak of its 'face' (*pānîm*) is conceivable, but that most probably means the broad side of the blade. To describe this face as 'blunt' as v. 10a does, is meaningless. The basis for interpreting *pānîm* as 'edge' lies in Ezek. 21.21, but it is far from clear that the word refers to the sword in that instance. Thus, the suggestion by K. Budde and Ginsberg, supported by Seow, that we should read *l*^{e}*pānîm,* 'beforehand', has merit, though it lacks other MS support. The term 'sharpened' is derived from the pilpel form *qilqal* describing something polished or honed (cf. Ezek. 1.7).

What, then, are we to make of this situation? If we consider the word order of the supplementary clause, the location of the word 'sharp' (*qilqal*) at the conclusion rather than after the negative particle would tend to favour the view that *pānîm* is adverbial rather than nominal, despite Loader's objection (1979: 64). Thus we perhaps should render the clause, '... and one (*hû'*) has not previously sharpened it'.

As for the apodosis (v. 10c), we note the use of an extremely terse expression, one not without its own difficulties. The plural *ḥ*^{a}*yālîm,* literally 'warriors' (1 Chron. 7.5), expresses the abstract idea of strength (see Williams, 1974, para. 7). If it is the subject of the verb *y*^{e}*gabbēr,* it is placed before it for emphasis. The piel form *y*^{e}*gabbēr* draws attention to the great amount of energy required to handle the implement (*barzel*). One of our difficulties is in knowing whether *ḥ*^{a}*yālîm* is subject or object. Most commentators regard it as object, rendering the verse, 'one must put forth greater effort', or something equivalent. This is acceptable, but is not necessarily the only interpretation. 'Strength will increase' is another possible reading. So we are thrown back on our understanding of the context for our exegesis. Thus, if the implement is blunt, more energy is expended to achieve one's purpose.

In the final clause (v. 10d) we meet again the word *yitrôn,* the key word in the programmatic question of 1.3 etc. Here it stands at the head of the clause as an absolute form. The ensuing hiphil infinitive construct *hakšēr* requires a conjoined term; thus we assume it is bound with the following *ḥokmāh,* 'wisdom'. As the concept of success is integral to the root *kšr,* we may suggest a translation, '*yitrôn* (will be) the reward/success of wisdom'. In this setting *yitrôn* appears to have a more traditional reference, that of the benefit which accrues from one's ability as an entrepreneur. The wise will be well prepared so as to increase efficiency, and with that will come greater profit. However, in view of the problems with this text noted above, one should admit that the interpretation suggested here can only be tentative, and caution against building theological 'castles' on an uncertain foundation.

10.11 The second of the two conditional clauses brings the unit to a close. It begins with a reference to the serpent biting (*'im yiššōk hannāḥāš*), the important inclusion which binds the unit together (cf. v. 8). Questions about the meaning of this verse are not inconsiderable.

The protasis, like that of v. 10, presents little difficulty; 'should the serpent bite before it is charmed' (*b*[e]*lō' lāḥaš*) is the scenario. Here the temporal sense is conveyed by the phrase *b*[e]*lō'*, 'without', thus 'when it has not yet...' The verb *lāḥaš,* 'charm', and the noun *nāḥāš*, 'serpent', present yet another example of assonance. Much is unclear about this terse statement. We might well ask, Is the serpent poisonous? Does it bite the charmer or a third person? Does the person bitten die as a result? To each of these questions there is no answer, so we have some difficulty controlling our interpretation. It would seem, however, that, as in vv. 8-9, several examples of risky undertakings were presented, so too here in v. 11, the charmer is attempting something which involves danger to his person. Perhaps we are meant to assume that the snake was poisonous, that it attacked the charmer, and with dire results (so Glasser, 1970: 15 7).

The apodosis simply notes that under these circumstances there was no *yitrôn* to the *ba'al hallāšôn,* 'charmer' (RSV). 'Charmer' is the most common translation given this term, yet it is subject to some question. Literally, 'master of the tongue' could portray one with the talent of speech (so Loader), but this interpretation does not appear to fit the context. Furthermore, as Lauha (p, 189) indicates, the tongue could be that of either the snake or the charmer. In v. 20 a similar form, *ba'al hakk*[a]*nāpîm,* refers to a bird. If we draw on this analogy, *ba'al hallāšôn* ought to refer to the snake. The difficulty created by this analogy is that to render *ba'al hallāšôn* as 'serpent' muddies the thesis of the sub-unit as well as of the secondary theme of risk in one's employment. If we take as our starting point the overall themes of the chapter, then we are led to accept the traditional view that *ba'al hallāšôn* depicts the charmer, not the snake. If then the charmer is bitten before making the snake perform in some way, this small reptile has frustrated the charmer's purpose.

We note in vv. 8-9 several examples of the vulnerability of the worker, the theme offered by 9.18. Verse 10 raises numerous problems for the interpreter, but despite them we can conclude that vv. 10-11 appear to present a contrast between two situations, one of which provides *yitrôn* or 'benefit', and the other, none. In the former (v. 10) there are connections with 9.17 in its advocacy of wisdom, while in v. 11 the theme is vulnerability as in 9.18. Both themes from 9.17-18 are present here.

The vulnerability theme, here and in 10.1, is expressed by means of small animals. We shall find the same feature in v. 20, and it represents an outstanding literary feature of this chapter. The world of nature was one of the objects of wisdom reflection (cf. Prov. 30.24-28; 1 Kgs 4.33), and we note Qoheleth's interest in it also.

10.12-15 Further Material on the Wise-Fool Contrast

Although there is some association between the tongue (v. 11) and speech, it does not alter the fact that vv. 12-15 bring us to a sub-unit, the theme of which differs from what precedes. As in vv. 2-3, the focus of attention is the fool (vv. 12, 13, 14, 15) and conduct typical of him. The unusual term *k^esîl* (cf. v. 2) occurs in vv. 12 and 15, encapsulating the term *sākāl* in vv. 13, and 14. The keywords throughout are *dābār* (vv. 12, 13, 14), and *peh*, 'mouth'. Associations with other parts of Qoheleth's record come particularly through the question in v. 14c (cf. 6.12), as well as the more general theme of much speech as typical of the fool (5.2-6[3-7]).

The superiority of wisdom is the important message being conveyed, as in 9.17, which relationship is obvious in the parallel phrases *dibrē-ḥ^akāmîm* (9.17) and *dibrē-pî-ḥākām* (10.12). The fool is one lacking knowledge (*lō' yāda'*). Qoheleth regularly points out that human knowledge on a wide variety of subjects is exceedingly limited, but here he refers specifically to the fool's ignorance of the future. Despite his ignorance, the fool nevertheless continues to make statements about the future (v. 14).

10.12 A contrast is drawn between the sage and the fool, the criterion being evident in what they say. On the one hand the sage's words are 'graciousness' (*ḥēn*), while the lips (*śiptôt*) of the fool will bring about his demise (*t^eball^e'ennû*). The noun *ḥēn* has appeared once already in 9.11 in the sense of popular acceptance or favour. Here it is descriptive of the speech of the wise person in its essential nature. The RSV translation 'win him favour' is an interpretation of that essence, under the influence of the parallel and contrasting effect of the fool's words (cf. Lauha: 191). However, Crenshaw notes that the sense here is a little ambiguous, meaning either that what the wise say can win them favour or 'bestow favor' on others. As for the fool, his comments have a destructive effect, the verb *bl'* suggesting 'swallow up, devour'. Whether it is the fool himself who is devoured (cf. 4.5), or 'graciousness', depends upon the interpretation of the pronominal suffix on *t^eball^e'ennû*. In light of the context, preference perhaps should be given to the latter interpretation, against that of the RSV.

10.13 From the above contrast, Qoheleth singles out the fool for closer attention. Again antithesis is employed, and it is that of two extremes, 'beginning' (*t^eḥillāh*) and 'end' (*'aḥ^arît*). As with the examples in the 'time'-poem in ch. 3, these extremes embrace all points in between, that is to say, the totality. Thus, the fool's comments on *every* issue are 'folly' (*siklût*) or an 'evil stupidity' (*hôlēlût rā'āh*), these latter being parallel terms. Once again it is clear that *rā'āh* does not denote a moral value, but is the equivalent of *hôlēlût*, 'folly', as in 1.17. The little-used term *t^eḥillāh*, 'beginning', occurs only this once in Qoheleth (cf. Gen. 13.3; Prov. 9.10); the more frequent term is *rē'šît* (cf. 3.11; 7.8).

10.14 Within the wisdom tradition, frequent expression was given to the idea that fools usually had far too much to say. The fool felt little embarrassment in demonstrating his ignorance; indeed, his major self-deception lay in believing that his words were worthy of a hearing (cf. 5.2-6[3-7]; Prov. 12.23; 14.3 etc.).

The specific criticism levelled against the fool, and thus an indication of Qoheleth's real concern, is that the fool pretends detailed knowledge about the future. At this point, several of the versions read a text which is the equivalent of *mah-šehāyāh* rather than *mah-šeyihyeh*. The MT is probably correct in reading the imperfect throughout this verse (cf. 8.7). We are already familiar with Qoheleth's definition from ch. 8 of the sage as one who recognizes what is unknowable, especially with regard to the future (8.7, 17).

Though v. 14bc is comprised of one statement and one rhetorical question, the theme of an unknown future is their common thread. That future, the *'aḥ^a^rît*, represents a play on words, for the same term in v. 13b refers to the 'end' of the fool's speech. In v. 14 the *'aḥ^a^rît* is temporal, descriptive of the future. There is a measure of ambiguity in this term since it can refer to whatever happens in one's own future or after one's own death. It could also refer to what transpires in society after one dies (6.12). Here there is a good possibility that Qoheleth's concern is with what transpires after one passes beyond death. The fool presumes to know and to proclaim that future, the unknown 'life' after death.

10.15 The sub-unit closes with a reference to the fool's labour (*'^a^mal hakk^e^sîlîm*) as that which 'wearies him' (*t^e^yagg^e'^ennû*). The grammatical peculiarities of this latter, namely a feminine verbal form following a masculine subject (*'āmāl*), may be due to a deliberate attempt to conclude the sub-unit with a verbal form similar in sound to that in v. 12 (*t^e^ball^e'^ennû*). It is then part of the inclusion which marks this section. Some scholars are tempted to emend (see Barton: 178, and Lauha: 190, for some possibilities), even though textual evidence is lacking. In addition we need to recall that Qoheleth operates with some freedom in respect of certain grammatical principles.

The nature of the fool's labour, if contextually defined, is his much speaking on matters about which he knows nothing. He talks and talks until even he himself is weary.

Use of a singular suffix on the verb *yg'*, 'grow weary', requires some comment, for as Barton points out, it is ambiguous. If, as in the case of *t^e^ball^e'^ennû* in v. 12, the suffix identifies the fool, the fact that in v. 15 the preceding term is in the plural (*k^e^sîlîm*) produces a slight difficulty, unless we consider it a singular with plural or corporate reference. Ehrlich, quoted by Loader (p. 77), suggests *hakk^e^sîl mātay y^e^yagg^e'^ennû,* 'when will it tire him?' Thus he removes the problematic plural. Another suggestion is that the suffix on *t^e^ball^e'^ennû* anticipates the singular expression in the following clause, though this only moves the problem back rather than solving it. If, as is suggested above, the particular form of the verb and its suffix in v. 15 is modelled on that of v. 12, then the suffix as singular is not a problem. In any event, that it relates to the fool is clear.

The criticism levelled against the fool in v. 15b is that he does not know 'to go to the city' (*laleket 'el-'îr*). How his uninformed chatter about the future and its associated fatigue relate to his ignorance about 'going to the city', is something of a mystery. We should avoid speculation when the text is so vague. That we are confronting an idiomatic saying in which not knowing how to 'go to the city' is a metaphor for being foolish is perhaps the best approach, rather than following Loader, who believes it 'cannot be understood'. Thus, v. 15b is a circumlocution for 'fool', the one indicated by the suffix on *yg'* in v. 15a. Fox has suggested (1999: 308) that this verse is 'an isolated and not quite relevant afterthought'. He links it back to the thought in v.3 and considers the possibility that it originally belonged together with that verse. In the absence of textual evidence we reject that possibility.

There can be little doubt about the general thesis of this subsection as it plays down the fool whose empty prattling, especially with regard to the future, is one of his distinctive characteristics. By avoiding this kind of behaviour, one exhibits wisdom. Thematically as well as linguistically, Qoheleth here upholds unequivocally the true value of wisdom, as in 9.17.

10.16-20 Advantages and Disadvantages of Royalty

At an initial glance there seems little obvious connection between this sub-unit and the material preceding. The varied content and the form in which the material comes to us makes the task of elucidating its meaning a problematic one, and its relationship to the context debatable. Yet that relationship can be explained.

Let us begin with the major literary feature of the unit. The closing verse, v. 20, draws upon nature for its illustration. A small bird may carry news of an unwise word to one in authority. The illustration from nature is a feature noted already in respect of vv. 1, 8 and 11, and forms one of the important inclusions for the chapter. The small creature symbolizes folly's threat to the greatness of wisdom. Additionally, the *ba'al-hallāšôn* that describes the charmer in v. 11, strikes an echo in v. 20 with the *ba'al-(hak)k^{a}nāpîm*.

Although one recognizes immediately that vv. 16-20 feature distinctive keywords (*melek, sār*) and lack those terms frequent in the preceding (such as *ḥkm, ksl/skl*), there is a point of connection to be made with that material. In the parallel sentences in vv. 16-17, there is a reference to a 'young man' (*na'ar*). In view of the contrast to *ben-ḥôrîm*, we conclude that *na'ar* and *'ebed* are here synonymous. This implies that the 'prince and servant' theme in v. 7 reappears in a novel context in vv. 16-17. So, while the connection between these verses and the foregoing is not immediately apparent, modest reflection can uncover evidence of the author's mind.

As for thematic, as opposed to literary, connections, we have seen in 9.17 that Qoheleth condemns the ruler (*môšēl*) who carouses with fools, as he does in 10.16-17. The idea that sloth or 'minor' indiscretions can destroy (10.18, 20), resonates with the theme of 9.18. Indeed, this conclusion to ch. 10 fits neatly within the framework of the twin themes of 9.17-18 about wisdom's power and vulnerability.

10.16-17 An identical or parallel structure characterizes these two verses, which consist of a 'woe'-form (v. 16) and its antithesis (v. 17). The 'woe'-form, regularly found in prophetic material (e.g. Isa. 5.8ff; see also March: 164-65), differs from the adapted form used by Qoheleth. This latter is devoid of the participial phrases which constitute one of its essential formal elements. The use of parallelism heightens the contrast between the two verses as they depict wise and foolish behaviour. This structure we may set out as follows:

'î-lāk	*'ereṣ šemmalkēk na'ar*	*weśārayik babbōqer*	*yō'kēlû*
'ašrēk	*'ereṣ šemmalkēk ben-ḥôrîm*	*weśārayik bā'ēt*	*yō'kēlû*

As these are general aphorisms, it is misguided to seek precise historical references in them.

10.16 The initial *'î*, 'woe', is found only here and in 4.10. It has associations with later Hebrew, and emendation to the more regular form *hôy* is not called for. The fact that we are dealing here with an adaptation of the 'woe'-form suggests that its function is not as an oracle of doom on the land, but rather as a statement of difficulties encountered whenever a land finds itself with a 'king' who is a *na'ar* (RSV, 'child'). The age of the monarch is not necessarily an index of his leadership abilities, so that youthfulness is not always detrimental, but it is generally to be related to immaturity and thus a lack of wisdom. We have already encountered several examples where Qoheleth equates wisdom and youth (e.g. 4.13-16), and Solomon was so described (1 Kgs 3.7). The antithetic parallelism provides a clue to the contextual meaning of *na'ar*—it stands opposite *ben-ḥôrîm,* 'free men'. That is to say, *na'ar* here means 'servant', the equivalent of *'ebed* in v. 7 (see Zimmerli, 1967: 237). Seow, however, argues for the emphasis to be laid on the fact of his immaturity.

The criticism levelled against the scenario in v. 16a must be predicated on an assumed failure on the part of the servant—that he is irresponsible (as in vv. 5-7). Confirmation of this view can be located in v. 16b. Parallel to 'king' is the term 'prince' (*śār*) as in Isa. 32.1. He is described as 'eating in the morning', and as an imperfect verb (*yō'kēlû*) is used, we presume that it is to denote frequency or habit. Again, the meaning must be drawn from the context. Eating in the morning is a universal custom, and carries no intrinsic moral reproof. We are dependent upon the explanatory clause at the end of v. 17 to infer that these 'princes' were indulging themselves, to the point that breakfast merely signalled the beginning of the day's gluttony. Such behaviour, says Qoheleth, is inappropriate, the action of a fool (cf. Isa. 5.11), and woe to any nation whose leaders are of that kind!

10.17 Verse 17 posits the antithesis of v. 16, the initial *'ašrē* signalling that contrast. *'Ašrē* is assumed by some to play a key role in the thought of the so-called wisdom psalms (though contrast Crenshaw, *OT Wisdom:* 185). Insofar as happiness, the ability to cope with life, was one of the goals of wisdom instruction, it is not surprising that Qoheleth should use the term. Regardless of its function within the wisdom psalms, in this instance Qoheleth employs *'ašrē* to picture the positive effect upon a land when its leader is the 'son of free men' (*ben-ḥôrîm*). This latter term is an Aramaism, from the root *ḥrr,* 'noble', frequently used in Nehemiah (e.g. 2.16). Being born and raised in a context familiar with the requirements of leadership Qoheleth considers a distinct advantage. Of course, there is no guarantee that one so raised will make a good stable leader any more than a servant/youth would be unable to rule by virtue of his youthfulness. However, we see reflected in this saying Qoheleth's view that one nobly born, if wise, ought to have the country's best interests at heart, and pursue that goal.

Knowing what is best and appropriate is also the thought behind the phrase 'eating at the appointed time' (*bā'ēt yō'kēlû*); discerning the appropriateness of the moment is one of the marks of the sage (cf. 3-1-8).

To this there is added an explanatory phrase (v. 17c) formed of two adverbial clauses. The first, 'for strength' (*bigᵉbûrāh*), indicates that the purpose of eating is to maintain physical energy. The second phrase, *wᵉlō' baššᵉtî,* 'not for drinking', expresses the debased purpose which eating and drinking can at times serve, as in the example cited in 7.2. The noun *šᵉtî,* used only here, presumably describes a drinking bout. Qoheleth cautions against indulgent feasting and what accompanied it.

These contrasting verses paint a forceful picture of the impact upon their respective countries which wise and foolish leaders have. Within the overall advice of ch. 10, they serve as arguments supportive of 9.17 and the value of wisdom.

10.18 Apart from its theme of the dangers of laziness (= folly = sin), connections between this verse and its context are not at first sight obvious, a fact magnified by the many *hapax legomena* or rare terms found here in concentration. The theme of v. 18 is not novel; we have met it in 4.5, and numerous sayings in Proverbs match its concern (10.4; 18.9 etc.). Textual problems are also present. The opening word *ʿᵃṣaltayim,* 'sloth', is a dual form calling for explanation, if not emendation. On the basis of a feminine noun *šiplūt*, 'indolence', and its attendant dual *yādayim* (v. 18b), there are those who would emend *ʿᵃṣaltayim* to read *ʿaṣlūt yādayim* (so Bickell, Siegfried, McNeile, Zimmerli), or read *ʿaṣlat* with Fox. Another approach is to regard the dual as an intensive (so Barton, Delitzsch, Gordis, Murphy). There is no extant MS evidence in support of emendation, so the latter interpretation is perhaps correct.

Consequent upon this laziness, 'the roof caves in'. The verb *yimmak* is niphal imperfect of *mkk*, 'be low, humiliated', and is one of only three OT examples. The roof timbers probably fall in on themselves, or sag and so leak. This reflexive sense is one of the niphal's original nuances. *Mᵉqāreh* describes the wooden rafters of a stone house, and does not appear elsewhere in the OT, though equivalent terms do.

In parallel with the above, Qoheleth reinforces the statement of the consequences of laziness. In v. 18b there occurs another *hapax legomenon, šiplût yādayim,* literally 'a falling of the hands'. There is a play on words here with the sagging or collapse of the roof in v. 18a and the lowering of one's hands (v. 18b) providing a vivid description of the consequences of sloth. Alongside *yimmak*, 'cave in', in the first stichos, is *yidlōp* in v. 18b. The root *dlp* in Prov. 10.4; 19.13; 27.15 describes rain dripping through the roof, so that in co-ordinating the 'falling of the hands' and the 'dripping (of rain)' we see further evidence of Qoheleth's literary skill. When Qoheleth says the house (*bayit*) leaks, he clearly means the roof leaks.

The purpose of the verse, expressing traditional wisdom, is to illustrate the tragic consequences of laziness; and as laziness is folly, he indicates the danger of folly (9.18). It offers an aphorism accounting for the deplorable situation portrayed in v. 16.

10.19 This verse bristles with problems for the interpreter. Though there is much in common with 9.7 and the general theme of enjoyment, it seems to bear very little association with its present context. However, there is no adequate reason to doubt the present text or its location (cf. Salters, 1977: 423-26). It is conceivable that the eating and drinking of which it speaks are not unrelated to the thought of v. 17. A second problem centres on the meaning of *'ānāh* in the final clause. Its many possible translations make precision difficult, leading to a division among commentators as to whether it speaks of something negative or positive.

The three clauses which form the verse vary slightly in structure. In v. 19a an initial infinitive construct with prefaced *l^e* indicates purpose—*liśḥôq* 'for laughter', that is, for pleasure (cf. 2.2). There follows a plural participle *'ōśîm*, which can only be rendered by the impersonal 'they make'. In compound with *leḥem*, 'bread', the phrase indicates the preparation of a meal, as in Ezek. 4.15.

The second clause places the subject *yayin*, 'wine', in front of the finite verb *y^{e}śammaḥ*, 'rejoice' (cf. the parallel use in 2.2). Wine, like bread, makes for a happy existence. The noun *ḥayyîm* can mean 'life', as in 9.3, or 'living' as in 9.4, but as this verse lacks contextual indicators, the interpreter cannot be dogmatic about the author's meaning. Wine would hardly bring pleasure to the dead, so perhaps we should render *ḥayyîm* in this instance as 'life' or 'living persons'.

The final clause is the one which poses the greatest difficulties, principally stemming from the verb *'ānāh*. Structurally, this third clause is identical with the second (v. 19b), but it is also distinguished by the sudden appearance of the definite article on both subject and object. Even allowing for Qoheleth's undisciplined use of the article, this sudden change is abrupt. It is the meaning of *'ānāh* which must concern us primarily. It covers a wide semantic range: answer, obey, submit, hear, testify, afflict. In 5.19(20) Qoheleth used this root with the sense of 'occupy' or 'provide for'. There is little reason to go beyond this in searching for a meaning here, though the versions made other choices. If *'ānāh* means 'provide for', then Qoheleth is merely saying that if one is to eat and drink one must have some money (*kesep*) with which to purchase bread and wine. That the money is 'squandered', as Barton opines, is an unwarranted assumption based on the relationship of this verse to v. 16. I have argued (see Ogden, 1980: 36) that a link is discernible between v. 17 and this verse, and that the nuance of v. 19 is at least neutral, though it is more likely to be a positive one; no criticism is implied in the verse. If criticism was intended then we would be required to render *'ānāh* as 'afflict'. Fox, on the other hand, rejects the meaning 'provide' as trivial. In his view, the verb is hiphil and refers to one being occupied with some task or being busy. This is close to Seow's suggestion that it means that the elite in the community are constantly 'preoccupied' with enjoying the good things of life.

The final term *'et-hakkōl*, 'all', as in 7.8 refers to the two listed items, food and wine. Without money, feasting or pleasure is not possible. Thus our preferred translation here is, 'and money provides them both' (cf. Lohfink, 1980: 78). Ironic or real, the point is clear.

10.20 A return to the theme of royalty indicates that there is a relationship between this verse and vv. 16, 17, the term 'king' functioning as the inclusion for the sub-unit.

In v. 20ab the two verbs are jussives, a feature present already in v. 4 above. The reiteration of *'al-tᵉqallēl*, 'do not curse', makes it emphatic. The objects of the potential curse in these two basically parallel clauses are the 'king' (*melek*) and the 'wealthy person' (*'āšir*). It is not clear why Qoheleth has not set the 'prince' of vv. 16, 17 in conjunction with 'king' but we can generally assume that the wealthy members of society held positions similar to those of royalty. The circumstances under which one should refrain from cursing these leaders are described in the attached adverbial phrases. The initial *gam*, 'even', adds emphasis by its suggestion that even under extreme circumstances one should not curse them. Specifically, in one's intimate conversation and secret thoughts one should not entertain potentially dangerous notions, as there is always the risk that one may be discovered by the authorities as harbouring such ideas. In ancient treaties, the vassal was always cautioned against critical language because this was an expression of rebellion. The first of the adverbial phrases, *bᵉmaddā'ᵃkā*, 'in your knowledge/thought' is related to he root *yd'*, 'know'. *Maddā'ᵃkā* itself is rarely used in Biblical Hebrew (2 Chron 1.10-12; Dan. 1.4, 17), but has Aramaic associations. 'In your mind' is probably an adequate translation (so Fox and many commentators), but Whybray has cautioned against it as purely conjectural. It is also problematic unless one gives expression to one's thoughts, since a person's thoughts are not normally known unless spoken of. Nor is it likely that Koehler's suggestion of 'bedroom' is entirely appropriate. His thesis depends on the sexual connotations of the verb *yd'* and this certainly provides an interesting parallel to the second adverbial phrase *b^{e}ḥadrē-miškāb^{e}kā*, 'bedchamber' (cf. 2 Kgs 6.12). Seow also links the term to the sexual connotations of the verb 'know', but rather than 'bedroom' he suggests 'intimacy' or what goes on in one's bedroom. Dahood, from an Ugaritic form *mnd,* suggests a meaning 'messenger' (1958: 312; 1965: 210-12). This latter seems to take us further from the sense of the second half of the verse.

Even one's most secret thoughts and intimate words have a way of becoming known publicly. Advice about being cautious in speech finds parallels in most world literature (cf. Ahiqar 7.96-99). Israel's legal code (Exod. 22.28) and its wisdom tradition (4 Ezra 5.6) all contain similar cautionary comments. On this occasion Qoheleth returns to his nature model, and speaks of the small bird (*'ôp, ba'al-hakk^{a}nāpîm*) carrying one's dangerous comments to the authorities. The bird may bring (*hôlîk*) one's voice, that is, carry the message to the royal person. In the final clause (v. 20d) the phrase is, the winged creature (*ba'al-hakk^{a}nāpîm* - Prov. 1.17) will 'tell the matter' (*yaggēd dābār*). The verbal form *yaggēd* is jussive, so we should perhaps read *yaggîd* the imperfect in lieu, as in v. 14 above. The reference to the bird is most probably a literal reference, consistent with the earlier references to a fly and snake. However, there is always the possibility that here the term is figurative for a servant or some member of the household who passes on domestic secrets to one in authority.

Thus, as the thematic statement in 9.18 intimated, one's career is forever at risk; it may be undermined at any time by lack of caution or by indiscretion. In this illustration of v. 20 it is a bird, in vv. 8, 11 it was a serpent, and in v. 1 it was a fly. All are small and apparently insignificant creatures, but each has the potential for harm. Folly is just like that. Despite wisdom's obvious and great power, yet a small measure of folly may do damage that could well be fatal.

This section 9.17—10.20 moves Qoheleth's discourse on wisdom from a focus on its power to the reality of its vulnerability. One of the many ironies which mark the human scene is found here, and Qoheleth draws our attention to it in his own utterly honest manner.

Chapter 11

Limits to Human Knowledge

Two motifs have characterized Qoheleth's closing discourse thus far. They are: the power of wisdom, and its vulnerability. Both are aspects of human wisdom which co-exist in tension. The next episode in Qoheleth's discourse raises two further issues, namely, what can and cannot be known. Human wisdom is significant for what it can discover to aid our attempt to master our world, but it also has severe limitations (see Good, 1981: 168-95).

The change in theme and topic from ch. 10 signals that in 11.1 we have come to a new literary unit. It is one marked by references to natural elements (water, wind, cloud, rain, tree, earth, seed), and by other features such as the recurrence of verbs in the imperative mood (vv. 1, 2, 6), the use of three paired sentences in parallel (vv. 1-4), and the reappearance of numerical statements (vv. 2, 6). Additionally, we note that vv. 1-2 carry the two themes of the unit, a literary convention created by Qoheleth and first used in 9.17-18. It will be used again in the following unit, 11.7-8. The themes prefigured in vv. 1, 2 will be expanded in vv. 3-5, with v. 6 serving as a concluding statement.

The structure of 11.1-6, the first unit in the chapter, is readily visible: an initial three sets of paired sentences (vv. 1-4), followed by one (v. 5) in ascending parallelism, and rounded off by a concluding verse which follows the pattern of vv. 1-3 (see Ogden, 1983: 222-30).

11.1-2 Our unit opens with two imperative clauses and their attendant adversative clauses, as the first in a series of three parallel sayings. The initial imperatives, *šallaḥ,* 'cast, send', and *ten,* 'give', are both distributive actions, the objects of which are respectively *leḥem* 'bread', and *ḥēleq,* 'portion'. To these is added an adverbial phrase denoting the place or persons to whom distribution is to be made: thus, *'al pᵉnē-hammayim,* 'on the waters', and *lᵉšib'āh wᵉgam lišmônāh,* 'to seven or eight'.

The saying in v. la appears to be a traditional saying, of which there is a comparable Arabic example: 'Do good, cast your bread upon the waters, and one day you will be rewarded'. Whether the Islamic proverb owes its genesis to Qoheleth, or whether both are from some common form, or whether Qoheleth has drawn the saying from an Arabic source is impossible to ascertain at this point.

The term 'bread' (*leḥem*) may be a metaphor for one's 'merchandise' (so Delitzsch, McNeile and others), a view which gives rise to a commercial interpretation, advocating overseas trade as a way of making money (so also Gordis, Whybray). It would appear that this interpretation is grounded on the assumption that 'waters' means 'ocean', and 'upon the waters' means 'overseas'. Both interpretations are difficult to substantiate. Loader's argument (1979: 67) in support is that *leḥem* in 9.11 is parallel to *'ōšer,* 'riches'. This is misleading, as *leḥem* in 9.11 is merely a further example of material benefit and is not a *parallel* term to 'riches'. Bauer has proposed that 'bread' actually means 'seed' and that the call is for one to sow seed in moist ground to assure a plentiful harvest. That *mayim* means 'moist ground' stretches the interpretation too far. Yet another view is that the metaphor 'casting bread' is a call for generosity or giving of alms (Barton, Ginsberg, Seow and others); it is the traditional Jewish interpretation. Gordis's argument against this view is that Qoheleth is never given to generosity, but his objection is debatable. The interpreter therefore appears to be at a loss to find a reasonably objective criterion for uncovering the verse's meaning. Murphy agrees with Galling and Hertzberg that it is a metaphor for doing something senseless (1992: 106) because even uncertainty is uncertain!

Hertzberg's view that the conjunction *kî* with which the final clause commences has an adversative function, 'yet', rather than as the motivating 'for', has merit. Seow prefers to regard it as a weakened asseverative and leaves it untranslated.

I want to suggest that the parallel structure of vv. 1, 2 and the common theme of their imperative elements ought to be the interpreter's starting point, for this structure appears deliberate. As both imperatives share the common theme of distribution, the concluding halves with their opposing positive (v. lb) and negative (v. 2b) verbs then become the operative clauses. Similar actions may have two contrary results: one distributive action produces results which we can 'find' (*māṣā'*) while another leads to something which we cannot know (*lō' tēda'*) or predetermine. Antithetical or conflicting statements are to be found throughout the wisdom material (cf. Prov. 26.4,5) because human experience and attendant advice are far too complex to be embraced within one pithy saying. Conditional or contextual factors are in large measure determinative of appropriate action, as well as of the results of any act.

That the first stichos of v. 1 is a traditional saying is almost certain. Whatever the terms *leḥem* and *mayim* once signified in that context is presently unknown and actually irrelevant to the present setting. So whether the saying originally spoke of foreign trade, generosity, or something else, is less important than to uncover what purpose it *presently* serves. The view taken here is that it is the foil to the second stichos in which Qoheleth makes the point that one may give something away, and yet find that after a period (*b*ᵉ*rôb hayyāmîm*), one gains that something back in return (*timṣā'ennû*).

We must still wrestle with the relationship of the second half of v. 1 to the preceding imperative. Does v. 1b provide the motive clause for heeding the call to 'cast bread'? Or does it, as Hertzberg suggests, provide a contrasting thought? Hertzberg appears correct, the reason being that by focusing Qoheleth's intention in the *kî*-clauses rather than in the imperatives, attention is drawn to the contrasting results of similar actions. Although wisdom advice frequently was grounded upon the ensuing reward or outcome of a certain kind of behaviour, the contrasting results of the distributive action in our present text are better highlighted by treating the *kî* as adversative (see also Lauha, 1979: 201) rather than motivating. Furthermore, if we consider that the second stichos of each verse is Qoheleth's own addition to a traditional saying, then the differing results of giving become more obvious.

In v. 1 the point made is that one is able to 'find out' certain information. In ch. 7 (esp. vv. 23-29) the concept of 'finding' was a dominant theme (see also 8.17). The conclusion there was that we have the potential to discover much about our world, but we are always frustrated in our longing for total comprehension. The verb *māṣā'* is one of Qoheleth's key verbs (used 16 times), indicating that the possibility of finding out about our world for the purpose of mastering it is one of the book's dominant concerns (see Wright, 1968: 323f). That such should feature in this closing discourse is to be expected. In this instance he sets it before his readers as one of two polarities around which the sage must work.

In the second verse, by following the principles established above, we note that a similar distributive action is commended, although on this occasion we are ignorant of its outcome; this makes v. 2 antithetical to v. 1.

We observe the term *ḥēleq,* 'portion' (see comments on 2.10) describing what it is that is to be widely distributed. This portion is to be given 'to seven or eight (persons)'. Use of numerals is an important literary device in the wisdom literature (see W. Roth, *Numerical Sayings,* 1965; *idem,* 'The Numerical Sequence x, x + 1 in the OT'; Ogden, 'Wisdom Sayings'), as well as in Qoheleth (cf. 4.1-12). Here, the x, x + 1 formula remains in vestigial form (cf. Amos 1.2). Numeration functions as an important inclusion in this unit (see v. 6).

The meaning of the saying in v. 2a seems now lost to us, so discussion as to whether it speaks of spreading one's investment portfolio for security purposes (so Loader, Gordis), or exporting merchandise (Crenshaw, Murphy), or whether it is a call to greater generosity or good deeds (Seow), is probably in the end a fruitless search. Although some commentators point out that a similar saying can be found in other cultures, there is no certainty that they have a similar meaning to that in the quote by Qoheleth. Whether one takes the 'bread' to be figurative or literal, the theme of uncertainty and of surprising results from an action seems to be the point being made. Verse 2a advocates a distributive action 'even though' (*kî*) one cannot know (*lō' tēda'*) what calamity (*rā'āh*) might eventuate. In light of the agricultural examples which follow, *rā'āh* presumably refers to potential failure, for various reasons, of the crop.

Although we must admit to the difficulty of determining precisely the original meaning of the two introductory aphorisms, the concepts of 'finding' and 'not knowing' are programmatic and central to the thought of vv. 1-2. These verses have a functional role in setting the unit's theme. Despite the fact that the material in vv. 3-4 which illustrates v. 1 does not repeat the verb *māṣā',* 'find', nevertheless that theme is abundantly evident. The second theme, what is unknowable, we find illustrated in v. 5: we see 'as through a glass darkly'. Together they express the second set of conditions which attach to the pursuit of wisdom, namely that wisdom has its limitations.

11.3 The second pair of sentences in this unit are each conditional clauses basically parallel in structure, in which illustrative material is drawn from the world of nature, the clouds and trees. The descriptive portion forms the protasis, and the apodosis carries the consequences of the situation described.

Storm clouds pregnant with moisture are seen in the heavens. The term *gešem,* 'rain', is accusative after the niphal imperfect *yimmālᵉ'û,* 'are filled (with)'. Heavy clouds rising on the moisture-laden winds from the Mediterranean are a certain sign of seasonal rains in Israel, and Qoheleth draws upon this natural phenomenon to indicate the reasonableness of the supposition that we can ascertain something from the world around us; we can determine that the clouds are about to 'pour out' (*yārîqû*) their moisture.

As for the second example in v. 3b, Qoheleth cites a simple case: a tree falls (*yippôl 'ēṣ*). Whether it falls towards the south (*baddārôm*) or towards the north (*baṣṣāpôn*), meaning, regardless of where it falls, there it will remain (*yᵉhû'*). Trees do not move after they are felled. This is another observable fact. *Dārôm*, 'north', is a late and poetic term especially frequent in Ezekiel's description of his Temple vision in chs. 40-42. The final verb *yᵉhû'* is probably a conflated reading; it ought to be the pronoun *hû'* as the copula, or *yihyeh*, the imperfect.

In the light of the stated theme of v. 1, we determine that the conditional clauses illustrate what practical wisdom can claim to find. Those who would argue that the theme of v. 3 is what humankind is unable to accomplish, that we cannot alter the laws of nature to prevent it raining (e.g. Barton, Loader, McNeile, Rankin), have not given adequate consideration to the function of v. 1 and the relationship v. 3 has to it. Lauha's contention (p. 201) that all events are predetermined (by God) is also not the emphasis which the verse carries. When Gordis suggests that human labour assures success, we are taken even further from the theme of what humankind can find out. While each verse, if viewed independently, can conceivably have the meanings ascribed to it by these commentators, their present context must be determinative, and such is provided by the opening thematic verses.

11.4 The trio of paired sentences in parallel ends with v. 4. Here we find the least complex of the forms, consisting of a participial phrase depicting one who observes the weather (*šōmēr rûaḥ* and *rō'eh be'ābîm*), and a negated imperfect verb indicating that one should refrain from action which the observation demonstrates to be inappropriate. The verse relates to the preceding v. 3 by virtue of a common interest in clouds and weather patterns.

Both ends of the cultivation process are mentioned: planting seeds (*zr'*) and harvesting (*qṣr*).

Qoheleth indicates that the farmer who pays close attention to the phenomena of wind and cloud as signals of approaching weather conditions, knows when it is unwise to sow the crop (*zr'*) or to attempt to harvest it (*qṣr*). Failure or success of the crop is dependent upon attention to these details (though contrast v. 6). The point being made again is that we are able to discover from observation and experience that there are ideal conditions for the performance of any task. The sage is the one who knows and can take advantage of this information. However, Murphy (1992: 109) presents a slightly different view, perhaps dependent upon the ambiguity of the text, though he does not mention that. It is that the farmer who watches the wind and clouds is looking for the 'right' time to sow or reap, and as a result becomes paralysed by a concern for that 'right time'. The result is that he does nothing. Seow's view is similar as he focuses on the farmer who will neither sow nor reap when viewing the weather for fear that the wind may be too strong, or that the rain will ruin what is about to be harvested.

Barton's view (p. 183), that here we have to do with lost opportunity, would be acceptable as a possible meaning for the verse if it were not in this present context. Although we are frequently troubled in interpreting wisdom statements because of their lack of context, here that context is provided. There are things which we may find out to our benefit. In this sense, Qoheleth is speaking to a principle enunciated in ch. 3, that there are appropriate (and inappropriate) times for all activities. If the goal of wisdom advice is to aid us in harmonizing with the divine order in our world, then we must be able to discern *sufficient* of that order to take the necessary steps towards that goal. Observing natural phenomena, as vv. 3 and 4 indicate, allows us a glimpse into the divine ordering of the world, to discover information which we might apply to add meaning to life.

11.5 Having dealt with what we can discover, Qoheleth now moves to take up the second theme, that of our restricted power to know or find out. The usual observation-reflection process implicit in vv. 3, 4 is again at work here.

Verse 5 illustrates the thesis of v. 2. It is linked cleverly with v. 4 by their shared term *rûaḥ,* which highlights both our power to comprehend and our woeful limitations.

Ascending parallelism is the major structural feature of v. 5: 'just as ... so also (*ka'ᵃšer* ... *kākāh*)'. The high point of this formal style is the thesis set in the second stichos, that we are denied the power to comprehend the actions of God. It is compared with the first stichos, which quotes the truism that we do not know 'the way of the wind/spirit' (*derek-hārûaḥ*). The key terms are *'ēnᵉkā yôdēa'* and *lō' tēda'*, which link directly with v. 2. The variant forms of this expression in v. 5 may be significant; the participial phrase describes a present situation, while *lō' tēda'* stresses that we are never able to find out more about it. We are impotent before God and his actions (*ma'ᵃśēh hā'ᵉlōhîm*). It is clearly not Qoheleth's view that we can know absolutely nothing about what God does; rather, that our grasp of it is only partial. This view also accords with the suggestion that the final *hakkōl* is best rendered 'both' rather then 'everything' (cf. 10.19). Here 'both' speaks of the breath/wind and the bones of the foetus.

Textual evidence from the versions suggests that we retain the reading *ka'ᵃṣāmîm* rather than emend to *ba'ᵃṣāmîm*. However, the present MT can only be explained in a very tortuous manner (see Barton), and then it still requires an additional conjunction 'and' to indicate the two elements of which we are ignorant. Emendation therefore is probably justified. 'Bones' (*'ᵃṣāmîm*) in the plural is a metaphor or diminutive for the whole person (e.g. Isa. 66.14; Prov. 14.30). The noun *hammᵉlē'āh*, denoting a 'pregnant (full) woman', is not found elsewhere in Biblical Hebrew. However, it is used here as a reflection of the description of the clouds that are 'full' of moisture (v.3).

We return again to the first stichos, to the term *derek-hārûaḥ*, to illustrate the interpreter's dilemma. We have already seen that *rûaḥ* binds together vv. 4 and 5, but what is the nature of that relationship? 'Wind' is without doubt the meaning of *rûaḥ* in v. 4, but in v. 5 we face a choice between 'wind' and 'breath/spirit of life'. The term 'path of the wind' is a perfectly acceptable rendering of the phrase in v. 5, and it is also contextually appropriate if we determine that Qoheleth intends a link back to v. 4. However, if he is speaking of the foetus in v. 5b, then *rûaḥ* probably means 'the way of the breath (of life)'. A truly objective solution is elusive, the more so when we realize that we are attempting to sunder a concept which in Hebrew represents a unity. Just as we cannot know how the life breath enters the growing foetus, so we cannot discover God's ways; they are alike a mystery.

11.6 Imperatives in this verse, recalling vv. 1, 2, urge the reader to action. Not only in the imperatival forms followed by a *kî*-clause, but also in the thematic association with 'not knowing' and the use of numerals, v. 6 takes our minds back immediately to vv. 1, 2. Additionally, v. 6 shares the 'sowing seed' imagery with v. 4. In these elements we are obliged to affirm the unity of both form and content.

Qoheleth's concluding call (v. 6ab) is cast as two balanced clauses in antithetical relationship. Both commence with a temporal phrase, 'in the morning' (*babbōqer*) and 'to/till evening' (*lā'ereb*), and are accompanied by two imperatives, 'sow' (*zera'*) and 'do not withhold' (*'al-tannaḥ*), similar actions expressed antithetically. The sowing of seed has its primary setting in an agricultural context, and this is perhaps its most obvious meaning here, given the focus throughout on the natural world. However, the Midrash has seen in these words a reference to begetting children, in light of v. 5. Both views are acceptable, and it is even possible that Qoheleth in using such a generalized expression intends the double meaning. However, if a choice is required, the agricultural interpretation is to be preferred.

In the second imperative, *'al-tannaḥ yādᵉkā*, as in 7.18, we meet a call for continuous activity. For this reason the temporal phrase *lā'ereb* is best rendered 'till evening', giving the impression of work from morn till night. This latter sense further endorses the agricultural interpretation of v. 6a against the Midrash! We might see another link here between v. 6 and the opening verses in that the imperative represents a similar distributive action.

As in vv. 1, 2, the *kî*-clause has been viewed differently here also. If, as appears likely, there is some deliberate attempt to structure v. 6 along lines similar to those of vv. 1, 2, then we ought to follow the above interpretation that the *kî* is the concessive 'yet'. From v. 4 we have noted that certain weather patterns are warnings to the farmer, who adjusts his activity accordingly. However, despite this knowledge, there is at the same time a remarkable ignorance on the farmer's part, in that he cannot know (*'ēnᵉkā yôdēa'*) what will produce results (*yikšār*). The root meaning of *kšr* is 'succeed' (see 2.21; 10.10) and it is used to indicate the potential for growth in the seeds sown. Qoheleth's point is that the farmer, for all his experience, has no certainty that the seed planted will germinate or that there will be a crop. That process and end-product are not within his power to know or control. It is akin to the thought of v. 5, as the manner in which the breath of life comes to the foetus is also something we cannot know. In both cases we are dealing with the 'secret' work of the divine Creator. Wherever our human activity intersects with the activity of God, we have no way of predetermining the outcome (v. 5b). Truly, our knowledge is severely limited, but we are fools if we permit this ignorance to reduce us to impotence. A sage is one who proceeds on the basis of what can be known, while affirming the maxim that before God our minds are profoundly limited.

In v. 6c there are some interesting expressions which require comment. The phrase *'ē zeh* is not found other than in Qoheleth, where we find it twice, here and in 2.3. Its sense is 'which (of two or more)'. The interrogative is made more weighty by the added question, *h^{a}zeh 'ô-zeh*, literally, 'is it this or this?' Emphasis is given to human ignorance by these phrases.

Verse 6d continues with the theme of our ignorance of the germination process and the growth of seeds, as Qoheleth makes the point that we cannot know which (of the seeds planted) will grow. Nor can we know if both of them (*š^{e}nēhem*) will be as good as the other (*k^{e}'eḥād ṭôbîm*). The numeral 'two' at this juncture carries the inclusive sense, 'all', while the term *k^{e}'eḥād* is an Aramaic expression 'like one another'. We have already noted the function of the numerical form as an inclusion (cf. 4.9-12).

Thus 11.1-6 with its dual theses—that wisdom is able to infer certain practical information about the world in which we live, but that it can never know all—brings us to the second qualification which Qoheleth makes to his strident claims about the power of wisdom in 9.1-16. The first qualification was that wisdom is vulnerable to small indiscretions (9.17—10.20). The discourse material in 11.1-6 reminds us that wisdom is always only partial, but for all that, it is still the most vital force in coping with life in this present. From here, we proceed to Qoheleth's final advice in 11.7-12.8.

Chapter 12

Enjoyment and Reflection

The final portion of Qoheleth's work begins with the closing verses of ch. 11, with v. 7, and extends to 12.8. Recognized almost universally as a distinct unit, we observe that it is marked by the same literary feature found in the two preceding sections, namely an introductory statement (11.7-8) setting out the twin themes of the unit as in 9.17-18 and 11.1-2. This feature of 11.7ff. was first noted by Glasser (1970: 167) and has been acknowledged by others (cf. Gilbert, 1981: 98; Witzenrath, 1979 etc.). *Śmḥ* ‘rejoice’, and *zkr*, ‘remember’, are the key words in this concluding section of the book, for the two themes which they mark are then elaborated in vv. 9-10 (*śmḥ*) and in 12.1-8 (*zkr*).

Apart from this major thematic and structural element of the verbs in the initial verse, there are other features of this section which we should note. First, that the second half of the section is further subdivided on the basis of three *‘ad ʾ^{a}šer lō’* phrases. Then there is the temporal element: *šānîm* and *yāmîm* in 11.8 are echoed in the phrases *bîmē b^{e}ḥûrôtekā in* 11.9 and 12.1, that is at the conclusion of the first stichos of both major portions of the section. In fact *yôm* is a principal term throughout (vv. 8, 9; 12.1, 3). Finally, the *hebel* phrase operates with its customary concluding function in 11.8, 10 and 12.8, that is, at the end of the theme-setting statement, and of both sub-sections which elaborate it.

We may set out the structure of the unit schematically as follows:

11.8	If a man lives many years	Time Phrase
	let him **rejoice**	Theme A
	and **remember**	Theme B
	the days of darkness will be many	Time Phrase
	all that comes is *hebel*	Conclusion

11.9-10	**Rejoice**	Theme A
	(in your youth) ... in the days of your youth	Time Phrase
	for youth ... is *hebel*	Conclusion
12.1	**Remember**	Theme B
	in the days of your youth before...	Time Phrase
12.2	before....	
12.6	before...	
12.8	*h^abēl h^abālîm*...all is *hebel*	Conclusion

11.7-8 It is Good to be Alive

As Qoheleth comes to the end of his discourse material (chs. 9-12), there is no further specific reference to wisdom. Having already made his point about the power as well as the vulnerability of wisdom, this change is understandable. His parting remarks now offer advice to all who would concur that wisdom is of such worth. But they do so in echoes of the advice given throughout the book, namely that we are to enjoy the life God gives even though it ends in death, the ultimate mystery. Thus, just as those earlier calls to enjoyment came at strategic moments in Qoheleth's presentation in chs. 1-8, so he now rounds off his remarks with the same basic advice: rejoice and remember.

Verse 7 opens with the adjective *mātôq*, 'sweet', as describing light (*hā'ôr*). That 'sweetness' is semantically apt to describe light is questionable, but Qoheleth uses it in what must be a metaphorical manner, as he did in 5.11 when referring to sleep. It certainly is intended as something positive. The second and parallel phrase suggests that 'seeing the sun' (*lirô't haššemeš*) is a good thing (*ṭôb*). Both 'light' and 'seeing the sun' have been used before (6.5; 7.11) to speak of life in the world. Qoheleth's opening gambit in this section is that it is indeed good to be alive, and this he insists is true despite life's frustrations and pain.

'Light' and its cognate expression are then contrasted with 'darkness' (*ḥōšek*), in nominal form in v. 8 and as a verb in 12.2, 3. As in 6.4, *ḥōšek* here also characterizes 'death'. However, it is also conceivable that darkness also carries the broader sense of that which is painful, that brings gloom and misery since that has also been the context for its use in 5.16[17]. However, as a final summary advice to the young, it remains that death is the primary sense here as it has been the dominating concern throughout, and that the gloom of old age will inevitably end in death.

Verse 8 relates to v. 7 by means of the initial *kî*, 'because'. It presents the evaluation of life spoken of in v. 7. Composed of two clauses, we find that each share common features, and so are to be seen as co-ordinates. Both have a temporal reference ('years' and 'days'), qualified by the adverb 'many' (*harbēh*). Of major significance, however, are the two jussive verbs *yiśmaḥ*, 'rejoice', and *yizkôr*, 'remember', the theme-setting verbs for the unit.

The possibility that one might enjoy a long life is the scenario for v. 8a, the precise expression being 'many years' (*šānîm harbēh*). Should that be realized, Qoheleth, by means of the jussive form, insists that one should derive most pleasure from them. We are by now quite familiar with Qoheleth's calls to enjoyment in 2.24; 3.12, 22; 5.17(18); 9.7-9, in each of which the root *śmḥ* plays the central role. In this concluding advice it is entirely fitting that the thought be present again.

The second jussive *yizkôr*, 'remember', is co-ordinated with 'rejoice', the result being that at the same time as one enjoys the life God gives, one should give consideration to the future. Remembrance, in this setting is not oriented to the past, as one might suppose, but to the future (cf. 5.17-19). It calls for the reader to give full consideration, not to what has happened in the past, but to bear in mind the issue he has striven throughout to bring to the fore, namely the inescapable fact that death will come, and that when it does it issues a permanent call (*y*^e^*mē haḥōšek... harbēh yihyû*). So we can better render the verb *zkr* in this context as 'ponder', 'never forget', or 'bear in mind'. The days of one's life may or may not be many, but death is assuredly permanent. For Fox, the fact of death urges us to 'lay hold of the pleasures that will divert our thoughts from death' (1999: 317). This view might carry some weight if the two key verbs, 'rejoice' and 'remember' were in the reverse order. However, it is surely significant that Qoheleth calls first for rejoicing. That is the priority advice. But such joy is to be balanced by the recognition that enjoyment is only to be had in the setting of a life that will ultimately come to a close in death. The call to 'remember' our end is not diversionary but is essential to forming a perspective on life here and now.

We may recognise the fact that death is a perpetual state, but what happens at that point and beyond (*kol šebā'*) is too much for our limited comprehension; it is *hebel*, a source of deep frustration, since we cannot know what lies before us.

11.9-10 Rejoice in Your Youth

Development of Theme A, 'Enjoyment', brings us to the imperative *śᵉmaḥ.* In moving from a jussive to an imperatival form, Qoheleth adds force to the call to enjoy life. We observe initially that v. 9a and v. 9b are parallel calls; this is the significance of the form *wîṭîbᵉkā,* an imperfect with simple *waw,* as the way by which the imperative is continued. As a wisdom instructor providing guidance for the younger generation, Qoheleth refers to his readers as *bāḥûr,* 'young person', literally 'one who is chosen'. Set alongside the term *bᵉtûlāh,* 'young woman' (Deut. 32.25; Isa. 23.4 etc.), it suggests a person in the full flush of youth, and logically so, as Qoheleth is offering advice on choosing a lifestyle. Such a choice is best made during one's youth (*bayyaldûtekā*) so as to establish good patterns of conduct. *Yaldût,* 'youthfulness', is an abstract term, late appearing in BH (only elsewhere in v. 10 and Ps. 110.3) and runs parallel to the phrase *bîmē bᵃḥûrôtekā,* 'in the time of your youth'. It is the time which Qoheleth describes as that in which one can find pleasure (*wîṭîbᵉkā libbᵉkā*). Purely hedonistic pursuits are not what Qoheleth envisages; this is clear from his earlier advice as well as here in the use of *lēb,* 'mind' (cf. also 10.2 etc.). We note again that the temporal phrase, 'in your youth', serves a structural function as well—it concludes the first stichos.

To the call for enjoyment, Qoheleth adds another imperative, *hallēk* (piel), as the first of four supporting injunctions. In urging the youth to 'walk in the ways of your mind' (*hallēk bᵉdarkē libbᵉkā*), we are reminded of Qoheleth's notion that pleasure-seeking is an *intellectual* pursuit, from which flows an appropriate lifestyle (see comments on 9.11-12). A second phrase, 'in the sight of your eyes' (v. 9d) is also associated with the idea of walking 'in the ways of your mind'. The former phrase, *bᵉmarē' 'ēnekā,* was used earlier in 6.9 in contrast to the 'wandering of desires', which was not commended. We presume it urges realism, striving for what is attainable, and is consistent with Qoheleth's pragmatism. The plural form *marē',* 'sight', is not so irregular that it requires emendation.

Divine judgment is correlated directly with one's response to the directives above, according to v. 9e. The imperative *da',* 'know', calls the reader to reflect on the divine attitude to the kind of lifestyle Qoheleth advocates. 'Concerning all these (*'al-kol-'ēlleh*)' we presume relates back to the immediately preceding 'ways' and ‘sights’. Why would God be interested in the way people responded to these imperatives? We can only surmise that it is because Qoheleth regards life and work as a gift from God, and therefore one’s response to that gift is important (cf. 5.17-19). A second reason is that if Qoheleth is exploring the possibility of a *yitrôn* extending beyond the limits of this present existence, then such a future must be predicated on God’s evaluation of our present. Any future ‘reward’ stands or falls upon our present response to God’s major gifts of life and work, and on his justice (cf. 2.24-25).

Two remaining imperatives are located in v. 10 in the form of parallel demands. Each expresses a ‘pruning’ or restrictive action: *ḥāsēr,* ‘remove’ and *haʿᵃbēr,* ‘put away’. Two negative values, *kaʿas,* ‘vexation’ and *rāʿāh,* ‘pain’ (RSV), are to be expunged from one’s mind (*libbekā*) and body (*bᵉśārekā*). Qoheleth has employed *kaʿas* previously (1.18; 2.23; 5.16[17]; 7.3) as that which hinders enjoyment or makes the task of the sage more burdensome. In 5.16(17) it is especially linked with the terms *yôm, ḥôšek,* and *harbēh,* terms which recur in 11.8. We have already drawn attention to the ties between the thoughts expressed in this unit and in 5.16-20(17-21). In many an instance the trials and difficulties conveyed under the terms *kaʿas* and *rāʿāh* are not within our control, and this makes for added problems.

The specific nature of the difficulties envisaged by Qoheleth here requires further exploration. At one level we can appreciate that Qoheleth is stating in negative form what he has presented positively in v. 9; that is to say, enjoyment of life in v. 9 is synonymous with avoiding pain in v. 10. Fox, however, prefers to call their relationship ‘complementary’ rather than synonymous. Yet, in light of comments in 1.18 and 5.16(17) another sense may be suggested, for Qoheleth has given expression to the pain the sage feels when he must give advice to someone trapped by difficult circumstances. On this view, v. 10ab urges the would-be sage to pursue enjoyment of life as God intended, and not to allow life’s darker side to deflect from this.

These cumulative calls to enjoyment are predicated on v. 10c, on the enigmatic nature of human experience, especially during those early adult years (*yaldût wᵉhaššaḥᵃrût*). Those years are crucial to the formation of good habits for living. Recognize early that life is enigmatic, and may be fleeting, but within that understanding pursue a meaningful life as God intended. *Śaḥᵃrût* is found only here in the OT. It presumably describes a stage of life or development similar to 'youth' (*yaldût*).

As in the opening thematic statement, so too this sub-section concludes with the *hebel*-phrase, by which Qoheleth comments on life's ironic dimension.

12.1-8 Remember Your Creator

Development of Theme B, 'remember', brings us to Qoheleth's ultimate advice. An initial imperative clause (12.1a) contains the time phrase *bîmē bᵃḥûrôtekā,* parallel to 11.9. The sub-unit is then broken into three unequal portions by the reiterated *'ad ʾᵃšer lō'* phrase (12.1bc, 2-5, 6-7). In conclusion, the *hebel*-concept rounds off both the unit and the book in 12.8.

An intriguing portion of Qoheleth's total work, 12.1-8 has occasioned a wide range of interpretations. The major issues are two: (1) is Qoheleth speaking of old age or of death; and (2) is 12.2-5 an allegory or some other form of writing? Literature relating to these debates is extensive.

That Qoheleth is discussing the issue of advancing age, being in that state himself, is a view held by numerous scholars including Crenshaw, Gordis, Lauha, Loader, Lohfink, Rankin, Wright, and Zimmerli. However, as Sawyer points out (1975: 523), Qoheleth has shown no interest to date in this problem. Not that it is conclusive proof that he does not now choose to raise the matter, but it would seem that in a final comment it is unlikely that a new topic should enter the discussion. For the interpreter, attention to the thematic statement in 11.7-8 and its contrast between life and death is imperative, not merely for the twin themes of rejoicing and remembering, but also for the focus established there, namely life and death. That theme is picked up in 12.2 which echoes seminal vocabulary from 11.7-8 (e.g. *ḥôšek, šemeš, 'ôr).* Additionally, the verbs in vv. 3-4 speak of activities which have come to an end (*bṭl,* 'cease', *ḥšk,* 'darken', *sgr,* 'shut', *šḥh,* 'weaken?').

The association with death is especially evident in v. 5, the *kî*-clause explaining the preceding presentation. Fox has suggested (1999: 321) that the key to understanding vv. 2-5 is to see them as depicting 'events that occur simultaneously with those of v. 5b which can only be on the day of the funeral'. However, Murphy has noted well that the mourning and funerary theme is specific with v. 5c only. With the theme of brokenness in v. 6, and the explicit statement of v. 7, it would seem beyond doubt that death is the primary subject of these verses. For these reasons the following interpretation will assume that after a brief reference to old age, the differing images in each of the three *ʿad ʾᵃšer lōʾ* sub-divisions all share a common theme, that of death (cf. Leahy, 1952; Witzenrath, 1979: 49; Murphy 1992: 121).

However, before turning to the second question, we should note that Seow (1999: 209-34) has offered another perspective on the passage, building on the suggestion of Fox (1988) that there are eschatological images present in the passage's background. Seow goes on to suggest that the poem is not about old age *per se*, but that it has to do with the end of human life 'in entirely eschatological terms'. The images are of the end of the world, of a cosmic catastrophe. All of the imagery that on the surface seems to reflect the situation faced by an old person, or by people within a society, Seow suggests has another level of meaning, the eschatological. In other words, the imagery of old age is used to point to cosmic doom and 'the end of human existence'. The fact that the poem calls upon the young to reflect and take into account important truths 'before it is too late to do so' would imply that any cosmic upheaval was imminent. But why, all of a sudden, Qoheleth should change from observations and advice directed towards a contemporary world and the universal fate of all in death to hint at some eschatological and cosmic end is difficult to explain and accept.

With regard to the second question, whether 12.2-5 is allegorical or of some other form of writing, the evidence is less clear, and most scholars are cognizant of this. An allegorical interpretation cannot be applied consistently throughout (see Sawyer, 1975: 519; Gordis, 1968: 338; Seow 1997: 372, Krüger, 2002: 199 etc.), and textual problems in vv. 4-5 add to the interpreter's difficulty. While an allegorical approach seems appropriate on occasion, such as 12.3, an allusion to the decline of physical strength, it cannot be applied in v. 5. That the terms in vv. 3ff. are related to an approaching thunder-storm which terrorizes a community, figuring the hour of death, is another view (Leahy, 1952: 299; also Ginsberg, Plumptre). For Gordis, the decline of a wealthy estate is the thought lying behind many of the terms used.

Against the allegorical interpretation is that of Sawyer, who prefers the word 'parable', and who believes 12.1-8 to refer to a house falling into ruin. Support for his view he draws from Proverbs 9, Job 27 and Matthew 7. However, this view is rejected by many other scholars who note that even Sawyer was not able to apply his approach consistently. His contribution was to highlight the tension between the allegorical and more literal parts of the text.

Given the difficulties in each of the above approaches, the following interpretation will recognize that there is present in the passage a variety of images, and that it is not possible to apply consistently any one view of its literary nature. We shall assume that there is a single theme—death—binding the material together. Thus, in trifold form Qoheleth urges readers to 'remember' before death closes the door on life.

12.1 Addressing the younger generation again, this second imperative *z^e^kôr,* 'remember', calls for reflection on *'et bôr'ekā*. In the OT generally, remembrance is an attempt to link the past with the present and future; no mere recollection of the past, it is a dynamic concept, appropriating the past into one's present (see Eising, *TDOT* IV: 64-82). Enjoyment of life is not to be divorced from reflection on its end in death. However, we note that in this verse the object of consideration is 'your creator' (*bôr'ekā*). Though a plural form, this is not unusual (see Job 3 5. 10; Ps. 149.2). Some would wish to emend to *bôr^e^kā,* 'your pit/ grave' (cf. Scott *et al.*), and others have suggested *b^e^rû'^e^kā,* 'your health', but no textual tradition supports these changes. Nevertheless, Crenshaw argues that reference to God as creator ill befits the context, and so he suggests that Qoheleth is calling for young people 'to reflect on the joys of female companionship before old age and death render one incapable of sensual pleasure' (1987: 185). In wisdom literature generally we find that the deity may be referred to as the Creator (Job 38ff., Prov., 20.12; 22.2) and Zimmerli has argued cogently that creation is the foundational concept in wisdom's theological perspective. Creation and death, the two extremities of existence, are bound together in Qoheleth's final comments.

The temporal phrase *bîmē-b^e^ḥûrôtekā* links us back directly with 11.9. The structural role which the phrase plays in expanding the two themes has been noted above. Qoheleth counsels the would-be sage to commence early and develop a life-style in which God as creator and sustainer is central.

Establishing this perspective on life 'before the evil days come' (*'ad '^a^šer lō' yabō'û y^e^mē-hārā'āh*) is commended. Here we encounter the first of the *'ad '^a^šer lō'* phrases Qoheleth uses to construct his argument. The phrase itself describes 'time until', hence 'before'. The concept 'evil days' requires further explication. From the context we note that *ṭôb* in 11.7 speaks of earthly life, so by implication *ra'* links with death. Secondly, the thematic jussive *yizkôr* in 11.8b is associated with 'days of darkness' and we may assume that *y*^{e}*mē-hārā'āh* is parallel. While Qoheleth generally uses *rā'āh* in descriptions of calamitous situations in society or in individual lives, so the phrase *y*^{e}*mē-hārā'āh* refers in a general way to the breaking in of any calamity. In this context it portrays the major problem concerning Qoheleth, death. 'Evil days' or better, 'a time of calamity', is Qoheleth's way of speaking of the shadowy existence one enters at that point. When we recall that this writer has already reminded us that our demise may come at any moment (e.g. 9.11-12), that it is not confined to the old, then it is clear that old age is not the focus issue in this section, but rather it is the end of human life whenever that might come.

Qoheleth calls the young reader to establish quickly the direction his/her life will take, for when death enters, it is already too late to give thought to it. Hence there is a note of urgency in the call.

Co-ordinated terms, 'days' and 'years', in the thematic verses recur in 12.1. 'Years' (*šānîm*) in 12.1c are similar to the 'days' of v. 1b, the link being made through the parallel ideas *yabō'û,* 'come' and *higgî'û,* 'approach'. Post-death concepts picture the individual as having lost all vibrance and vitality. In Qoheleth's terms, during this time (*šānîm*) one can expect no *ḥēpeṣ* (3.1, 17; 5.3, 7; 8.6). Use of the term *ḥēpeṣ* in other contexts helps us to set its meaning here. To translate it as 'pleasure' (RSV) makes for easy misunderstanding. In 3.1 *ḥēpeṣ* denotes 'thing, matter', and has a special connection with time, with the appropriateness of an action for the occasion. An inappropriate act is one which deviates from the divine pleasure (5.3[4]). Bringing these ideas together leads to a translation as follows: 'there is no acceptable time for me in them', that is to say, 'it is too late to do anything now'. This sees the phrase as a confession of lost opportunity. An alternative view is to preserve the 'days' and 'years' as equally referring to the after-life, and the quotation *'ēn-lî bāhem ḥēpeṣ* as describing that time as having nothing attractive to offer.

12.2 The second *'ad '*^{a}*šer lō'* phrase brings us to the longest of the temporal passages setting the time frame for 'remembering'. It is marked by the need for haste in decision making. The best time to make it is 'before the sun darkens' (*'ad '*^{a}*šer lō' teḥšak* *haššemeš*). We have noted above that interpretation of this passage is debated, but that we shall assume it is referring to death, not to old age nor to climate change as some have proposed.

The link with 11.8b is abundantly evident, as is the vocabulary of 'light' and 'sun' with 11.7, and this is one basis for our view that here the issues are life and death. In 12.2 four nouns describe life: 'sun', 'moon', 'light', 'stars'. Extinction of these would plunge the world into darkness, symbolic of death's arrival (cf. Mt. 24.29ff.). Again we have the theme of remembering before it is too late to do anything about it.

The second half of v. 2 is less easily determined, for the images of cloud and rain seem not directly related to v. 2a. It is the verb *šûb* whose meaning is crucial to the interpretation. Already in 11.3 Qoheleth has spoken of clouds (*'ābîm*) as signs of impending precipitation (*gešem*). Here the matter is slightly different, for the rain has come and gone. The question then is, what are the clouds doing when they *šûb*? For Fredericks (1991) the clouds 'return' and so signal 'a certain despair'. But do they return in the sense of 'reappear', as most commentators suggest? If so, does their return have the effect of blotting out sun and warmth? Or do they simply 'turn away', going back whence they came? Objectively setting the meaning of the verb is far from easy. Yet, even if we determine that the clouds reappear after the rain, that is, bringing more rain, we still must evaluate what happens: is it a benefit, or not? Likewise, if the clouds return whence they came, is that detrimental or not? Seow, following Scott (1949), argued that the preposition 'after' (*'aḥar*) here carries the sense of 'with' rather than having a temporal sense, so that the clouds return 'with the rain'. That view he has since modified (1999: 212, note 17), accepting the more traditional view that it means 'after the rain'. However, we are still puzzled by the verb 'return' as used in this context. Perhaps all we can safely say is that there has been rain and the weather has changed. It is the point of transition, which in v. 2a is the passing to death/darkness which Qoheleth emphasizes. Each of the time locators in vv. 1, 2, 6 focuses upon the moment beyond which a desired course of action becomes impossible, thus urging the young reader to all speed in making his decision. The precise content of v. 2b seems now irrecoverable, beyond seeing it as marking a point of transition.

12.3-5 The introductory phrase, 'in the day when...' (*bayyôm še...*), and its following clauses suggest a separate sub-unit. The independence of this unit and its structure have received much attention (cf. e.g. Sawyer, 1975: 524-25), yet the interpretation of its component parts and general theme is still debated.

Formally, we divide this sub-section into a series of six phrases in which four perfect verbs with prefixed *waw* follow an introductory imperfect, *yāzuʿû*, 'tremble'. In the final phrase we meet an adverbial clause with an infinitive construct. There follows a series of imperfect verbs with prefixed *waw,* and the unit is rounded off with a motive clause (v. 5c) prefaced by *kî*, 'because'. The significance of this verbal pattern, according to Sawyer (p. 524), is that it allows a contrast to be drawn between the degeneration of the human body and the indifference of nature to an individual's demise. Before reaching any conclusions, no matter how tentative, about the meaning of this section, let us turn to the text.

12.3 Qoheleth has urged 'remembrance' upon the youthful reader as something to be done 'before the darkness of death overtakes one' (v. 2). The temporal phrase with which v. 3 commences must be related to the preceding *'ad 'ᵃšer lō'* phrase and bear similar reference. Although on the surface it appears that vv. 3-5 are formally distinct from the preceding, it can hardly be so divorced in meaning. That will be our supposition in what follows. Thus 'before darkness descends' is equivalent to 'on the day when ...' The initial pair of sentences (vv. 3a, b) appear to run parallel in sense, as is suggested by the similarity of their verbs (*zwʿ*, 'tremble', and *ʿwh,* 'bent') as well as their subjects, *šōmᵉrē-habbayit,* 'keepers of the house', and *'anše-heḥāyil,* 'men of strength'. 'Trembling' and 'being bent over' are expressed using imperfect verbal forms and their equivalent following the pattern of the preceding imperfect *teḥšak,* 'become dark' (v. 2a). The description here is of a situation not yet realized. Diminished powers are the thought conveyed by these verbs; but are they typical of old age as the Talmud would have it, of a declining estate, or some other situation? Are the 'keepers of the house' and 'men of strength' allegorical references to one's arms and legs? Bearing in mind that wisdom material is generally couched in non-specific language, we see here a portrayal of several possible and related conditions. There is no contextual evidence permitting an exclusive interpretation. The strong are bent and the custodians of a house quake, whether in fear or for other reasons is a mystery. However, the tasks they should perform are not done. This is about as far as our interpretation can legitimately go; speculating about the reasons why the strong are bent, for example, goes beyond what the text says. Qoheleth's underlying principle in the various images used is to assert that one should remember the Creator before reaching that stage or time when one can no longer do so.

That 'before it is too late'-theme runs through into v. 3c, d, where again we note two verbs, 'cease' (*bṭl*) and 'darken' (*ḥšk*), in which the thought is of activity completed. As these phrases are also bound to the initial *bayyōm še...*, Qoheleth is once more urging reflection on the issue before it is too late to act upon it. On this occasion the terms 'grinders' (*ṭōḥ*^{a}*nōṭ*) and 'seers/eyes' (*rō'ōt*) are participial forms, as was 'keepers' (*šōm*^{e}*rē*) in v. 3a. Whether they describe those who grind, or peer out at the world, or speak literally of the teeth and eyes themselves, is again a question the answer to which depends upon our initial reading of the text as allegory, literal description, or 'parable'. Perhaps deliberately, Qoheleth uses terms which serve only to indicate that certain basic human functions will have ceased 'on that day'. Verse 3c adds a motive clause which states that grinders have ceased 'because they have become so few' (*kî mi'ēṭû*). Again degeneration to a point where activity ceases seems to be the thrust of the image. In v. 3d, *ba'*^{a}*rubbôt* is the word for an aperture or opening, perhaps a window through which one looks out at the world (cf. Gen. 7.11; Hos. 13.3; Isa. 60.8). The verb *ḥšk* speaks of darkness having fallen; therefore nothing can be seen.

12.4 Locked doors no longer opening onto the street is the image used in v. 4a. The dual form *d*^{e}*lātayim* points to double doors, while most houses apparently had only single panel doors. Seow suggests that the dual form may refer to the city gates, but Fox also notes that some houses had double doors (Josh 2.19). The doors (*d*^{e}*lātayim*) have been shut (*suggar,* pual). That a house opening onto the *šûq*—the modern Arab equivalent, the *sûq*, is the crowded bazaar where activity seems frantic and incessant—would be closed is suggestive of some special circumstance. For Fox, it is closed for the funeral he suggests as the overall context for the passage. Whybray suggests they are closed perhaps because of a storm (see his views on v. 2), or because normal household activity has ceased. Crenshaw sees it as the deterioration of a building. Normally the hub of life in an eastern city (like the night markets of Asia), the doors have been closed 'against the bazaar' (*baššûq*). In our view, the imagery here is a poetic representation of death, of a closing off against the throb of life, and as such it is a most expressive picture.

This reading of the text of v. 4a differs from the allegorical interpretation, but one should note that those who choose the allegorical approach do not agree about the symbolic meaning of 'doors'. Is it 'feet' (Targum), 'lips' (e.g. Ewald), 'eyes' (Hengstenberg), or 'ears' (Wildboer)? The dual form *d*^{e}*lātayim* could apply to all four, or to none.

In v. 4b a slightly differing form of presentation from the previous five cameos is used. It features an infinitive construct (*š*^{e}*pal*) with the preposition *b*^{e} to express a temporal sense. The root *špl*, 'become low, abased', may be seen as part of the deterioration theme. The implication is that the moment of decline has come. What has declined is the 'sound of the mill' (*qōl haṭṭaḥ*^{a}*nāh*). Its silence could result from one of several factors, but unmistakable is the fact that no grinding of flour or other grain is being done. Domestic life, food preparation for the household, has come to a halt.

At this point in v. 4 Qoheleth moves from primarily perfect consecutive verb forms to imperfects with *waw* conjunction. Sawyer argues that this grammatical shift hints at a new emphasis, that nature is now the focus of attention. Fading sounds of human activity are replaced by the incessant sounds of nature.

A basic question with regard to v. 4cd has to do with its subject. The RSV renders '*one* rises up', and commentators who opt for an allegorical approach to these verses would interpret 'one' as the aged person. That such a person would 'rise up' at the sound of the birds (*l*^{e}*qôl haṣṣippôr*) is generally agreed to be its meaning, but this creates a possible inconsistency. The degenerating person is not likely to be rejuvenated by the chirping of a bird. The verb *qûm* suggests an awakening, and is in stark contrast to the verbs of v. 4ab where attention is focused on the degeneration of certain functions. Alternatively, the subject of the verb 'rises' is the sound made by the birds (Seow) in contrast to the declining sound of the mill.

No explanation or translation of v. 4b has found consensus among scholars, making any interpretation problematic. One possible solution that we find attractive is that Qoheleth has been urging the young person to give early thought to the Creator and to a wise lifestyle (v. 1). So in this long second 'before'-clause beginning in v. 2, getting up early when the birds begin to sing may serve as yet another image for youthfulness. By contrast, v. 4d comments that the song birds, literally 'all the daughters of song' (*kol-b*^{e}*nōt-haššîr*), are silenced (*yiššāḥû*), suggesting death. The phrase 'daughters of song' stands parallel to the term 'birds' and so may be synonymous, giving two quite contrasting activities, the one rising and the other falling. The rare verb *šāḥāh* occurs in this sense in Isa. 29.4 (note also the parallel verb *špl* as in our verse here). The contrast between the two phrases in v. 4cd is further indicated by the assonance *qôl*/*kol*. As for the unusual phrase 'daughters of song', there are examples of the word *bt* being applied to birds (see Job 30.29). Thus the birds have ended their song, presumably because they have died. Fox, on the other hand, has suggested that the 'daughters of song' are professional mourners, related to the funeral context he sees throughout, while Crenshaw views them as possibly dancers or entertainers. It is obvious that there can be no agreement as to the verse's meaning.

12.5 A further example of Qoheleth's present theme is introduced in v. 5 by the initial *gam*, 'also'. According to Sawyer the subject of the verb here is the birds of v. 4d (so also Seow). However, given the sudden change of imagery throughout this section, that conclusion is far from certain. Others have continued with the view that old age is the background concept and so believe that old people are afraid of heights (so Crenshaw, for example) Perhaps Qoheleth's generalized expression should be mirrored in our interpretation.

According to the RSV and the versions, the text reads *yārē'*, 'fear', though the LXX *opsontai* indicates a reading *rā'āh*, 'see'. If this is the correct reading, then the suggestion appears to be that the birds look down from a height (*miggābōah*) to espy the dangers and terrors (*ḥatḥattîm*) on the road. Grammatically, this translation has more to commend it than the RSV, though its meaning is also difficult to establish, especially if v. 4d speaks about death under the image of the birds being silenced. Fox, on the other hand retains the view that the verb here is 'fear' and speaks of the emotional outpourings 'compounded of misery and fear' by those songstresses who are part of the funeral procession.

It may be best to regard v. 5a as yet another independent example of Qoheleth's theme of death. Murphy sees the theme here as that of an aged person who is unsteady on his feet and so keeps to his room. Whybray also links the thought with an old person's fear of heights and steep slopes, as well as of imaginary obstacles on the road. The 'terrors on the road' (*ḥatḥattîm badderek*) is clearly where the emphasis of the verse resides, so it is vital that we ascertain its meaning. Not only here, but also in the rest of v. 5, there is a direct connection with the *kî*-clause at the end. This implies that each clause in the verse speaks about death. From this perspective, the terrors are akin to the 'evil days' of v. 1, portraying the prospect of death at the end. The plural *ḥatḥattîm* indicates that death and ruin are common obstacles (cf. Prov. 10.14).

There follow yet three other examples from nature, each speaking about a changed status. In the first, the almond tree (*šāqēd*) puts forth blossoms (*n'ṣ*); cf. Num. 17.8. That here we are dealing with a symbol of resuscitating nature is the view of Buzy, Glasser and Sawyer—almonds blossom, locusts eat their fill, and berries burst with juices. Numerous ancient versions hint that the original text read *yānēṣ,* from the root *nṣṣ*. This points to an original 'be reviled' and a possible translation, 'he will despise...'. One view based on this reading is that in old age one is unable to eat the almond nut, or more generally with Crenshaw, that old people have trouble digesting their food.

In seeking an acceptable exegesis of v. 5, we hold to the fact that the concluding motive clause asserts that death has come. The preceding clauses must together provide the evidence for such a finale. With this as our starting point, the almond, which blossoms in the winter, perhaps symbolizes the dormant season. On an allegorical reading its blossoms symbolize the white hair of the aged. The grasshopper (*ḥāgāb*) is symbolic throughout the OT for destruction, as they come in plague proportions and with devastation (cf. Joel 1.4). The hithpael *yistabbēl* means 'to become a burden', or even, 'bear its own load' (Gen. 49.15), suggesting that we have here an allusion to the burden of loss brought about by these creatures. Seow, however, argues that the term *ḥāgāb* may refer to a plant called 'locust', and speaks of it as drooping, a situation similar to that of the almond. As for the third example, *w^{e}tāpēr hā'^{a}biyyōnāh,* 'desire fails' (RSV), again we face difficulties though some have seen in this a reference to the declining sexual energy of the old. *'^{a}biyyōnāh,* a *hapax legomenon,* may mean 'desire', from the root *'bh,* or refer to the caper-berry (BDB: 2-3). Even if we are unable to resolve this problem, the verb *prr,* 'break', 'frustrate', indicates that the situation or subject is effete (cf. 2 Sam. 15.34). Again, death is the allusion. Allowing the motive clause to function as the controlling exegetical device enables us to draw out the sense of this verse.

The concluding motive clause, as was suggested above, undergirds the entire section vv. 3-5, which means that we are dealing throughout with the matter of death. The motive clause itself consists of two elements, the first picturing humankind's progress towards an 'eternal home' (*bēt-ʿôlāmô*). The nature of the participle *hōlēk* is that it describes an on-going action; thus humankind's progress is always towards that final goal, the grave (9.3). Its second element speaks of the company of mourners (*sōp^{e}dîm*) walking about in the streets (*šûq*;.cf. v. 4a) of the city. The return to a perfect consecutive form (*w^{e}sāb^{e}bû*) links us back to the verbs of vv. 3-4a, as well as indicating an imperfect equivalent. The sense is that mourners are a frequent and common sight in the streets; they are tangible reminders that death has once more visited the community.

12.6-7 The third 'time-before-which' sub-unit (cf. vv. 1, 2), imposes yet other limits upon the task of remembering.

A group of six phrases lends weight to the single thought threading its way through these illustrations, that of brokenness, of having come to the end of a useful life. Gilbert points out (p. 106) that the six elements are in orderly arrangement, such that 'silver' and 'gold', 'pitcher' and 'wheel', 'dust' and 'spirit' each form a natural pair. This is purely a stylistic device. He also draws attention to the repetition in the vocabulary—*rṣṣ, gll*, (v. 6ab), *ʿal, ʾel* (vv. 6b, 7a), *šûb* (v. 7a, b)—devices which serve to bind the verses together. However, the question for our interpretation is whether, in the case of the paired terms, we are to see them as three examples or simply as a series of six different and only marginally related examples. That is to say, is the bowl suspended on the cord? Is the pitcher tied to a cord that runs through the pulley wheel? Are 'dust' and 'spirit' more or less synonymous? The view we shall take is that we are dealing with six different examples that are arranged in pairs because of their similarity, rather than as three integrated illustrations.

12.6 Qoheleth hopes the young reader will remember, call something to mind, 'before the silver cord breaks' (*yērāḥēq ḥebel-hakkesep)* and 'before the golden bowl is broken' (*tāruṣ gullat-hazzāhāb*). The semantic and structural similarity of these two phrases is clear. *Yērāḥēq* is a piel imperfect portraying separation, the breaking of a rope (*ḥebel*) by which something is suspended. In the second clause, *taruṣ* depicts the shattering of a bowl (*gullāh*). By means of these verbs Qoheleth indicates clearly that two precious objects, a silver cord and a golden bowl, have been rendered useless. Commentators have discussed the meaning of *gullāh* at some length—is it a 'bowl' (1 Kgs *7.41-42)* or 'reservoir' (Zech. 4.2-3) or even a 'counterweight' (Gordis: 348)? Perhaps it refers to the oil container of a lampstand (Seow). It does seem unlikely that a counterweight would be made of silver, unless by chance Qoheleth is instead thinking of a necklace as some suggest; there is also a question as to whether a golden bowl could be broken in the sense of 'smashed', as the metal is quite soft, so 'crushed' might be the better rendering. This kind of speculation is actually of little relevance, for the emphasis in the text seems to be confined to two elements: (1) a valuable or useful object is (2) broken beyond all usefulness. These two objects, the cord that has snapped and the bowl that is crushed, symbolize the awful impact of death as a state from which there is no repair, and so serve to dramatize the call to 'remember' before death comes.

The theme of shattered objects continues into v. 6c with two further examples. The verb *šbr* in the niphal imperfect envisages a vessel (*kad*) lying in pieces beside the fountain (*mabbûa'*, cf. Isa. 35.7), no longer of use in drawing water. Similarly, the object described as a *galgal* no longer functions; consequently the water in the pit (*bōr*) or cistern cannot be raised. The *galgal*, usually rendered as 'wheel' (RSV) or pulley, more likely refers to a type of container (so Dahood, Fox and Seow). Each example is of an object of some practical value that can no longer serve its purpose because it lies broken. As analogies of human life ending in the 'brokenness' of death, each is potent, and more so in combination. Do not wait until death makes remembering your Creator (v. 1) impossible, is Qoheleth's solemn warning.

12.7 Continuing the call to 'remember', Qoheleth now supplies an even clearer reference to death as the incentive for following his advice. He speaks of 'dust' (*'āpār*) returning to the earth, and of the human spirit/breath (*rûaḥ*) finding its way back to the Creator who gave it. The thought is a direct allusion to Gen. 2-3 (cf. Ps. 146.4). God's creature, made from dust and enlivened with God's breath, will return whence it came. Before that moment arrives, it is vital that one give serious consideration to the Creator.

So we reach the end of the concluding advice which Qoheleth offers. Enjoyment of life, as defined by Qoheleth, is his constant theme, made the more urgent in this scenario because of the fact that death might intrude at any moment, robbing the young of their chance to establish their life-style in accordance with wisdom's guidelines. The two themes represented in the verbs *śmḥ* and *zkr* summarize those guidelines. In 9.1-16 he has underscored wisdom's supreme value, qualified it by pointing to its vulnerability (9.17-10.20) and limitations (11.1-6). Life under the shadow of death is for our enjoyment, and this thought is the 'silver cord' which binds the total work together. Additionally, by suggesting that at death the human spirit/breath returns to God, Qoheleth is again theorizing on the post-death possibility of *yitrôn*. Reversing the process of original creation would seem to imply that Qoheleth reasons that death will not separate us from God; rather, at that moment we return to his presence. Though the term *yitrôn* is not cited, this return to God is fundamental to Qoheleth's hope for the future.

12.8 The curtain falls on Qoheleth's dissertation in the same manner as it opened in 1.2, with a chorus line—the *h*^{a}*bēl h*^{a}*bālîm* phrase. It is the literary inclusion which frames the entire work, though the 12.8 version is shorter than that of 1.2, lacking the duplicated phrase of the initial example. This phrase summarizes a most realistic appraisal of the human experience, for the world in which we live is so deeply enigmatic. Despite this fact, Qoheleth has demonstrated in 1.3-12.7 his own affirmative approach to life in this kind of world, and the enjoyment theme is the medium for that.

The notion that *hebel* equals 'vanity' and that it is a catchword for a pessimistic view of the world is a long way from the truth as we have seen it. Qoheleth would have us recognize the enigmas and frustrations of the human experience, but at the same time calls for one to grasp life as a divine gift and enjoy it in all its mystery. Only this honest and theological approach qualifies as the truly sagacious one, and he urges it wholeheartedly on all who will hear.

12.9-14 In Conclusion

The peculiar features of 12.9-14 have long been an object of scholarly interest, for they move from first-person address by Qoheleth to third-person reference about him (esp. vv. 9, 10). There is a general consensus among scholars that these verses are from the hand of an Editor or Editors. However, Seow (1998) has argued that vv. 9-13a belong to the original work being 'in complete harmony with the rest of the book'. Some scholars have additionally alleged that there are some novel thoughts introduced in vv. 13, 14, by which is usually meant that an orthodox addition has sought to bring Qoheleth's work into line with acceptable religious attitudes (e.g. Lauha). There have also been attempts to link the Epilogue with the wider sapiential tradition of Sirach and Proverbs (cf. Sheppard, 1977, and Wilson, 1984).

Our analysis will begin with the broad division of the Epilogue into two sub-sections, both introduced by *w^e^yōtēr*—that is vv. 9-11 and vv. 12-14—then examine their peculiarities and implications for our understanding of the relationship between the Epilogue and the main body of the work.

The division of vv. 9-14 into two sub-sections is based upon the following literary evidence:

1. The use of *w^e^yōtēr* to head vv. 9 and 12. The term *yōtēr* elsewhere (6.8, 11. 7.11, 16) is from the same root stock as *yitrôn*, one of the key terms in Qoheleth's vocabulary. Here we suggest a translation, 'something additional', in keeping with Mishnaic usage. It serves to mark two addenda to Qoheleth's work.

2. Verses 9-11 speak about Qoheleth in the third person, and respect his learning and role in the wisdom community. Verses 12-14 are imperatival, concluding with two motive clauses typical of admonitory material.

3. *Dibrē* in vv. 9-11, used three times, refers to wisdom material including that of Qoheleth, while *dabar* in v. 13 carries the general meaning, 'matter'.

4. Qoheleth and his contribution are the theme of vv. 9-11; vv. 12-14 address the faithful, their search for wisdom, and tender advice on how and why one should aspire to wisdom.

Thus we may conclude that these two appended notes stem from another author(s). Their purpose is to commend Qoheleth's work to a wider audience. We cannot know whether 1.1, the Superscription, is added by this Editor or not, or whether it predates him.

12.9 If we are satisfied that 12.9-14 is an editorial postlude, then we may presume that the term *yōtēr* is the means by which these additions have been signalled. The Mishnaic meaning is that of something additional (cf. 1 Sam. 15.15). The introductory *w^e^yōtēr* can be a noun, 'an addition', or adverb, 'in addition, additionally'. The relative *š^e^* which follows introduces the editorial note regarding Qoheleth.

Verse 9a affirms that Qoheleth was a sage (*ḥākām*). It is an objective assessment by a third person that what Qoheleth was striving to do and be (cf. chs. 1-2) was evidence of his standing in the community of wise men. Furthermore, he was a popular teacher (*limmad... 'et-hā'ām*). This statement was prefaced with the adverb *'ôd*, here probably with the meaning 'constantly', indicating the persistence or regularity with which he taught. 'Knowledge' *(da'at)* correlates with Qoheleth's qualification as a *ḥākām*. The conjoining of three piel verb forms, *'izzēn, ḥiqqēr, tiqqēn,* in v. 9b is a rhetorically powerful way to amplify the preceding general description of Qoheleth's work, highlighting the care and diligence with which it was undertaken. Important information about aspects of the process whereby the tradition was preserved and handed on lies within these three verbs: *'zn* links with the Arabic *wazan,* 'to weigh' (BDB: 24; Gordis, Whybray etc.), often descriptive of the measuring or scanning process in poetry. However, as Whitley (1979) has noted, the verb should be understood as 'listened to' (so also Fox and Seow). The verb *ḥqr,* 'search out' (it occurs as a piel only in this instance) portrays the examining of life situations and the gathering together of like sayings; *tqn* is a verb Qoheleth himself has employed in 1.15 and 7.13, though it appears to have a different nuance, that of making straight. In this editorial example it means 'to order, arrange', pointing to the editorial process we know from other collections of proverbial material (e.g. Prov. 22.17—23.11). Here then we meet the sage as preserver, teacher, and transmitter of wisdom.

The RSV'S 'with great care' is an attempt to render the adverb *harbēh.* However, it would seem from other instances of its use, for example v. 12 (*s^epārîm harbēh*), that the word *harbēh* is an adjective qualifying *m^ešālîm,* thus 'many proverbs' is the correct translation. The proverbs spoken of may be restricted to Qoheleth's own work, though there is some evidence (cf. Wilson, 1984) that his could well include the canonical book of Proverbs.

12.10 Quoting from Qoheleth's own autobiography (7.25ff.), the editor comments on Qoheleth's search (*bqš*) 'to find words of pleasure' (*dibrē-ḥēpeṣ*). Rendering *ḥēpeṣ* as 'pleasure' is consistent with Qoheleth's own usage (5.3). 'Words of pleasure' connotes sayings, proverbs, and the like which are both elegant in form (Barton: 199) as well as able to convey deep and satisfying meaning. We encounter a slight textual difficulty with the passive participle *w^ekātûb.* Manuscript evidence varies, indicating the textual problem to be an early one. Emendation seems in order (though see Lohfink: 86), but in what direction is not easily determined. Whether it should be an infinitive construct *liktôb* similar to the form *limṣō'*, or whether it is qal perfect *kātab*, must for the time being rest on subjective judgments. However, it is transparently clear that the editor is at pains to show that what Qoheleth struggled to do, he did successfully: he was able to draw honest and worthy (*yōšer*) conclusions, which justify their being called 'words of truth' (*dibrē-'ᵉmet*), which is to say, advice that could be trusted and was deserving of acceptance.

12.11 A more general statement about sapiential writing (*dibrē-ḥᵃkāmîm*) includes all that Qoheleth had to say, but is also wider in its embrace. What it does is to dispel all doubt that Qoheleth is a recognized figure within Wisdom circles. Although 'words of pleasure' were sought (v. 10), in actual fact there was always something uncomfortable about wisdom sayings, for they confronted reality without shrinking from dealing with life's darker side. Thus the message which Qoheleth so often laboured—that a given situation was an enigma (*hebel*)—is supported by the Editor's expression that the sage's words were akin to goads (*kaddor bōnôt*). Common in Aramaic, this latter term derives from an Arabic root describing the prodding or goading of cattle. The goad is a painful but necessary tool for direction and instruction. Parallel with this is a second simile, *kᵉmaśmᵉrôt nᵉṭû'îm*, 'like nails secured', duplicating the observation that sometimes true wisdom and insight are gained only via a relatively painful process, the crucible of life. While *nt'* regularly applies to 'planting', it may also describe the driving of tent pegs into the ground (Dan. 11.45).

The second phrase is in chiastic relationship to v. 11a, thus the unusual term *ba'ᵃlē 'ᵃsuppôt*, a *hapax legomenon*, is synonymous with *dibrē-ḥᵃkāmîm*. This provides some guide for our interpretation, though it does not mean that the term is any the less obscure in itself. *Ba'al*, 'master', may also denote one who participates in an activity, thus 'one of...' a group (see Wilson: 176). The process of collating materials lies within the root *'sp*, so here the rare word *'ᵃsuppôt* (in Neh. 12.25; 1 Chron. 26.15, 17 it occurs as masculine) speaks of a gathering, whether of sages (Delitzsch, Barton etc.) or of their distilled wisdom (Fox), is not obvious.

The niphal perfect *nittᵉnû*, 'were given' requires a subject. We presume it is 'the sayings of the wise', the accumulated proverbs mentioned in v. 12b. By associating this entire process with 'one shepherd' (*rō'eh 'eḥād*) we are prompted to seek his identity. Is it Qoheleth? Solomon? God? Most scholars would opine that it is

God who is in mind here (cf. Barton, Gordis, Plumptre, Zimmerli etc.). On this reading our Editor appears to be making some important comments about the process of inspiration, claiming that the observation-reflection method typical of the sage and philosopher qualifies as a method by which the divine will and purpose may be ascertained. This then gives the sage's words an authority as revelation, as scripture (cf. Jer. 18.18). However, Fox has argued cogently that the phrase 'one shepherd' simply refers to any person who is actually a shepherd. The shepherd is a real shepherd just as the goads are real goads.

12.12-14 A second postscript also is introduced by *w^e^yōtēr* (cf. v. 9). Its main features are a series of imperative verbs in vv. 12a, 13ab, and a change of subject from observations about Qoheleth and the sages, to advice to a young reader on a wise person's duty before God. Whether this section is the work of yet another sub-editor (so Galling: 124-25; Zimmerli: 250 etc.), or from the same hand as penned vv. 9-11, is impossible to determine conclusively.

12.12 If our view is correct that *w^e^yōtēr* is an editorial marker, then we may render this verse as: 'P.S. From these things, my son, be instructed...' ' The phrase *mēhēmmāh* signals the preceding v. 11, that is, what Qoheleth and sages like him have taught. The phrase may also be understood as 'beyond these things...' warning the student in a formulaic conclusion that it is not necessary to go beyond the advice contained in the document to which the warning is attached. It speaks of the adequacy of the advice contained within.

Addressing the reader as 'my son', we note that the Editor chooses a form of speech not used at all by Qoheleth. The Editor is commending Qoheleth's work to his own students. The imperative (niphal) *hizzāhēr* carries overtones of admonition and warning, but is nevertheless a call to learn from the experience and reflection embodied in the tradition. It occurs in 4.13 in the sense of instruction which can make the foolish king wise—it has powerful transforming effect, and is not simply some additional information which will add to one's wisdom.

What is it that this footnote seeks to convey? Tone of voice and nuance cannot be easily represented in written form, and here in v. 12bc we have a classic example of the interpreter's dilemma. The infinitive absolute, *'^a^śôt*, carries a nominal sense, 'the composing of...' Our postscript offers the truism that gathering proverbs into a collection, or doing as Qoheleth has done and expressing in written form his years of observation and reflection on the human condition, is an endless task (*'ēn qēṣ*). Not only the multi-faceted nature of human experience, but also changing social and historical conditions, the growth of knowledge, all require constant reflection and assessment. Furthermore, each generation, each individual, must come to terms with life for himself/herself. Is this comment from our Editor intended to convey something negative, that the task of thinking and writing is tedious and ultimately of little value? Does he imply that what Qoheleth wrote falls into this category, that perhaps we might well be better off without this extra document? Surely not! He is advising the student that what Qoheleth has done is the same endeavour that any who would be wise must undertake for themselves. True, there is a warning here, but it is a warning that pure wisdom comes only at the end of an arduous, demanding, all consuming search. *Lahag,* a late noun, describes such dedication to a task, here probably with the narrower focus of devotion to the life and work of a sage. The term *harbēh,* 'much', again underscores the extent of the task ahead, for it is physically and mentally exhausting (*yᵉgiʿat bāśār).* Qoheleth has already given evidence of this aspect of the work in chs. 1-2, and our Editor presents it in stark terms for his young readers to ponder. Wisdom is not to be sought lightly.

On this interpretation, v. 12 is certainly not a warning to avoid the writing of more books and endless study, as some have proposed (cf. Gordis, Lohfink etc.); nor is it a warning against reading literature from other religious traditions (so Barton), nor even a warning to Qoheleth to moderate his views (as Rankin). Crenshaw's suggestion (1987: 191) that it is a 'warning against an open attitude towards the canon' seems to extend the warning far beyond the immediate context. It is, on the contrary, a solemn counsel to any who would follow the sage that such a decision calls for a sincere commitment to an endless and all-consuming task. There can be no turning back.

12.13 In a final note *(sôp dābār),* the Editor comments that 'all is heard' (*hakkōl nišmaʿ*), meaning that there is only one further thing to say by way of conclusion. As in v. 12, we note here two imperatives, *Yᵉrā',* and *šᵉmôr,* calls to fear God and keep his commands. This is, of course, advice which is fully consonant with orthodoxy, though never are the two phrases brought together as here except in Sirach (cf. Sir. 1.25-26). Our interpretation has suggested that despite deep questioning, Qoheleth has never cast doubt on the fundamental tenets of Israelite faith and practice (cf. ch. 5). The editorial comment reminds the reader again of those basic principles which undergird Israelite faith and wisdom. Verse 13 calls the reader to fear God, not Yahweh as in Proverbs. This preference for 'God' rather than the divine name is consistent with Qoheleth's usage throughout.

The motive clause upon which this demand is grounded is the highly condensed idiom *kî zeh kol-hā'ādām,* literally, 'for this is all of humanity'. Delitzsch (1920) pointed out that the saying means that all people share this responsibility. Similar grammatical constructions are to be found in Pss. 109.4; 110.3; 120.7; Job 5.25; 8.9. The Editor is appealing to common religious duty, as does the deuteronomic tradition. He links wisdom's form of that obligation, fear, with the more common call to 'obey', saying that these are not two separate, but rather like, actions.

12.14 Yet another reason is given for upholding the tradition. The accusative phrase *'et-kol-ma'ᵃśeh* has been used by Qoheleth in 7.13 and 8.17, so its lack of the definite article here by the Editor is not surprising. Every deed will be brought under divine scrutiny; Qoheleth's phrase from 11.9, *yābi' bᵉmišpāṭ,* reappears here. The notion of God as judge and arbiter of all that is done on earth is crucial to Qoheleth's theology. Here the Editor extends that judgment to embrace even things done secretly. The root meaning of the niphal participle *n'lm* is 'to conceal'. Normally, we might assume that such actions were perhaps perverse, but the final clause *'im ṭôb wᵉ'im rā'* makes it clear that even good deeds might be done secretly. What this verse pronounces is confidence in the ultimate justice of God with regard to every human endeavour. Qoheleth left this issue hanging in 3.17-18, owing to the fact that on occasions divine justice is not seen to be done in this life. Yet his ambivalence is clear from other statements such as 8.12 and 11.9 in which he clings to the notion of a just God, for without that he would sink into the mire of cynicism and pessimism. The tension in Qoheleth's own personal view is not evident in the Editor's note, but it may not be correct to follow Childs (1979) and agree that this now places Qoheleth under an overarching eschatological rubric.

Thus concludes the second editorial appendage to Qoheleth's work. Like the first note in vv. 9-11, this one also commends the work of the sage in the hope that students will emulate the deep personal wrestling with the meaning of life so evident in Qoheleth's writing (cf. Polk, 1976: 15). If God is the final arbiter of all deeds, then surely he will look with compassion and kindness on all who, following Qoheleth, devote themselves at whatever personal cost to the struggle to bring faith and life experience into some measure of harmony.

There is within this statement from the Editor an apologetic note, as he expresses support for Qoheleth against those who presumed to judge his work as lacking authority and acceptability.

The purpose of the Epilogue then is clear. It is not an orthodox 'corrective' to Qoheleth's work to bring it into line with acceptable theology. Qoheleth, according to the commendation of the Editor, already stands within the broad theological parameters of the pluriform Judaism of the post-Exilic period. The Editor has recognized that, and the purpose in adding these two notes is none other than to commend it to others, perhaps in particular to his own students. However, his purpose does not stop there. The apologetic tone commends it further, to those Jewish groups who may have felt very uncomfortable with a work which questions so deeply but honestly some of the attitudes and theological concepts which were also part of traditional faith. That debate is reflected in the problem of the canonical qualifications of the book which marked first century rabbinic discussions.

The Superscription (1.1) and Epilogue (12.9-14) may be from the same hand, though it would seem more logical to suppose that the Superscription was added early on in the life of the document. The date of the Epilogue cannot be affirmed, so that we can only suggest that within late BCE Judaism two wisdom groups, Qoheleth's own and that of the Editor, whether contemporary or generationally separate, found in these words a value for life which enriched their experience of God. For this reason the original document was preserved and handed on to successive generations, now with a wider commendation, a sign of a growing appreciation of its validity and authority within the pluriform faith community of its day.

Excursus

Chinese Wisdom and Biblical Revelation

1. Every cultural group known to humankind has its own developed wisdom tradition. Whether in sophisticated literary form, or in pithy sayings persisting orally, or both, the distilled wisdom of each community abides. It is one of the key elements in defining the uniqueness of particular cultural families.

Insofar as our experience of life transcends barriers of geography, language, and other divisive factors, there is much in the wisdom of any one group of people linking it directly with the wider human family. We do not need to confine our study of Israelite wisdom's parallels to that of her near neighbours, the Egyptians and Babylonians, to demonstrate this fact. If there is any common ground between Israel and other members of the human community, it should not surprise us to find that biblical wisdom shares much in common with the wisdom of nations with which it had no formal political or geographical contact. Indeed, it should surprise us if this were not the case, for it would suggest that somehow the experience of the people of Israel was not representative of the rest of humanity. This we know to be far from the truth.

Those of us who identify with the Judeo-Christian tradition are accustomed to affirming that the Scriptures are God's word to all humanity. Without abandoning this faith position, we have nevertheless to determine how such a view relates to material in Africa or Asia which manifests so much common ground with what we regard as sacred Scripture.

One response to this phenomenon has been to ignore the non-biblical material altogether. This is what Sanders describes as the 'tribalisation of Scripture' (1984, p. 66). Another has been to place all wisdom material, biblical and other, on a lower level than the rest of Scripture, to dub it 'general revelation' and so to distinguish it from the so-called higher level 'special revelation'. Neither of these two approaches is adequate.

2. Israelite wisdom material had posed difficulties for the historical approach to OT theology. This was because it apparently was uninterested in some of the themes serving as the major foci for her historical traditions, such as the exodus and covenant themes. It also showed little interest in specific historical personages, preferring the generic treatment of people. A second reason was no doubt that Israelite wisdom was seen to overlap with the material available from Israel's neighbours, meaning that it was not sufficiently distinctive to carry the 'Made in Israel' stamp. It was thus difficult to accommodate the wisdom material to the definition of 'revelation' as propounded (see C.F.D. Moule, 'Revelation', *IDB,* IV). That definition of 'revelation' was based on a narrow range of biblical materials only. Thirdly, wisdom depended much more on human reflection, on philosophizing, than it did on the 'supernatural' as the vehicle for receiving divine truth. For reasons such as these, wisdom material in the OT was not given its rightful theological place alongside other materials. By dubbing it 'general' revelation, it was given a discounted theological value. So-called 'special revelation' was descriptive of the word communicated to and through prophets, priests, and the like, and was considered more valid and theologically substantive. Clearly, the theological presuppositions of this view prevented its adherents from coming to terms fully with the issue of wisdom's, and the sage's, place in the overall theological scheme of the OT.

In more recent years OT scholars have shown an increasing interest in biblical wisdom material and its importance for the constructing of a fuller OT Theology (see Emerton. 1979). The 'history-as-the-medium-of-revelation' approach of the 1950s, though standing in the centuries-old *Heilsgeschichte* tradition of von Hoffmann, is now recognised as having grossly overstated its case (see D. Knight, 1977, pp. 173-74). In its zeal to demonstrate that the OT was both unique and supremely reliable as a means of knowing God, it went too far, and effectively isolated wisdom material from theological consideration. Zimmerli and others have now helped us return to a more honest position, and have defended the need to find a place for wisdom in a truly comprehensive OT Theology. See also more recently, B. W. Anderson's *Contours of Old Testament Theology* (Fortress; 1999).

3. This commentary was written in Taiwan, against the background of many years in East Asia, and in the context of a cultural community which proudly draws attention to its 5,000 years of recorded history. The Chinese wisdom tradition is ancient, paralleling that of the OT both in its longevity and content. It is not only practically impossible, it is also theologically irresponsible and naive, to ignore some of the issues raised by the juxtaposition of these two great wisdom traditions.

Although in the body of the commentary itself there are no explicit references to Chinese sayings, some reflections are called for here by way of a postscript.

4. Numerical Sayings are a well-known phenomenon in the OT and have been studied in some depth by W. Roth (1962, 1965). It is less well known that formally similar sayings can be found in the Confucian Analects (see Ogden, *TJT*, 1981). Here we find both the Simple Numerical Saying consisting of the title line, numeral, and list of attributes or items, and the Double Numerical Saying with contrasting positive and negative components. The Graded Numerical Saying of the OT, that is the X, X + 1 type, is not found in Confucian writing. Form-critically, as well as in content, Chinese wisdom writing stands very close to Israelite wisdom.

Other examples are available (see Ogden *TJT,* 1982) which further illustrate the wide overlap between Chinese wisdom and that preserved in the OT. Similar social and personal problems have been the object of reflection in both cases, and conclusions reached are almost identical. A moment's consideration of the common humanity we share, the similarity of all human experience, should remind us that this phenomenon is to be expected. Qoh. 4.1-12 includes several numerical sayings, and although their form does not follow exactly that of the 'standard' Israelite forms, nevertheless the fact is that Qoheleth has made use of an ancient and universal wisdom model.

In terms of methodology, both Israelite and Chinese wisdom traditions adopt the same observation-reflection approach which we saw was so typical of Qoheleth. From this common approach to reality there flow numerous shared conclusions about life. Both sense the need for justice and equity, for considerate behaviour, for a loving attitude to others, for courage, selflessness, humility, loyalty, truthfulness, and all that makes for gracious and harmonious relationships. Even when one makes allowance for divergences between the two traditions' cultural and religious backgrounds and presuppositions, one nevertheless must acknowledge that they overlap to an amazing degree.

Yet it would be injudicious to treat too lightly the real differences which exist between the various cultures and their wisdom. The fact that when Israel borrowed from her neighbours, those new ideas came under the sway of Yahwistic faith, were uprooted from their original setting and indigenized, indicates just how each tradition is contextually oriented. However, the modifications which may apply to what is borrowed are just that—they are modifications rather than wholly distinct ideas, and as such can never transcend that which is common to both. Obviously, the interpreter, in doing any comparative study cross-culturally, must be duly aware of the specific factors which impinge upon the contextual understanding of common phenomena. Yet that which is indeed common must be affirmed.

5. If we recognize that wisdom material outside the OT, some of which was directly known to Israel, obtains in forms and ideas parallel to what is preserved in the OT, then we are forced to ask about the method(s) by which revelation comes. Does revelation to the OT sages come in ways similar to or dissimilar from that given to non-Israelite sages? Is revelation found in 'foreign' wisdom material of a different order from that which God showed his prophets and other agents in Israel? When we examine the biblical texts we discover frequent references to God's word coming to his agents through mysterious supersensory methods: dreams, visions, auditions. How does God's revelation come to his people?

If we borrow the terminology of the biblical writers, and the testimony of Hebrews 1.1, we can state that revelation comes in many extraordinary ways. Yet there is a sense in which these 'special' methods of communication are merely literary conventions for referring to communication from the deity; in fact, the reality is that revelation is given in what are closer to 'normal' methods of discovering information. Among these 'normal' methods are meditation, pondering, philosophizing, reflecting. We mention also in passing, the revelation which comes to us through the natural world in which God has placed us (Psa. 19; Rom. 1.18-20). Despite the fact that so many western theologians have balked at accepting the created world as a source of revelation (e.g. K. Barth, G.S. Hendry etc.), the Asian would find the natural world a most obvious place to expect God to make himself known. Perhaps, then, our tendency has been to stress supernatural methods of revelation at the expense of other, 'natural' methods, methods which accord with the experience of most Christians today. If God continues to make himself known to the believing community, it is most likely to be through quite mundane channels. That it was so in the past must be allowed also.

Think, for a moment, of some of the great biblical prophets. Among the variety of ways in which God made himself known to them, there is the observation of one's surroundings and reflection thereon. In Amos 7 and 8, the prophet mentions a number of things he saw. Whether they were actual or metaphorical sightings may be a significant question in the visions of 7.1, 4 and 9.1. However, there can be little question about what 8.1 describes. The basket of summer fruit was something which caught Amos's eye as he strolled through the local market, or as he passed the vendor by the roadside. What he saw prompted reflection; in the homonym *qēṣ-qayiṣ* he found the text for his next sermon. The process of revelation began with his noticing some ordinary object; it touched off an association in his mind, and reflection on that turned a mere sighting into revelation. The same holds true for the general prophetic observation of social conditions, of the behaviour of groups and individuals, of their values and the like. What they themselves witnessed became the raw material of revelation. What set them apart from those who merely saw but did not behold, was that under God their reflection on those observed phenomena introduced them to a knowledge of the divine mind.

The prophets saw that people's lives did not measure up to the divine demands. But how 'supernatural' must revelation be before they could reach that conclusion? Is it only the prophet who can discern that fact? Surely not! Most members of the community would have known that, given their awareness of those requirements as taught by priest and elder. Perhaps there are some aspects of revelation which lie outside the 'ordinary' method of discerning truth, and it may not apply to everything that the prophets said, but it certainly can describe much of what the prophets felt constrained to say. The point of all this is to affirm that the observation-reflection method is obviously one of the major ways in which God made known his will to his people and to his particular spokespersons.

As we turn to the Israelite sage, we may wonder how and where 'revelation' came. Similar to the testimony of Amos, we note the sage focusing attention on daily life and intercourse. What happened in the courts, in the marketplace, in the home, wherever people related to one another or to their environment, there the sage was, observing, noting, checking with previous observations and with what he had been taught of the tradition. This inductive method was the way in which the tradition he inherited, the 'revelation', was validated (Knight, 1977, p. 174). It could also be supplemented by new insights, but as far as the methodology is concerned, he depended on his keen observation of the world around him.

Interestingly enough, we have exactly this situation portrayed for us in Prov. 24.30-34. We are there told of a wise man walking by a field. He describes what he saw: an uncared-for field overgrown with weeds, its protective wall broken down, allowing predators and others easy access. This observation provoked reflection (v. 32), which in turn led to 'revelation'. The spiritual insight he was given is expressed in a typical wisdom speech-form in vv. 33-34. We are close to the truth if we assume that this represents a typical procedure for all sages. It certainly can account for most if not all of the material in Qoheleth. That it differs significantly from the means of revelation known to many prophets must be denied. We conclude therefore, that observation and reflection was and is one of the major avenues by which God communicates with his people. That we should set it on some lower plane, simply because we think of it as 'philosophy' can only raise questions about our definition of revelation.

The method we have described above is not confined to Israel. Israelite sages felt free to borrow material from neighbouring cultures and incorporate it into what we now term 'God's Word' because they recognized in that alien material the voice of God. They thereby acknowledged the God-givenness of their neighbours' insight either explicitly or implicitly, and affirmed its authority for them. This was the liberating attitude which a stress upon God as Creator could give. The traditions of China ought to be evaluated in the same manner as the sages of Israel viewed the wisdom traditions of their neighbours. That is to say, we can only affirm that here too is God's word revealed to those ancient sages who meditated on the experience of communal life in China. We should read it in what Sanders calls 'the prophetic mode' (1977, pp. 66-67).

6. Our question then is, how significant is the fact that material in the OT which we regard as Scripture may also be found outside in the literature of China? What are the *theological* implications of this fact?

Surely, there can only be one intelligent response, and that is to acknowledge that outside the Scriptures as Christians traditionally define them, there exists other material which is part of the totality of God's revelation. That is to say, God's revelation is not confined to the Scriptures as we know them. If material which in our Scriptures we honour as the revealed wisdom of God is paralleled elsewhere, the latter must also be respected as coming from the same and only God, the Lord of all (cf. 1 Cor. 2.12). We are inevitably led to the conclusion that God is actively present in and within cultural groups other than the people of Israel. His revelation is not bound only to one group of people, for his love and saving concern extend to all his creatures.

This permits, indeed encourages, us to look to the two wisdom traditions of the OT and China as the obvious point at which to seek a bridge from the Church to the local community, from the Christian to the person who adheres to another faith system. The OT is far less an alien document to the East Asian world than the NT, and this is due partly to their shared intellectual or wisdom traditions.

Within the Christian family, the Scriptures remain the primary touchstone by which we evaluate not only our lives but also the lives of groups and individuals with whom we are in contact. The Scriptures provide us with a screen through which to view the world, a paradigm by which we can identify God's saving activity, and included in that world and activity is the revelation which God has made known to others who do not at this present identify with the Christian community.

The view that the Scriptures are the canon by which we weigh other materials, is akin to the 'canon within the canon'-theory propounded by von Rad. We are taking a portion of God's total revelation, in this case the Judeo-Christian Scriptures, and applying it to the wider body of revealed knowledge. This is an unavoidable situation. It is justifiable on the grounds that whatever God has revealed will not be inconsistent with what is contained within the Scriptures, though it may well be different in perspective or emphasis, and even content, given the national dimensions of much of the OT and NT material.

Whether setting priorities for evangelism, teaching, or Bible translation, the Christian is not only theologically justified, but practically required, to begin with the revelation we share with others, our common wisdom.

Bibliography

Commentaries and Monographs

Barr, J., *The Semantics of Biblical Language* (London: Oxford University Press, 1961).

Barré, M. (ed.), *Wisdom, You are my Sister: Studies in Honor of Roland E. Murphy, O. Carm., on the Occasion of his Eightieth Birthday* (CBQMS, 29; Washington, DC: The Catholic Biblical Association of America, 1997).

Barton, G.A., *Ecclesiastes* (ICC, New York: Charles Scribner's Sons, 1908).

Bea, A., *Liber Ecclesiastae* (Scripta Pontificii Instituti Biblici, 100; Rome: Pontifical Biblical Institute, 1950).

Beck, A.B., *et al.* (eds.), *Fortunate the Eyes that See: Essays in Honor of David Noel Freedman in Celebration of his Seventieth Birthday* (Grand Rapids, MI: Eerdmans, 1995).

Bickell, G., *Der Prediger über den Wert des Daseins* (Innsbruck: Wagner'sche Universitäts-Buchhandlung, 1884).

Braun, R., *Kohelet und die frühhellenistische Popularphilosophie* (ed. G. Fohrer; BZAW,130; Berlin: de Gruyter, 1973).

Brown, W.P., *Ecclesiastes* (Interpretation; Louisville: Westminster John Knox, 2000).

Budde, K., *Der Prediger* (HSAT, 2; Tübingen, 1910).

Childs, *B.S., Introduction to the Old Testament as Scripture* (Philadelphia: Fortress, 1979).

Christianson, E.S., *A Time To Tell: Narrative Strategies in Ecclesiastes*, (JSOTSup, 280; Sheffield: Sheffield Academic Press, 1998).

Crenshaw, J.L., *Old Testament Wisdom: An Introduction* (London: SCM 1981).

—, *Ecclesiastes: A Commentary* (OTL; Philadelphia: Westminster, 1987).

—, 'Ecclesiastes,' in *Harper's Bible Commentary* (ed. J.L. Mays; San Francisco: Harper Collins, 1999), pp. 518-524.

Davidson. R, *The Courage to Doubt* (London: SCM, 1983).

Delitzsch, F., *Commentary on the Song of Songs and Ecclesiastes* (trans. M.G. Easton; Edinburgh: T. & T. Clark, 1877).

Dubarle, A-M., *Les sages d'Israël* (Lectio Divina, 1; Paris: Les Éditions du Cerf, 1946).
Eichhorn. D.M., *Musings of the Old Professor* (New York: J. David, 1963).
Eissfeldt, O., *The Old Testament: An Introduction* (trans. by P. Ackroyd; Oxford: Blackwell, 1965).
—, *Der Maschal im alten Testament* (BZAW, 24; Giessen: Töpelmann, 1913).
Ellermeier, F., *Qohelet* (Hertzberg am Harz: E. Jungfer, 1967).
Fichtner, J., *Die altorientalische Weisheit in ihrer israelitsch-jüdischen Ausprägung* (BZAW, 62; Giessen: Töpelmann, 1933).
Farmer, K.A., *Who Knows What is Good? A Commentary on the Books of Proverbs and Ecclesiastes* (ITC; Grand Rapids: Eerdmans, 1991).
Fohrer, G., *Introduction to the Old Testament* (trans. by D. Green; Nashville: Abingdon Press, 1968).
Fox, M.V., *Qoheleth and his Contradictions* (JSOTSup, 71; Sheffield: Sheffield Academic Press, 1989).
Fredricks, D.C., *Coping with Transience: Ecclesiastes on Brevity in Life* (The Biblical Seminar, 18; Sheffield: Sheffield Academic Press, 1993).
Galling. K., *Der Prediger* (HAT, 18; Tübingen: J.C.B. Mohr, 1969).
Gammie, J.G., *et al.* (eds.), *Israelite Wisdom: Theological and Literary Essays in Honor of Samuel Terrien* (New York: Scholars, 1978).
Genung. J.F., *The Words of Qoheleth* (Boston: Houghton Mifflin, 1904).
Gese. H., *Lehre und Wirklichkeit in der alten Weisheit* (Tübingen: J.C.B. Mohr, 1958).
Ginsberg, H.L., *Studies in Koheleth* (New York: Jewish Theological Seminary, 1950).
Glasser, É., *Le procès du bonheur par Qohelet* (Lectio Divina, 61; Paris: Les Éditions du Cerf, 1970).
Good, E., *Irony in the Old Testament* (Sheffield: Almond, 2nd edn, 1981).
Gordis, R., *Koheleth. The Man and his World* (New York: Schocken Books, 3rd edn, 1971).
Hayes, J.H. (ed.), *Old Testament Form Criticism* (TUMS, 2; San Antonio: Trinity University Press, 1974).
Hertzberg, H.W., *Der Prediger* (KAT, 17; Gütersloh: Gerd Mohn, 1963).
Jastrow, M., *The Gentle Cynic* (Philadelphia: Lippincott, 1919).
Jones, E., *Proverbs and Ecclesiastes* (New York: Macmillan, 1961).
Knight, D.A., *Tradition and Theology in the Old Testament* (Philadelphia: Fortress, 1977).
Kroeber, R., *Der Prediger* (Berlin: Akademie, 1963).

Lauha, A., *Kohelet* (BKAT, 19; Neukirchen: Neukirchener Verlag, 1978).
Loader, J.A., *Polar Structures in the Book Of Qohelet* (BZAW, 152; Berlin: de Gruyter, 1979).
Lohfink, N., *Kohelet* (Stuttgart: Echter Verlag, 1980).
Lohfink, N., *Qoheleth* (A Continental Commentary; trans. by Sean McEvenue; Minneapolis: Augsburg Fortress, 2003).
Longman, T., *The Book of Ecclesiastes* (NICOT; Grand Rapids: Eerdmans, 1998).
Loretz, O., *Qohelet und der alte Orient* (Freiburg: Herder, 1964).
McNeile, A.H., *An Introduction to Ecclesiastes* (Cambridge: Cambridge University Press, 1904).
Miller, D.B., *Symbol and Rhetoric in Ecclesiastes: The Place of Hebel in Qohelet's Work* (Atlanta: SBL, 2002).
Murphy. R.E., 'Ecclesiastes', in *Jerome Biblical Commentary,* ed. R.E. Brown *et al.,* (Englewood Cliffs, NJ: Prentice Hall, 1968), pp. 534-40.
—, *Ecclesiastes*, (WBC, 23; Dallas, TX: Word, 1992).
Perdue, L., *Wisdom and Cult* (Missoula, Montana: Scholars, 1977).
Plumptre, E.H., *Ecclesiastes* (Cambridge: The University Press, 1887).
Podechard, E., *L'Ecclésiaste* (Paris: Lecoffre, 1912).
Rad. G. von., *Wisdom in Israel* (trans. by J.D. Martin; London: SCM, 1972).
Rankin, O.S., 'Ecclesiastes', in *Interpreter's Bible* (ed. G. Buttrick; Vol. V, New York: Abingdon, 1956).
Roth, W.M.W., *Numerical Sayings in the Old Testament* (SVT, 13; Leiden: Brill, 1965).
Rudman, D., *Determinism in the Book of Ecclesiastes* (JSOTSup, 316; Sheffield: Sheffield Academic Press, 2001).
Rudolph, W., *Vom Buch Kohelet*, (Münster: Aschendorf, 1959).
Salyer, G., *Vain Rhetoric: Private Insight and Public Debate in Ecclesiastes* (JSOTSup, 327; Sheffield: Sheffield Academic Press, 2001).
Sanders, J., *Canon and Community* (Philadelphia: Fortress, 1984).
Schoors, A., (ed.) *Qohelet in the Context of Wisdom* (Leuven: Leuven University Press, 1998).
Scott, R.B.Y., *Proverbs; Ecclesiastes* (AB, 18; New York: Doubleday, 1965).
Seow, C-L., *Ecclesiastes* (AB, 18c; New York: Doubleday, 1997).
Stone, M., *Scriptures, Sects, and Visions* (Philadelphia: Fortress. 1980).
Strobel, A., *Das Buch Prediger* (Düsseldorf: Patmos, 1967).
Towner, W.S., 'The Book of Ecclesiastes', in *The New Interpreter's Bible* (Nashville: Abingdon, 1997), pp. 265-360.
Volz, P., *Weisheit* (Göttingen: Vandenhoeck & Ruprecht, 1911).

Weiser, A., *The Old Testament* (trans. by D. Barton; New York: Association Press, 1961).
Whitley, C.F., *Koheleth: His Language and Thought* (Berlin: de Gruyter, 1979).
Whybray, R. N., *The Intellectual Tradition in the Old Testament* (BZAW, 135; Berlin: de Gruyter, 1974).
—, *Ecclesiastes* (NCB; Grand Rapids: Eerdmans, 1989).
Williams, R.J., *Hebrew Syntax: An Outline* (Toronto: University of Toronto Press, 1967).
Witzenrath, H., *Süss ist das Licht* (St. Ottilien: EOS Verlag, 1979).
Wright, A.G., 'Ecclesiastes (Qoheleth)', in *The New Jerome Biblical Commentary* (ed. R.E. Brown *et al.*; Englewood Cliffs, NJ: Prentice Hall, 1990), pp. 489-495.
Zimmerli, W., *Das Buch des Predigers Salomo* (ATD, 16; 2nd edn, Göttingen: Vandenhoeck & Ruprecht, 1967).

Articles in Journals and Collections

Ackroyd, P.R., 'Two Hebrew Notes', *ASTI* 5 (1966-67), pp. 84-86.
Anderson, W.H.U., 'The Curse of Work in Qoheleth: An Exposé of Genesis 3:17-19 in Ecclesiastes', *Evangelical Quarterly* 70 (1998), pp. 99-113.
Andre, G., 'Heq', in *TDOT,* IV (ed. G.J. Botterweck and H. Ringgren; trans. by D. Green; Grand Rapids: Eerdmans, 1980), pp. 356-58.
Baumgärtel, F., 'Die Ochsentachel und die Nagel in Koh. 12.11', *ZAW* 81 (1969), p. 8.
Baumgartner, W., 'The Wisdom Literature', in *The Old Testament and Modern Study* (ed. H.H. Rowley; Oxford: Clarendon Press, 1951), pp. 210-37.
Blank, S.H., 'Ecclesiastes', in *Interpreter's Dictionary of the Bible* II, ed. G.A. Buttrick (Nashville: Abingdon, 1962), pp. 7-13.
Blenkinsopp, J., 'Ecclesiastes 3.1-15: Another Interpretation', *JSOT* 66 (1995), pp. 55-64.
Boer, P.A.H. de, 'The Counsellor', in *Wisdom in Israel and in the Ancient Near East,* ed. M. Noth and D.W. Thomas (VTSup 3; Leiden: Brill, 1955), pp. 138-49.
Breton, S., 'Qoheleth Studies', *BTB* 3 (1973), pp. 22-50.
Bruns, J.E., 'The Imagery of Ecclesiastes 12.6a', *JBL* 84 (1965), pp. 428-30.
Bryce, G.E., '"Better"-Proverbs: An Historical and Structural Study', in *Society of Biblical Literature Seminar Papers,* 1 (Missoula, MT: Society of Biblical Literature, 1972), pp. 343-54.
Buzy, D., 'La notion du bonheur dans l'Ecclésiaste', *RB* 43 (1943), pp. 494-511.
Carasik, M., 'Qohelet's Twists and Turns', *JSOT* 28.2 (2003), pp. 192-209.
Castellino, G.R., 'Qoheleth and His Wisdom', *CBQ* 30 (1968), pp. 15-28.

Choi, J.H., 'The Doctrine of the Golden Mean in Qoh 7, 15-18', *Bib* 83, (2002), pp. 358-374.

Crenshaw, J.L., 'Popular Questioning of the Justice of God in Ancient Israel', *ZAW* 82 (1970), pp. 380-95.

—, 'The Eternal Gospel (Eccl. 3.11)', in *Essays in Old Testament Ethics,* ed. J.L. Crenshaw and J.T. Willis (New York: Ktav, 1974), pp. 23-55.

—, 'The Shadow of Death in Qoheleth', in *Israelite Wisdom: Theological and Literary Essays in Honor of Samuel Terrien,* ed. J. Gammie *et al.* (Missoula: Scholars, 1978), pp. 205-16.

—, 'Wisdom', in *Old Testament Form Criticism,* ed. J. Hayes (San Antonio: Trinity University Press, 1974), pp. 225-64.

Dahood, M., 'Canaanite-Phoenician Influence in Qoheleth', *Bib* 33 (1952), pp. 30-52, 191-221.

—, 'Hebrew-Ugaritic Lexicography IV, V, VIII, X', *Bib* 47 (1966), pp. 403-19; 48 (1967), pp. 421-38; 51 (1970), pp. 391-404; 53 (1972), pp. 386-403.

—, 'Qoheleth and Recent Discoveries', *Bib* 39 (1958), pp. 302-18.

—, 'The Language of Qoheleth', *CBQ* 14 (1952), pp. 227-32.

—, 'Canaanite Words in Qoheleth 10.20', *Bib* 46 (1965), pp. 210-12.

Davies, G.H., 'Vow',in *IDB* IV, ed. G. Buttrick (Nashville: Abingdon, 1962), pp. 792-93.

De Vries, S.J., 'Observations on Quantitative and Qualitative Time in Wisdom and Apocalyptic', in *Israelite Wisdom,* ed. J. Gammie *et al.* (Missoula: Scholars, 1978), pp. 263-76.

Donald, T., 'The Semantic Field of "Folly" in Proverbs, Job, Psalms, and Ecclesiastes', *VT* 13 (1963), pp. 285-92.

Eising, H., '*Zkr*', in *TDOT* IV, ed. G. Botterweck and H. Ringgren; trans. D. Green (Grand Rapids: Eerdmans, 1980), pp. 64-82.

Ellermeier, F., 'Die Entmachtung der Weisheit im Denken Qohelets', *ZThK* 60 (1963), pp. 1-20.

—, 'Das Verbum *Ḥûš* in Koh 2,25', *ZAW* 75 (1963), pp. 197-217.

Emerton, J.A., 'Wisdom', in *Tradition and Interpretation,* ed. G.W. Anderson (Oxford: Blackwell, 1979), pp. 214-37.

Forman, C.C., 'Koheleth's Use of Genesis', *JSS* 5 (1960), pp. 256-63.

—, 'The Pessimism of Ecclesiastes', *JSS* 3 (1958), pp. 336-43.

Fox, M.V., 'Frame-Narrative and Composition in the Book of Qohelet', *HUCA* 48 (1977), pp. 83-106.

—, 'Aging and Death in Qohelet 12', *JSOT* 42 (1988), pp. 55-77.

Fredericks, D.C., 'Chiasm and Parallel Structures in Qoheleth 5:6—6.9', *JBL* 108 (1989), pp. 17-35.

—, 'Life's Storms and Structural Unity in Qoheleth 11.1—12.8', *JSOT* 52 (1991), pp. 95-114.

Galling, K., 'Kohelet-Studien', *ZAW* 50 (1932), pp. 276-99.

—, 'Predigerbuch', *RGG* (3rd edn; Tübingen: J.C.B. Mohr, 1961), pp. 510-14.

—, 'Das Rätsel der Zeit im Urteil Koheleths (Koh. 3.1-15)', *ZThK* 58 (1961), pp. 1-15.

Garcia Bachmann, M., 'A Study of Qoheleth (Ecclesiastes) 9:1-12', *International Review of Mission*, 91 (2002), pp. 382-394.

Gese, H., 'Die Krisis der Weisheit bei Koheleth', *Les sagesses du proche-orient ancien* (Paris: Presses Universitaires de France, 1963), pp. 139-51.

Gianto, A., 'The Theme of Enjoyment in Qohelet', *Bib* 73 (1992), pp. 528-532.

Gilbert, M., 'La description de la vieillesse en Qoheleth 12.1-7, est-elle allégorique?', VTSup 32 (1981), pp. 96-109.

Ginsberg, H.L., 'The Quintessence of Koheleth', in *Biblical and Other Studies,* ed. A. Altmann (Cambridge, MA: Harvard University Press, 1963), pp. 47-59.

—, 'The Structure and Contents of the Book of Koheleth', in *Wisdom in Israel and in the Ancient Near East,* ed. M. Noth and D.W. Thomas (VTSup 3; Leiden: Brill, 1955), pp. 138-49.

—, 'Ecclesiastes', in *Encyclopaedia Judaica* VI (Jerusalem: Keter, 1971), pp. 349-55.

Good, E., 'The Unfulfilled Sea: Style and Meaning in Eccles. 1.2-11', in *Israelite Wisdom,* ed. J. Gammie *et al.* (Missoula: Scholars, 1978), pp. 59-73.

Gordis, R., 'Ecclesiastes 1.17—Its Text and Interpretation', *JBL* 56 (1937), pp. 322-30.

—, 'Quotations in Wisdom Literature', *JQR* 30 (1939-40), pp. 123-47.

—, 'The Wisdom of Koheleth', in *Poets, Prophets, and Sages: Essays in Biblical Interpretation* (Bloomington, Ind.: Indiana University Press, 1971), pp. 325-56.

—, 'Was Koheleth a Phoenician?', *JBL* 74 (1955), pp. 103-44.

Hasel, G., 'Za'aq', in *TDOT* IV, ed. G. Botterweck and H. Ringgren (Grand Rapids: Eerdmans, 1980), pp. 112-22.

Haupt, P., 'The Book of Ecclesiastes', *Oriental Studies* (Boston: Ginn, 1894), pp. 242-78.

Hayman, A.P., 'Qohelet and the Book of Creation', *JSOT* 50 (1991), pp. 93-111.

Hentschke, R., 'Gbh',in *TDOT* II, ed. G. Botterweck and H. Ringgren; trans. by D. Green (Grand Rapids: Eerdmans, 1975), pp. 356-60.

Hessler, B., 'Kohelet: The Veiled God', *The Bridge* 1 (1955), pp. 191-206.

Holm-Nielsen, S., 'On the Interpretation of Qoheleth in Early Christianity', *VT* 24 (1974), pp. 168-77.

Horton, E.H., 'Koheleth's Concept of Opposites', *Numen* 19 (1972), pp. 1-21.

Humbert, P., 'Qoheleth', *RThPh,* n.s. 3 (1915), pp. 253-77.

Irwin, W.A., 'Ecclesiastes 4.13-16', *JNES* 3 (1944), pp. 255-57.

—, 'Ecclesiastes 3.18', *AJSL* 56 (1939), pp. 298-99.

—,, 'Ecclesiastes 8.2-9', *JNES* 4 (1945), pp. 130-31.
—, 'A Rejoinder (3.18)', *AJSL* 58 (1941), pp. 100-101.
Jarick, J., 'An "Allegory of Age" as Apocalypse (Ecclesiastes 12:1-7)', *Colloquium* 22 (1990), pp. 19-27.
Jasper, F.N., 'Ecclesiastes: A Note for our Times', *Interpretation* 21 (1967), pp. 259-73.
Johnston, R.K., '"Confessions of a Workaholic": A Reappraisal of Qoheleth', *CBQ* 38 (1976), pp. 14-28.
Johnstone, W., '"The Preacher" as Scientist', *SJT* 20 (1967), pp. 210-21.
Kamhi, D.J., 'The Root *Hlq* in the Bible', *VT* 23 (1973), pp. 235-39.
Klopfenstein, M.A., 'Die Skepsis des Qohelet', *ThZ* 28 (1972), pp. 97-109.
Knight, D.A., 'Revelation through Tradition', in *Tradition and Theology in the Old Testament,* ed. D.A. Knight (Philadelphia: Fortress, 1977), pp. 143-80.
Knopf, C.S., 'The Optimism of Koheleth', *JBL 49* (1930), pp. 195-99.
Koch, K., 'Gibt es ein Vergeltungsdogma im Alten Testament?', *ZThK* 52 (1955), pp. 1-42.
Kugel, J.L., 'Ecclesiastes', in *Harper's Bible Dictionary,* ed. P.J. Achtemeier (San Francisco: Harper and Row, 1985), pp. 236-67.
—, 'Qohelet and Money', *CBQ* 51 (1989), pp. 32-49.
Lauha, A., 'Die Krise des religiösen Glaubens bei Kohelet', in *Wisdom in Israel and in the Ancient Near East,* ed. M. Noth and D.W. Thomas (VTSup 3; Leiden: Brill, 1955), pp. 183-91.
Leahy, M., 'The Meaning of Qoh 10.15', *ITQ* 18 (1951), p. 288.
—, 'The Meaning of Eccles. 12.1-5', *ITQ* 19 (1952), pp. 297-300.
Loader, J.A., 'Qoh. 3.2-8 – A "Sonnet" in the OT', *ZAW* 81 (1969), pp. 240-42.
Lohfink, N., 'Technik und Tod nach Kohelet', in *Strukturen christlicher Existenz,* ed. H. Schlier, *et al.* (Würzburg: Echter Verlag, 1968), pp. 27-35.
—, 'War Kohelet ein Frauenfeind?', in *La sagesse de l'Ancien Testament,* ed. M. Gilbert (Leuven: Leuven University Press, 1979), pp. 259-87.
—, 'Qoheleth 5:17-19—revelation by joy', *CBQ* 52 (1990), pp. 625-635.
Lys, D., 'Par le temps qui court (Eccl. 3.1-8)', *ETRel* 48 (1973), pp. 299-316.
McKenna, J.E., 'The Concept of Hebel in the Book of Ecclesiastes', *SJOT* 45 (1992), pp. 19-28.
March, W.E., 'Prophecy', in *Old Testament Form Criticism,* ed. J.H. Hayes (San Antonio: Trinity University Press, 1974), pp. 141-77.
Miller, D.B., 'Qohelet's Symbolic Use of *hbl*', *JBL* 117 (1998), pp. 437-454.
—, 'What the Preacher Forgot: The Rhetoric of Ecclesiastes', *CBQ* 62 (2000), pp. 215-235.
Mitchell, H.G., '"Work" in Ecclesiastes', *JBL* 32 (1913), pp. 123-38.
Montgomery, J.A., 'Notes on Ecclesiastes', *JBL 43* (1924), pp. 241-44.

Muilenburg. J., 'A Qoheleth Scroll from Qumran', *BASOR* 135 (1954), pp. 20-28.
Müller, H-P., 'Wie sprach Qohälät von Gott?', *VT* 18 (1968), pp. 507-21.
Murphy, R.E., 'Form Criticism and Wisdom Literature', *CBQ* 31 (1969), pp. 475-83.
—, 'The Pensées of Qoheleth', *CBQ* 17 (1955), pp. 304-14.
Ogden, G.S., 'The "Better"-Proverb *(Tob-Spruch),* Rhetorical Criticism, and Qoheleth', *JBL* 96 (1977), pp. 489-505.
—, 'Qoheleth's Use of the "Nothing is Better"-Form', *JBL* 98 (1979), pp. 339-50.
—, 'Qoheleth ix 17—x 20: Variations on the Theme of Wisdom's Strength and Vulnerability', *VT* 30 (1980), pp. 27-37.
—, 'Historical Allusion in Qoh. iv 13-16?', *VT* 30 (1980), pp. 309-15.
—, 'Qoheleth ix 1-16', *VT* 32 (1982), pp. 158-69.
—, 'Qoheleth xi 1-6', *VT* 33 (1983), pp. 222-30.
—, 'Qoheleth xi 7—xii 8', *VT* 34 (1984), pp. 27-38.
—, 'The Mathematics of Wisdom: Qoheleth iv 1-12', *VT* 34 (1984), pp. 446-53.
—, 'The Interpretation of *Dôr* in Ecclesiastes 1.4', *JSOT* 34 (1986), pp. 91-92.
Pedersen. J., 'Scepticisme lsraélite', *RHPhR* 10 (1930), pp. 317-70.
Polk, T., 'The Wisdom of Irony: A Study of *Hebel* and its Relation to Joy and the Fear of God in Ecclesiastes', *SBT* 6 (1976), pp. 3-17.
Rainey, A., 'A Study of Ecclesiastes', *CTM* 35 (1964), pp. 148-57.
—, 'A Second Look at *Amal* in Qoheleth', *CTM* 36 (1965), p. 805.
Reines, C.W., 'Koheleth on Wisdom and Wealth', *JJS* 5 (1954), pp. 80-84.
—, 'Koheleth 8.10', *JJS* 5 (1954), p. 86.
Reitman, J.S., 'The Structure and Unity of Ecclesiastes', *Bibliotheca sacra* 154 (1997), pp. 297-319.
Roth, W., 'The Numerical Sequence x/x + 1 in the Old Testament', *VT* 12 (1962), pp. 301-308.
Rousseau. F., 'Structure de Qohelet i 4-11 et plan du livre', *VT* 31 (1981), pp. 200-17.
Rowley. H.H., 'The Problems of Ecclesiastes', *JQR* 42 (1951/52), pp. 87-90.
Rudman, D., 'A Contextual Reading of Ecclesiastes 4:13-16', *JBL* 116 (1997), pp. 57-73.
—, 'Woman as Divine Agent in Ecclesiastes' *JBL* 116 (1997), pp. 411-427.
Ryder. E.T., 'Ecclesiastes', in *Peake's Commentary on the Bible,* ed. M. Black and H.H. Rowley (London: Thomas Nelson, 1962), pp. 458-67.
Rylaarsdam, J.C., 'Hebrew Wisdom', in *Peake's Commentary on the Bible,* ed. M. Black and H.H. Rowley (London: Thomas Nelson, 1962), pp. 386-90.
Salters, R.B., 'A Note on the Exegesis of Ecclesiastes 3.15b', *ZAW* 88 (1976), pp. 419-22.

—, 'Notes on the History of the Interpretation of Koh 5.5', *ZAW* 90 (1978), pp. 95-101.
—, 'Notes on the Interpretation of Qoh 6.2', *ZAW* 91 (1979), pp. 282-89.
—, 'Text and Exegesis in Koh 10.19', *ZAW* 89 (1977), pp. 423-26.
Sanders, J.A., 'Hermeneutics in True and False Prophecy', in *Canon and Authority,* ed. G.W. Coats and B.O. Long (Philadelphia: Fortress, 1977), pp. 21-41.
Savignac, J. de, 'La sagesse du Qoheleth et l'épopée de Gilgamesh', *VT* 28 (1978), pp. 318-23.
Sawyer, J. F., 'The Ruined House in Ecclesiastes 12: A Reconstruction of the Original Parable', *JBL 94* (1975), pp. 519-31.
Seow, C.L., 'Linguistic Evidence and the Dating of Qohelet', *JBL* 115 (1996), pp. 643-666.
—, 'Qohelet's Eschatological Poem', *JBL* 118 (1999) pp. 209-234.
Serrano, J.J., 'I Saw the Wicked Buried (Eccl. 8.10)', *CBQ* 16 (1954), pp. 168-70.
Shead, A.G., 'Reading Ecclesiastes "Epiologically"', *Tyndale Bulletin,* 48 (1997), pp. 67-91.
Sheppard, G.T., 'The Epilogue to Qoheleth as Theological Commentary', *CBQ* 39 (1977), pp. 182-89.
Shields, M.A., 'Ecclesiastes and the End of Wisdom', *Tyndale Bulletin* 50 (1999), pp. 117-139.
Sneed, M., 'A Note on Qoh 8,12b-13', *Bib* 84 (2003), pp. 412-416.
Spanenberg, I.J.J., 'Irony in the Book of Qohelet', *JSOT* 72 (1996), pp. 57-69.
—, 'A Century of Wrestling with Qohelet: The Research History of the Book Illustrated with a Discussion of Qoh 4:17—5:6', in A. Schoors, ed., *Qohelet in the Context of Wisdom* (Leuven: Leuven University Press, 1998), pp. 61-91.
Staples, W.E., 'The "Vanity" of Ecclesiastes', *JNES* 2 (1943), pp. 95-104.
—, '"Profit" in Ecclesiastes', *JNES* 4 (1945), pp. 87-96.
—, 'Vanity of Vanities', *CJT* 1 (1955), pp. 141-56.
—, 'The Meaning of *hēpets* in Ecclesiastes', *JNES* 24 (1965), pp. 110-12.
Szikszai, S., 'Anoint', in *Interpreter's Dictionary of the Bible,* ed. G. Buttrick (Nashville: Abingdon, 1962), pp. 138-39.
Thomas, D.W., 'A Note on *bmd'k* in Ecclesiastes 10.20', *JTS* 50 (1949), p. 177.
—, 'Kelebh "Dog": Its Origin and Some Usages of It in the OT', *VT* 10 (1969), pp. 410-27.
Torrey, C.C., 'The Problem of Eccles. 4.13-16', *VT* 2 (1952), pp. 175-77.
Ullendorf, E., 'The Meaning of *qhlt*', *VT* 12 (1962), p. 215.
Ulrich, E., 'Our Sharper Focus on the Bible and Theology Thanks to the Dead Sea Scrolls', *CBQ* 66 (2004), pp. 1-24.
Verheij, A., 'Paradise Retried: On Qohelet 2.4-6', *JSOT* 50 (1991), pp. 113-115.

Vogel, D., 'Koheleth and the Modern Temper', *Tradition* 2 (1959), pp. 82-92.
Waldman, N.M., 'The *Dabar Ra'* of Eccl 8.3', *JBL* 98 (1979), pp. 407-408.
Whybray, R.N., 'Qoheleth the Immoralist? (Qoh 7.16-17)', in *Israelite Wisdom,* ed. J. Gammie *et al.* (Missoula: Scholars, 1978), pp. 191-204.
—, 'The Identification and Use of Quotations in Ecclesiastes', *VTSup* 32 (1981), pp. 435-51.
—, 'Ecclesiastes 1:5-7 and the Wonders of Nature', *JSOT* 41 (1988), pp. 105-112.
Williams, J.G., 'The Prophetic "Father"', *JBL* 85 (1966), pp. 344-48.
—, 'What Does it Profit a Man? The Wisdom of Koheleth', *Judaism* 20 (1971), pp. 179-93.
Wilson, L., 'Artful Ambiguity in Ecclesiastes 1:1-11', in A. Schoors, ed., *Qohelet in the Context of Wisdom* (Leuven: Leuven University Press, 1998), pp. 225-238.
Wise, M., 'A Calque from Aramaic in Qoheleth 6:12; 7:12 and 8:13', *JBL* 109 (1990), pp. 249-257.
Wright, A.G., 'The Riddle of the Sphinx: The Structure of the Book of Qohelet', *CBQ* 30 (1968), pp. 313-34.
—, 'The Riddle of the Sphinx Revisited: Numerical Patterns in the Book of Qoheleth', *CBQ* 42 (1980), pp. 38-51.
—, 'Additional Numerical Patterns in Qoheleth', *CBQ* 45 (1983), pp. 32-43.
Zimmerli, W., 'Das Buch Kohelet—Traktat oder Sentenzensammlung?', *VT* 24 (1974), pp. 221-30.
—, 'The Place and Limit of the Wisdom in the Framework of the Old Testament Theology', *SJT* 17 (1964), pp. 145-58.
Zimmerman, F., 'Kohelet', *JQR 52* (1961), pp. 273-78.

Index of Authors

Lightning Source UK Ltd.
Milton Keynes UK
UKHW02f0854060118
315625UK00002B/254/P

9 781906 055097